Methods for Social Analysis in Developing Countries

Recent Titles in the
Social Impact Assessment Series

Methods for Social Analysis in Developing Countries

EDITED BY

Kurt Finsterbusch,
Jasper Ingersoll,
and Lynn Llewellyn

Westview Press
BOULDER, SAN FRANCISCO, & OXFORD

Social Impact Assessment Series

The opinions and interpretations expressed in this volume are those of the individual contributors rather than the positions or policies of the varied organizations for which they work.

Table 8.1 reproduced by permission of the Society for Applied Anthropology from *Human Organization* 43(1):27–37. Chapter 9 was published previously in *Evaluation Review,* vol. 13, no. 3, June 1989. Reprinted by permission of Sage Publications.

Published in 1990 in the United States of America by Westview Press, Inc., 5500 Central Avenue, Boulder, Colorado 80301, and in the United Kingdom by Westview Press, Inc., 36 Lonsdale Road, Summertown, Oxford OX2 7EW

Library of Congress Cataloging-in-Publication Data
Methods for social analysis in developing countries / edited by Kurt
Finsterbusch, Jasper Ingersoll, and Lynn Llewellyn.
   p. cm. — (Social impact assessment series ; 17)
Includes bibliographical references.
ISBN 0-8133-7829-X
   1. Economic development projects—Social aspects—Developing
countries. 2. Economic development programs—Developing countries—
Cost effectiveness. I. Finsterbusch, Kurt, 1935–   .
II. Ingersoll, Jasper. III. Llewellyn, Lynn G. IV. Series: Social
impact assessment series ; no. 17.
HD75.8.M48   1990
338.9′009172′4—dc20   90-33658
                                         CIP

Printed and bound in the United States of America

The paper used in this publication meets the requirements
of the American National Standard for Permanence of Paper
for Printed Library Materials Z39.48-1984.

10   9   8   7   6   5   4   3   2   1

Contents

Part Three
Special Approaches and Methods

Part Four
An Application

Preface and Acknowledgments

Two lines of development in social science methodology are brought together in this volume. First, social impact assessment methods for development projects and programs developed rapidly in the United States in the 1970s and have continued to develop under the leadership of Canada and Western Europe in the 1980s. Second, methods for cost effective social analyses of development projects and programs in Third World countries have gained greater acceptance over the past decade. It is gratifying to be able to bring together the fruition of these advances in one volume through the contributions of some of the leading innovators and practitioners among applied social researchers working in the Third World.

This volume fills the gap between standard social science methodology books and the realities of conducting social research under Third World conditions. The authors presume that the reader has access to a methodology book for the details of standard methods. Relieved of the responsibility of detailing these methods, the authors give information on how to do social research in Third World settings. The articles discuss critical methodological issues and explain how basic and innovative methods can be applied. This volume, therefore, should be valuable for graduate students, development practitioners, and applied researchers in the Third World.

Social analysis for development activities entails both specific methods and general approaches. The first major section of the book presents four general approaches. Jasper Ingersoll reviews the general approaches of AID and the World Bank, Nicholas Taylor and Hobson Bryan describe a more participatory approach practiced in New Zealand, and Kurt Finsterbusch and William Partridge describe the development anthropology approach. Each of these approaches derives from a different institutional perspective. Since they are more idealistic than are the actual practices in the field, they converge more than they diverge. Nevertheless, they provide the applied social researchers with alternatives from which they can piece together their own approaches and vary them for different contexts.

The two other major sections describe specific methods. The second major section discusses the three standard or basic methods of surveys

(Shirley Buzzard), demographic analysis (Cynthia Cook), and informant interviewing (William Derman). These standard methods, however, require extensive adaptation when used in difficult Third World settings and constrained by the typical time and resource limits found there. The third major section describes a number of special approaches and methods. Kurt Finsterbusch provides a rationale for using several inexpensive methods that add up to fairly trustworthy conclusions and describes several specific methods that can be used in this approach. David Gow describes the rapid rural appraisal approach that is becoming quite popular and the methods it utilizes. Annette Binnendijk describes the extensive developments in monitoring and evaluation that have taken place in her division in AID. Finally, George Honadle and Lauren Cooper present a new methodology for evaluating development programs that could have widespread applications beyond evaluation.

The book begins with a description of the context for social analysis in the Third World provided by Jasper Ingersoll. It ends with Lynn Llewellyn's application of many of the methodological suggestions of the book to the problem of tropical deforestation.

The editors wish to thank Geraldine Todd for mastering the instructions for producing disks in the proper format, a challenge that each of us failed, and for typing the manuscript while maintaining an extraordinarily good spirit. We also gratefully acknowledge support from the Sociology Department of the University of Maryland for producing the manuscript. Finally, we appreciate the patience and encouragement of Dean Birkenkamp and Ellen Williams of Westview Press, which were vital to the birth of this book.

Kurt Finsterbusch
Jasper Ingersoll
Lynn Llewellyn

Introduction: Social Impact Assessment— For Richer and for Poorer

Jasper Ingersoll

This book presents brief summaries of contemporary methods for doing social impact assessment (SIA) of development projects. Our focus is on SIA of projects in developing countries in Latin America, Africa, and Asia, based on two decades of experience. Our emphasis is on *methods* because our intent is to help improve this recent experience of assessing the human implications of proposed projects *in time* to make their outcomes more humane. We, editors and contributors, hope that the book finds its way into the hands of people of many countries who are and will be working on, or connected with, social analysis of projects in developing countries. Previous books have reviewed problems of doing SIA in developing countries (Cernea, 1985; Derman, 1985; Green, 1986; Partridge, 1984). Others have presented methods for doing SIA in industrial countries (Branch et al., 1984; Canter et al., 1985; Finsterbusch and Wolf, 1977; Finsterbusch et al., 1983; Millsap, 1984). This book focuses on methods (what to assess and how to do it) in agrarian countries.

This chapter focuses on two diverse but interrelated trends: the "faces" of SIA, and its working environment (professional and political) in developing countries. Our purpose here is to show that SIA is both essential and possible in poor countries as well as rich countries. First, it is *essential* because people's social and cultural organization presents significant resources as well as constraints for development efforts. The features of their social landscape are as real—if less apparent to outsiders—as features of their natural, technical, or economic landscape. Second, SIA is *possible* because methods exist for trying to optimize these human resources and cope with these constraints. In the face of grinding poverty, development officials usually move too quickly to

1

some technological "quick fix," ignoring subtle social issues, which are always closely interconnected with the natural, technical, and economic landscape (Goulet, 1977). In conditions of poverty, people's social and cultural organization are always part of the solution, as well as part of the problem to be solved.

The Many Faces of Social Impact Assessment

Social impact assessment shows kinship with several recent, disparate yet related traditions of action and analysis:

1. The environmental protection movement: citizens and government
2. A social science R & D approach: views and values
3. The project cycle: large and small projects
4. Projects as systems: theory and practice
5. Social criticism: projections and prophecies

The Environmental Protection Movement: Citizens and Government

Human interest in the environment is at least as old as Chinese Taoist sages seeking to live in harmony with the flow of nature, in the current of the Tao. But it was only in the 1960s that popular concern with destruction of that flow by pollution and degradation resulted in political pressure for government action to safeguard the natural environment. The pressure emerged first in industrial countries, the most badly polluted, and spread gradually to agrarian countries. Several governments have responded with various policies and programs to establish such safeguards. In the United States, Congress passed the National Environmental Policy Act (NEPA) in 1969, and amended it in 1970, in response to mounting public concern with environmental pollution and degradation. NEPA established a legal requirement for environmental impact assessment (EIA) of the possible environmental implications of proposed, federally funded projects or programs, in order to anticipate and improve their environmental outcomes. The intent of SIA was the same regarding the social environment; however, the NEPA legislation dealt explicitly and comprehensively with the natural environment but only incidentally with the social environment.

The general form and procedures of SIA thus derive from the more widely mandated activity of EIA: detailed government standards for assessing proposed projects before funding in order to achieve environmental protection outcomes. Popular and official concern, however, was much more focused on particular, glaring sites of natural pollution than on diffuse, subtle social impacts—such as loss of community vitality, social cohesion, or adverse effects on minority groups. Cases of bio-chemical pollution were compelling because they were site-specific, observable and measurable; but social impacts seemed much less evident, "objective," or compelling.

Although the idea (and the calculation) of social costs gained currency (Kapp, 1971; Little and Horowitz, 1987), a social equivalent of "carrying capacity" or "pollution" has not yet been formulated. Governmental attempts to regulate threats to the environment grew in quantity and quality during the 1970s, against mounting vested interests and ideological opposition in the late 1970s. The practice of EIA nevertheless became established, with SIA as a modest component.

Several other countries built on this innovative American experience, and have continued to develop it, in some cases, well beyond the American original. Canada, European countries, New Zealand and others have been particularly active in establishing and carrying out EIA and SIA (see Bowles [1981] on Canada and Taylor and Hobson [Chapter 2 in this volume] on New Zealand). These countries are predominately industrialized and wealthy. Rather than trying to profit from this belated and very costly experience of the North, governments of the poorer, agrarian countries of the South initially regarded it with suspicion.

Some saw it as a new, covert form of Western imperialism: retarding industrialization in the agrarian world in the name of environmental preservation. A skeptical Sri Lankan official, for example, told a visitor who admired the pristine beaches in the 1970s that his country could not delay industrialization. He declared that Sri Lankans first had to acquire the same kind of industrial strength that had so enriched the North; only *then* would they have enough money to clean up their industrial mess. Such skepticism was based on general unawareness of environmental pollution.

Joel Halpern observed a group of Bulgarian garden workers distraught and crying at the sudden loss of roses and strawberries which they were lovingly cultivating in Sofia in the mid 1970s. Barbara Halpern recognized their cries as very similar in form to some of their dirges for the dead. Both Halperns noted that despite the gardeners' strong love for the soil and for cultivation of beauty, they appeared unconcerned about toxic wastes being dumped in a very close dump, or about the burning of all household wastes in the neighborhood. Their love for nature was not accompanied by awareness of threats to nature (Halpern, 1989).

Increasing pollution in *all* countries has made people and governments far more aware of the dangers ahead, but governments in the

South have not yet *generally* established their own official environmental standards or procedures. Some governments, however, have begun. India has drawn up quite thorough standards and regulations; and the Maharashtra state government did so on its own earlier than New Delhi; but implementation capacity lags well behind the policy standards. The Philippines has established environmental standards. Other countries have taken action in response to particular emergencies. On the western edge of central Thailand, for example, sugar refineries helped promote a regional cash crop in the early 1970s, but at the expense of dumping sludge into the Maekhlong River ("The River Kwai") choking off fishing downstream. When fishermen complained to Bangkok, the government imposed controls on sludge. Sugar refining and fishing have coexisted since then.

Such measures of control, however, have usually been reactions to emergencies. Most preventive EIA and SIA (*before* project funding) in developing countries have been carried out in the course of project assistance from multilateral and bilateral assistance programs. Although environmental and social scientists in developing countries have gained valuable experience in this process, their governments have not yet generally *institutionalized* such policy and program assessment on their own. The authors of this book hope to strengthen the interest in social analysis on the part of governments in developing countries, and also the capacities of social scientists in those countries to do the job.

In the United States, SIA rose with EIA in the 1970s and declined with it in the 1980s. Opposition to both was symbolized in the 1980 election campaign by entrepreneurs determined to exploit natural resources free of government control. The Reagan administration in 1981 drastically cut back environmental protection funds, as well as EIA and SIA, but did not quite demolish them: popular and congressional political strength were enough to prevent complete demolition. Although popular concern with environmental protection has survived (forced by recognition of ever-growing environmental degradation) federal support for environmental assessment and control has weakened. At the beginning of the 1990s, EIA and SIA are diminished in the face of federal government support for privatization and deregulation, at the expense of environmental protection for today and tomorrow.

In many individual states, however, EIA and some SIA continue as state-funded requirements. Further, a new practice has emerged in recent years. Private firms planning new investments have commissioned their own EIA and SIA studies, partly to justify their plans to the public, and partly to protect their own interests by critically checking the implications of their proposed investments (Preister, 1987).

In the current fragile political climate, it is up to analysts conducting SIA to demonstrate convincingly that the condition of the social environment can, does, and *should* influence project design and implementation, in practical ways which people can appreciate and officials can use. In addition to this book, several studies have demonstrated such influence (Cernea, 1985; Derman, 1985; Green, 1986; Salmen, 1987). Despite obvious differences between the political atmosphere in London and Lagos, or Stockholm and Sierra Leone, industrial and agrarian nations share a profound similarity: they both regard technical and economic issues as more "real" and compelling than social issues. Thus, social analysts in every country must be public advocates of the need and usefulness of SIA, as well as professional practitioners of the art.

NEPA required EIA for *all* U.S. federal projects that would affect the environment significantly. Most government agencies adopted a generally uniform format for EIA and somewhat less uniform formats for SIA. The Agency for International Development (AID) incorporated the ideas of EIA and SIA in its own project planning system in the 1970s. The World Bank and other development agencies also devised somewhat similar procedures for their project planning. We shall examine them in the next chapter. Even though designed for generally large projects, these guidelines can be usefully adapted for small, low-cost projects as well. The basic ideas of SIA are fully as appropriate for very modest projects as for very large projects.

A Social Science R & D Approach: Views and Values

SIA was born as a government response: a procedure to help guide government decisions and investment. Following the lead of environmental scientists, social scientists began responding to the new opportunity in the 1970s; but they also began trying to incorporate this activity into social science theory and practice. They began to professionalize SIA as an applied social science approach. A progression of conferences, newsletters, journal articles, and books appeared during the 1970s. A new tradition of social science R & D has emerged.

SIA contributes to applied research and planning and also draws on basic data regarding social conditions: two interdependent but separate realms. SIA also addresses social settings of diverse, sometimes conflicting, political interests and values. SIA must thus adapt to the urgent demands of action programs and to the professional demands for analysis of complex social situations. Two practitioners have developed complementary approaches, each oriented to one of these two demands.

C. P. Wolf designed an approach for SIA, modified from EIA, to meet the demands of action programs: defining the nature and scope of the development problem needing a solution; drawing out the main features of the proposed project design; profiling the types of people who would be affected by these proposed project features; projecting the main probable project outcomes; assessing the social implications of these outcomes for the people concerned; evaluating the positive and adverse impacts on the people; proposing mitigating measures for adverse impacts; and monitoring project results to improve project implementation (Finsterbusch et al., 1983:15–34).

Finsterbusch designed an approach for SIA, to address analysis of complex social settings. He focused on the types of people ("social units") to be affected by a proposed project: identifying the types of people affected; distinguishing the impacts by the types of people; and specifying the appropriate social science methods for estimating impacts on each type of people. He advocated identifying impacts on (1) individuals, (2) organizations, and (3) communities—in order to move beyond identifying impacts to measuring (or estimating) them. He proposed that impacts of projects (1) on individuals should be studied as quantitative indicators and as qualitative descriptions of the meaning of these conditions to the individuals; (2) on organizations should include their formal goals, survival and autonomy, and their mobilization of resources; and (3) on communities should include changes in community inputs (resources), organization, activities and outputs (quality of life the community can provide) (Finsterbusch and Wolf, 1977:13–20).

SIA addresses many aspects of the social and cultural organization of project populations. It employs a wide variety of study methods, both quantitative and qualitative, which are the main contents of this book. SIA began as examination and appraisal of proposed projects, but some analysts have extended it to appraisal of proposed policies, a particular kind of policy analysis. Wulff, for example, used the SIA approach to analyze impacts on prospective borrowers of banking regulations proposed by the U.S. Housing and Urban Development Department (Wulff, 1989). He then proposed modifications, making the regulations more consumer-centered and less banking-centered. Finsterbusch reviewed ways to use SIA for selecting, designing, and implementing policies (Finsterbusch and Wolf, 1977). In the fifth part of this section, we examine a further extension of SIA into critical assessment of long term social trends.

Any form of impact assessment (IA)—environmental, social, economic, technical, managerial—can be seen as value-free investigation. IA can be done of proposed pesticide factories or pesticide bans, highways, health clinics, or nuclear plants. IA can offer estimates of impacts of projects whatever their ideological hue, and it usually includes assessing implications of "no-go"—of doing nothing. But the basic rationale for doing IA is *not* value neutral. The rationale is, indeed, a value judgment: it is possible to offer informed guidance to future decisions with carefully gathered data and judicious projections; and it is desirable to anticipate the implications of possible outcomes early enough to mitigate the adverse ones and enhance the positive ones. IA is premised on a rational view of the world, and on "rational" governance (identifying and solving problems) rather than "pressure group" governance (responding to the interests of powerful, organized groups). SIA is also premised on humane values—making clear the impacts on people, including the poor, powerless, and silent—often left out of project planning. Actual SIA work, however, often runs into contrary ideological forces: powerful vested interests, preference for short-term gains, and indifference to long-term risks or secondary effects, whether personal or public. Issues of basic values and objective research are both at the heart of SIA (Hyman et al., 1986).

A practical advantage of SIA is that people can adapt its essential approach to any project, enterprise, movement, or activity in which they are interested professionally or personally—from very large to very small. A basic tenet of this book is that the logic and basic approach of SIA—although mainly invented in the course of assessing large, expensive projects—can be well used in greatly simplified form for very small, inexpensive projects. What kinds of people or groups would a proposed project affect? How would it do so? These questions can be equally useful to answer (for the people affected) whether the project is a village fish pond or a large hydro dam.

The Project Cycle: Large and Small Projects

SIA is one *phase* in the life cycle of projects. Most projects (especially large ones) pass through a succession of (variously named) phases, such as: identification, planning or design, assessment or appraisal (of the possible implications of the design), funding, implementation, monitoring, and evaluation (Baum and Tolbert, 1985). Some projects seem to unfold in fairly separate, discrete stages; but for most projects the phases seem less clear-cut, at times overlapping. Projects may revert to an earlier phase (e.g., for redesign) as they continue to grow in, at best, an iterative process of accumulating learning and experience. In the best of projects, social analysis occurs at each phase of the cycle, not just the assessment phase. Most experienced social scientists feel that if social analysis is to succeed in human terms, it must occur very early in the project cycle, and recur in the subsequent phases (Cernea, 1985; Partridge, 1984). Although we agree with this position, we have focused, for economy of presentation, in this book mainly on the assessment or appraisal stage.

Projects as Systems: Theory and Practice

Projects are complex systems of action (resources mobilized to achieve goals) that are interventions into existing natural and human systems in the locality or region. A project system typically includes interacting technical, economic, environmental, social and managerial components. Technical outputs may have impacts on all the other elements of the project system and thus on the preexisting natural and human systems. Mechanical pumps, for example, might contribute to: increased crop yields, greater soil erosion, reduced local employment of water carriers, emigration of unemployed former water carriers and new problems of allocating a greater volume of water. Similarly, outputs of every dimension will have complementary repercussions on the other, related dimensions. By trying to identify these *sets* of interrelated impacts, we gain a more realistic understanding of the systemic nature of projects and a more realistic grasp of their potential outcomes. An advantage of SIA, for project success *and* for general sociocultural understanding, is that social impacts of projects—like the social aspects of life—emerge with much greater clarity when we search for them as integral dimensions of some "real-world" systems (irrigation, health care, educational systems . . .) rather than as isolated sociocultural phenomena. The deeper significance of social impacts lies in their subtle interaction with "non-social" factors (technical, economic, environmental, managerial . . .).

The point here is that professional analysts tend to categorize experience in disciplinary terms (technical, environmental, political, economic, or social), but ordinary people experience life in "real-world" *compound* systems: shifting cultivation, fishing, irrigation, transportation, marketing, family maintenance, child raising, education, health care, and the like. We should thus seek the social implications of the complex operation of real-world compound systems, rather than trying to isolate discipline-centered "social systems" (Palinkas, 1985; Rossini, 1983).

Social Criticism: Projections and Prophecies

Some analysts have extended the logic and format of SIA beyond examining the social implications of proposed projects or proposed policies to examining the implications of basic future directions of societal change. Their focus is on fundamental social ends rather than particular means, on where society seems to be heading rather than particular (project) mechanisms to get there. Tester, for example, builds on Merton's trenchant critique: "Ours is a progressively technical civilization committed to the quest for continually improved means to carelessly examined ends" (Merton, 1964). Tester, following D'Amore, defined SIA very broadly as an effort

> to predict the future effects of policy decisions (including the initiation of specific projects) upon people: their physical and psychological health, well-being and welfare, their traditions, lifestyles, institutions and interpersonal relationships (Tester, 1980:4).

Tester distinguished between a micro and macro version of SIA. His micro version is "fine tuning" the many projects which comprise the basic course of the ship (society)—identifying appropriate technical adjustments in decision-making, and proposing incremental improvements in that course. His macro version is one of *questioning* the basic course of the ship, seeking

> *fundamental social change,* by creating an *active informed public* through the *processes* involved in conducting assessment and by demonstrating the social costs, benefits and consequences of certain types of decisions (Tester, 1980:5).

Tester's point is that the elementary logic and procedures of SIA should be used to explore critically the implications of the longer, wider trends of change. Based on his work in the Canadian frontier, he is skeptical of the generally optimistic assumptions regarding capitalist growth. Tester wants to apply this critical approach to such general societal trends as: centralization, deforestation, deregulation, privatization, industrialization, renewable/nonrenewable energy budgets, and the like. His critical skepticism seems well placed in the face of official optimism regarding growth. His professional skepticism, however, would not guarantee (1) that his projections of objectionable future trends would be complete, or (2) that "an active, informed public" would want the same things that he would favor.

Tester and others are nevertheless right in pressing for making use of the basic logic and procedure of SIA for macro social criticism. Rather than projecting future trends in ideological terms or presuming to make "objective, value-free" projections Tester would seek a third alternative. He would question the assumptions and values underlying the current course of the ship of society by identifying the current beneficiaries, benefactors, and victims of contemporary projects, programs, and policies. He would then try to engage them all in serious consideration of more humane alternative societal courses. Such efforts are desirable in rich societies like Canada, with marginalized impoverished minorities. In poor societies with marginalized impoverished masses of people, however, such careful examination of alternative future courses is essential to their survival.

This first section has reviewed the many faces and uses of SIA. Like the old Hindu deities, it presents itself in many guises but has an underlying unity of purpose: anticipation of the social implications of a proposed project or policy in time to modify those implications for the well-being of the people concerned. It is an analytical procedure, a humane undertaking, and in the long run, a generally cost-effective practice. It is cost-effective because social costs are almost always ignored or underestimated, despite decades of experience (Kottak, 1985). Social costs are the effects (for which "other people" must pay or suffer) of projects or enterprises which are not fully accountable for their results, which are always greater after the fact (Kapp, 1971).

The Working Environment of SIA

The first section has suggested some of the professional and political constraints to SIA in its first two decades, mainly in the industrialized world. This section considers three scattered examples of the current working environment of SIA in the developing countries. The very conditions of poverty which would make SIA so useful—by making development projects more socially sound—also tend to inhibit the general acceptance and wide use of SIA. We focus here on "supply" and "demand" issues: on the availability of social analysts in Third World countries able to conduct SIA, and on the effective demand for their services by governments and other agencies.

In the industrialized countries, the social sciences are moderately accepted (and modestly employed) for their analyses of the process of modernization, the problems of modernity, and (to a much lesser extent) their proposed solutions. In most agrarian countries, social scientists have been "outside," academic critics of the severe problems of modernization rather than "inside" policy, program, or project analysts. In both the industrialized and agrarian countries, however, it is much easier to prepare competent social analysts (supply side) than to employ them (demand side). We examine here these supply and demand factors in Africa, Brazil, and the Philippines.

On the supply side, African universities are now producing substantial numbers of social science undergraduates who enter administration and other professions. Lacking textbooks, library books, and field data on African conditions, social science training in these institutions may sensitize students to social and cultural issues, if not prepare them to carry out social analysis. Moreover, these universities offer an abstract education for a prestigious elite rather than a methodological training for a professionally competent middle class (World Bank).

Apart from a very few graduate centers—such as the Ahmadu Bello University in Nigeria and the University of Nairobi in Kenya—graduate study in social science entails travel to foreign universities, most of them remote from African studies and field data. Furthermore, African social scientists educated in France are more thoroughly prepared in philosophical and ideological discourse than in empirical field research or analytical skills. Although the authors of this book strongly support theoretical criticism of the injustice of poverty, our intent here is to strengthen the practical ability of social scientists to identify the social implications of project designs and better adapt them to the lives of the people concerned.

On the demand side, African governments have not conducted very much social analysis of their development projects except when required to do so by external development agencies. The reasons are numerous: (1) The governments have defined development projects as primarily technical and have sought engineers, economists, and 'practical' people to make technocratic contributions; (2) governments are very sensitive to political unrest—often first expressed by students—and they would not encourage close field study of rural poverty by social science students; (3) governments fear that social analysis of any particular local group might become a weapon to promote the interests of that group rather than of the country as a whole, and (4) many governments are grappling with the sensitive issue of tribal loyalties in a delicate balancing act which they would not want made explicit in formal social analysis and reporting. All development projects in Africa involve allocating very limited resources (financial, power, administrative, material, human, informational . . .) among many needy, contending groups. SIA that is to make any real difference in development projects, especially those sponsored by governments, takes place in highly politicized social environments.

Despite these political constraints, which are widely shared in other continents, a substantial amount of social analysis is being done in Africa. Official international development agencies require various kinds of pre-project and post-project social analysis, using African and expatriate analysts. Many international and domestic private voluntary groups also conduct informal social analysis which enable them to construct more socially sensitive project designs. Project monitoring and evaluation also include social issues, engaging and enhancing the skills of local university and consulting staff.

In some African countries, primarily Kenya, and secondarily Senegal and others, a number of social analysts are at work, for domestic academic, consulting, and voluntary groups. Since the governments, however, have not yet included social analysis as an *explicit* and *required* part of development planning and implementation, these human skills are employed on an ad hoc basis and are not part of official government policy or practice. In African countries, as in all countries, social analysis does not become a regular part of project planning and implementation unless a government makes it a routine requirement, expresses it in formal guidelines, and enforces it strenuously. We shall see two examples of such guidelines in the next chapter.

In Brazil, the picture is different in particular, but similar in general. The supply of professional social scientists has risen dramatically; the demand for their services has been mainly academic; their numbers are now greater than the jobs for them; they are increasingly interested in working on development programs; but that demand for them has not yet fully emerged.

Social science training in Brazil began in the 1930s. Students could get only B.A. degrees in social science until recently. The University of Sao Paulo offered the M.A. in anthropology only in the 1960s. Other universities followed. Students can now earn Ph.D. degrees in social science disciplines at Sao Paulo, Brasilia, Campinas, Rio de Janeiro and other universities. The Brazilian Association of Anthropology estimated about 400 graduates with M.A. and Ph.D. degrees in 1981 and about 2000 in 1989. The number of sociologists is substantially higher. For both disciplines, the number of graduates is much greater than the number of jobs, mostly academic. Interest has turned to applied social science, but training programs do not yet include social analysis of projects.

The demand for social scientists has been mainly limited to employment in universities. Within the Ministry of Interior, an agency for indigenous Indian affairs (FUNAI) employed anthropologists until the military takeover in 1964. Anthropologists gradually left FUNAI; they resigned in 1970 after basic disputes with military leaders; but they are now returning after the restoration of civilian government. A few social scientists have worked in official agencies dealing with health, education and culture; but none have found places in the numerous private voluntary organizations. A very few Brazilian anthropologists have worked as consultants for the World Bank and for AID; and none have worked for the other international development organizations.

In the late 1980s the Brazilian government required a report of impacts on the environment of all proposed government projects. Such requirements normally take several years to become fully enforced. The stakes for exploitation (and degradation) of the environment by both the rich and poor are so high and so pervasive that enforcement of this requirement is as uncertain as it is essential to sustainable future development. The current rate of destruction of Amazon tropical rain forests is beyond imagination (discussed in the concluding chapter). Settlers burned some eight million hectares of rain forests in 1987, about the size of Austria, and probably more in 1988 (Brown 1989:4).

It is also uncertain if the new government impact report will include the social environment. Amazonian Indians have recently complained that they were the first environmentalists, and that Brazilian and North American environmental groups have ignored them as a vital part of their own environment.

This new government requirement offers an opportunity, but not yet an assurance, that human impacts might be assessed in the future. The issue is of fundamental importance in that enormous country. Brazil has some 27 large hydroelectric projects under construction or projected, displacing perhaps as many as 500,000 people. By 2010 Brazil is considering some 80 hydroelectric and other large projects. This mega program would vastly increase electricity and other resources for the cities, at the cost of displacing a very large portion of the indigenous, marginalized, impoverished Indians from the only livelihood they know.

Political constraints to impartial SIA are still severe although less rigid than under the military government. The military perspective was, and remains, that border areas are particularly sensitive and must be defended with air strips and occupation by Brazilians for "national security." These border areas contain most of the potential dam sites and most of the forest-dwelling Indians. Study of Indians requires FUNAI permission, not always granted. Military officers regard anthropologists and missionaries as threatening to their control in the border areas. Here too, SIA occurs in a politicized environment (Ramagem, 1989).

The picture in the Philippines exhibits several parallels with that of Brazil: (1) poverty, extreme population pressures, and official corruption have resulted in catastrophic destruction of tropical forests; (2) the supply of competent social analysts well exceeds the demand for their services; (3) the recent end of the Marcos regime (like that of the Brazilian military regime) has modestly increased official interest in social analysis and in the willingness of social analysts to participate.

On the supply side, the University of the Philippines, both in Manila and on Mindanao, and also the Ateneo de Manila, have granted M.A. and Ph.D. degrees for the last ten years or more. Their training has included work in development projects. They have done both basic and project-related research, for example de los Reyes in communal irrigation (1980) and in agrarian reform (1989).

On the demand side, despite the ample supply of competent professionals in universities, research institutes, and consulting firms, the government has not made regular use of social analysts. International development agencies have tended to bring in their own social analysts for project work. These agencies and the government have continued, by default rather than by intent, a colonial practice of favoring outside analysts.

The Aquino government has recently established a regular environmental impact statement. It has only begun to be implemented, after decades of denuding the forested hills and silting the river basins. In 1900 the estimated forest cover was about 70% of the country; American colonial agriculture and rising population pressure greatly reduced the forest cover; the "cronies" of the Marcos regime accelerated this destructive process to a tragic level; and a recent projection was for "forest extinction" by 2000 (Anderson 1987:250). It is not yet clear here, as in Brazil, whether or not the new environmental standard will include analysis of the social environment (Guerrero-Abellera, 1989).

Governmental political constraints are diminished since Marcos's fall, but continuing poverty, landless people, and insurgency cast a shadow on rural development planning and action. Insurgents, struggling to remain the champions of rural poor people, do not welcome social analysts in areas under their control. "Marcos left the country looted, indebted, divided, and the government dismantled" (Anderson 1987:263). The Aquino government's emergency priorities are too strenuous to permit adequate focus on the implications of future development projects for the natural and social environment.

These three brief examples—Africa, Brazil, and the Philippines— suggest a common dilemma. The very conditions of poverty and fragile natural environments, which make impact assessment so essential, also make it politically very difficult to conduct and manage. Social analysts in poor countries, like those in the rich countries, must join in the effort to educate official and public opinion on the practical advantages of doing SIA and making use of the results.

References

Anderson, James, N. "Lands at Risk, People at Risk: Perspectives on Tropical Forest Transformations in the Philippines." In *Lands at Risk in the Third World: Local Level Perspectives.* Edited by Peter D. Little and Michael M. Horowitz. Boulder. Colo. and London: Westview Press, 1987.

Baum, Warren C. and Tolbert, Stokes M. *Investing in Development: Lessons of World Bank Experience.* New York: Oxford University Press, 1985.

Berger, Peter L. *Pyramids of Sacrifice: Political Ethics and Social Change.* New York: Basic Books, Inc., 1974.

Bowles, Roy. *Social Impact Assessment in Small Communities.* Scarborough, Ontario: Butterworths, 1981.

Branch, Kristi; Hooper, Douglas A.; Thompson, James; and Creighton, James. *Guide to Social Impact Assessment.* Boulder, Colo. and London: Westview Press, 1984.

Brown, Lester R. et al. *The State of the World, 1989.* New York and London: W. W. Norton & Company, 1989.

Canter, Larry W.; Athinson, Samuel F.; and Leistritz, F. Larry. *Impact of Growth: A Guide for Socio-Economic Impact Assessment and Planning.* Chelsea, Michigan: Lewis Publisher, 1985.

Cernea, Michael (ed.). *Putting People First: Sociological Variables in Rural Development.* New York: Oxford University Press, 1985.

Cook, Cynthia. Personal communication regarding social analysis of projects in several countries, 1989.

de los Reyes, Romana. *Managing Communal Gravity Systems.* Quezon City: Institute of Philippine Culture, Ateneo de Manila University, 1980.

——— . *Claims to Land: Lessons from Haciendas in Negros Occidental,* Quezon City: Institute of Philippine Culture, Ateneo de Manila University, 1989.

Derman, William, and Whiteford, Scott (eds.). *Social Impact Analysis and Development Planning in the Third World.* Boulder, Colo. and London: Westview Press, 1985.

Finsterbusch, Kurt, and Wolf, C. P. (eds.). *Methodology of Social Impact Assessment.* Stroudsburg, Pa.: Dowden, Hutchinson and Ross, 1977.

Finsterbusch, Kurt; Llewellyn, Lynn G.; and Wolf, C. P. (eds.). *Social Impact Assessment Methods.* Beverly Hills, Calif.: Sage, 1984.

Guerrero-Abellera, Victoria. Personal communication regarding social analysis in the Philippines, 1989.

Goulet, Dennis. *The Uncertain Promise: Value Conflicts in Technology Transfer.* Washington, D.C.: Overseas Development Council, 1977.

Green, Edward C. *Practicing Development Anthropology.* Boulder, Colo. and London: Westview Press, 1986.

Halpern, Joel, and Halpern, Barbara. Personal communication regarding ecological awareness in Bulgaria, 1989.

Hyman, Eric L., and Stiftel, Bruce with Moreau, David H., and Nichols, Robert C. *Combining Facts and Values in Environmental Impact Assessment: Theories and Techniques.* Boulder, Colo. and London: Westview Press, 1986.

Kapp, William. *The Social Costs of Private Enterprise.* New York: Schocken Books, 1971.

Kottak, Conrad Phillip. "When People Don't Come First: Some Sociological Lessons from Completed Projects." In *Putting People First: Sociological Variables in Rural Development.* Edited by Michael M. Cernea. New York: Oxford University Press, 1985.

Little, Peter D., and Horowitz, Michael M. (eds.). *Lands at Risk in the Third World: Local Level Perspectives.* Boulder, Colo. and London: Westview Press, 1987.

Merton, Robert. "Foreword" in Jacques Ellul, *The Technological Society.* New York: Alfred Knopf, 1964.

Millsap, William (ed.). *Applied Social Science for Environmental Planning.* Boulder, Colo. and London: Westview Press, 1984.

Palinkas, Lawrence A.; Harris, Bruce Murray; and Peterson, John S. *A System Approach to Social Impact Assessment: Two Alaskan Case Studies.* Boulder, Colo. and London: Westview Press, 1985.

Partridge, William L. (ed.). *Training Manual in Development Anthropology.* Washington, D.C.: American Anthropological Association, 1984.

Preister, Kevin. "Issue-Centered Social Impact Assessment." In *Praxis: Translating Knowledge into Action,* edited by Robert M. Wulff and Shirley J. Fiske. Boulder Colo. and London: Westview Press, 1987.

Ramagem, Sonia Bloomfield. Personal communication regarding social analysis in Brazil, 1989.

Rossini, Fredrick A., and Porter, Alan L. (eds.). *Integrated Impact Assessment.* Boulder, Colo. and London: Westview Press, 1983.

Salmen, Lawrence F. *Listen to the People: Participant-Observer Evaluation of Development Projects.* New York: Oxford University Press, 1987.

Tester, Frank J. "Social Impact Assessment: Coping with the Context of our Times." In C. P. Wolf (ed.), *Social Impact Assessment Newsletter 53/54,* May-June, 1980.

World Bank. *Education in Sub-Saharan Africa: Policies for Adjustment, Revitalization, and Expansion,* 1988.

Wulff, Robert M. Personal communication regarding policy analysis, 1989.

Part 1

General Approaches

1
Social Analysis in AID and the World Bank

Jasper Ingersoll

This chapter emphasizes "what to ask"—the most significant social issues to be covered in SIA. Later chapters emphasize "how to do it"— the methods social analysts use in conducting SIA. "What" is prior to "how." The choice of methods must follow from the social issues raised by the project in relation to the project population. This chapter examines the guidelines of what to assess, as formulated by two development agencies. The great diversity of development projects makes it impossible to standardize completely the contents of SIAs, so these guidelines are suggestions rather than directives.

The fundamental SIA task of anticipating the human implications of proposed projects, however, is always the same. That task is (1) to identify the main features of the proposed project, (2) to identify the types and numbers of people who would be affected by those main project features (the project population), and (3) to identify the main impacts the project would have on the various segments of the project population. A project population usually includes various types of beneficiaries (who would benefit from the project), benefactors (who would pay for it), and victims (who would suffer from it).

During the 1950s and 1960s most international and bilateral development assistance to Third World countries was carried out *as if* development were essentially a process of increasing gross national product by transferring infrastructure to promote technological change. Prospective projects were routinely examined and designed exclusively for their technical and economic aspects. That conventional view of development assistance changed very substantially in the early 1970s, toward one of alleviating the poverty of the majority of the people in the poor countries. This new view of development focused more directly on poor people and on the many constraints to their escape from poverty.

It was in this new policy environment that social issues became part of regular project analysis. Two development assistance organizations led the way by formulating the social aspects of project analysis and design. In the early 1970s the U.S. Agency for International Development (AID) added environmental analysis to its older technical and economic analysis of proposed projects. In 1975 AID issued guidelines for social soundness analysis and also required that administrative or institutional analysis also be carried out for all prospective projects. In 1981 the World Bank issued guidelines for the social aspects of project appraisal as part of its routine analysis of the various aspects of a proposed project. Both the AID and Bank guidelines were presented in the form of topics or themes for investigation. I have restated them here in the form of *questions* to be posed, in order to make them clearer and more concise.

The AID guidelines suggest an analytical and planning strategy for assessing: (1) compatibility between the way of life of the people concerned and the project, and looking for ways to improve the mutual fit; (2) prospects for wider and longer diffusion of project results beyond the initial intended beneficiaries; and (3) potential contributions of project results to alleviation of poverty and to wider social equity.

I have made five modest changes in the AID guidelines, to make them more useful for social analysis, without changing their substance. (1) Project "victims" and "benefactors" are added to "beneficiaries," to make clear that the people involved may be quite heterogeneous and diversely affected by the project. (2) Emphasis here is shifted from a rather static "compatibility" between project and people to a more dynamic "mutual adaptability" between people and project, implying mutual adaptations by both sides in the course of project implementation. (3) The temporal idea of durability of project results in the future is added to the spatial and social issues of spread effects. (4) The idea of equity is made more explicit in the third section on social impacts. (5) A question is added to each of the three main aspects of social soundness regarding how improved project design might improve that aspect.

AID Guidelines for Social Soundness Analysis

Sociocultural Compatibility

- Who are the intended *beneficiaries* of the proposed project? Who are the possible *victims* (who might suffer)? Who are the possible *benefactors* (who might pay)?

- In what ways are the main features of these peoples' lives and the main features of the proposed project *mutually adaptable?* In what ways are they *not?*
- What could be done to enhance mutual adaptability?

Suggested Inquiries for Analysis of Sociocultural Compatibility

- *Who lives where?* Location and numbers of affected groups.
- *How are they organized?* What sort of social and power relationships do they have? Should development be promoted through existing or newly created organizations?
- *How do they allocate their time?* How do people in different roles spend their time among their tasks (e.g., how much time on subsistence and how much on commercial tasks)? How are they occupied at different times during the year? How does their allocation of their time influence their incentives?
- *What are the characteristics of participators?* What are the requirements or requisites for people to participate in the project (e.g., minimum resources, education, skills, attitudes, exposure to innovation, sustained exposure . . .)? What are the levels above which people are not likely to participate (not inclined or not eligible)?
- *Who are the most likely stakeholders?* Combining information from the four items above, who are the most likely participants: victims, beneficiaries, and benefactors? How would these groups be affected?
- *What social obstacles or opposition may arise?* What types of people may oppose the project? What types of non-participants might oppose or disapprove of the project? What social gaps exist between project personnel and beneficiaries?
- *What are the people's motivations?* What are their reasons for participating in the proposed project? How much similarity and difference exist in the motivations (and definitions of interests) by the intended beneficiaries and various government officials? How compatible are the motivations of the people with the development goals of the project as we see it? As they see it?
- *What sort of communication strategy should be used?* What information should be communicated to potential beneficiaries in the initial and the wider populations? How early should this effort begin? How should information be communicated to diverse people across social cultural gaps so that they can understand the intents of the project and its potential advantage for them?

Spread Effects: Diffusion of Innovation

- How likely are the proposed project results to diffuse beyond the initial intended beneficiaries without further project inputs? With additional inputs?
- How durable are the proposed project results likely to be among the initial intended beneficiaries? Among later, wider populations?
- What might be done in the initial project to enhance spread and durability of its results?

Suggested Inquiries for Analysis of Spread Effects

- *What are the patterns of leadership and authority?* Who are the leaders (modern or traditional) or opinion shapers in the wider area, whose cooperation may be vital to project diffusion? Can indigenous leaders be influential in project diffusion? How can such leaders be supported in this process?
- *What are the patterns of mobility and migration?* What is the area of mobility within which people live, work, worship, trade, and visit within the year? What sort of seasonal movements, mobility, or migration do they have? What is the area of mobility of officials, and their range of contacts with people? What is the geographical area (horizontal) and the social area (vertical) within which people receive information? Thus, what are the areas within which people get information, learn and adopt innovations?
- *What about previous projects in the region?* What influence might previous or other projects in the area have on diffusion of this project (roads, schools, institutions . . .)?
- *How long does information dissemination require?* What information has to spread? Knowledge, techniques, methods, skills, attitudes, values, behavior patterns, products . . . ? How long is it likely to take people in the area of spread to acquire and absorb the information and learning necessary? How long is it likely to take the desired spread effects to move enough to have a reasonable chance of continuing? Can any spread effects be anticipated, or encouraged, without new project inputs?

Social Impact: Equity

- How would the main benefits and burdens of the project be distributed among the types and strata of people affected (e.g., rich and poor, farmers and landless . . .)?
- How could the project benefits be distributed more effectively among the poorer people in the intended beneficiary population?

- What might be done to lessen the burdens on project victims or benefactors, especially poor people?

Suggested Inquiries for Analysis of Equity

- *How unequally is access to resources and opportunities distributed?* How unequally is access to land, capital, credit, education, information, markets, etc. distributed? Would the project broaden or narrow this access, especially of the poorest people?
- *How unequally are employment opportunities distributed?* Would the project increase or reduce the inequality of employment opportunities? How much employment would the project generate? For whom? Would the project involve labor-using or labor-replacing practices?
- *Whom would the project displace or uproot?* Would the project remove any groups from the land, or displace any groups from their current livelihood? Where would they go? What would they do?
- *How might the project affect people's power positions and participation?* Would the project change the *relative* capacity of intended beneficiaries to influence public policy?

These AID guidelines for social analysis were used mainly at the final stage of design, but many social analysts complained that social analysis should be part of project study and design from the beginning. It did occur in some projects, and in the early 1980s AID issued brief guidelines for social analysis at the project identification phase. They required brief descriptions of: (1) the general sociocultural context of the project and people; (2) the beneficiaries who would be affected; (3) their potential participation during project planning and implementation; (4) the sociocultural feasibility of the project; and (5) the anticipated social impacts of the project.

World Bank Guidelines for Social Analysis

The five major components of World Bank guidelines for social analysis also comprise a general strategy for fitting projects into peoples' ways of life and for adapting peoples' ways of life to projects: (1) identifying the general sociocultural and demographic character of the people concerned (the "project population"); (2) characterizing the social organization of their productive activities; (3) assessing the cultural acceptability of the proposed project to them; (4) devising a social strategy to improve that acceptability; and (5) considering any special or vulnerable populations. A summary and adaptation of the guidelines follow.

Sociocultural and Demographic Character of the Project Population

The initial task is to identify major characteristics of the people who would be affected by the proposed project, starting with those characteristics directly related to the project. The best way to begin is to examine the project design as it relates to the people's lives:

1. What are the particular problems of poverty and development which the project is designed to help solve?
2. What are the basic goals and assumptions of the project regarding the project population?
3. What are the primary intended project outcomes (outputs)?
4. Who are the main types of people who would be affected by each project outcome, as beneficiaries, benefactors, victims, and project staff?

Answers to the four questions above are crucial but easily overlooked. Indeed, many project designs ignore the initial questions to be solved and move too quickly to proposed techniques for solutions. A national rural development project in Thailand avoided this design gap by carefully examining the nature of rural poverty and then formulating a system of bottom-up planning in which people would identify local poverty problems and plan local solutions, and a system of top-down, integrated responses by government to these local plans. In social analysis the focus is on "the project population" rather than "the people in the project area" because some projects (irrigation) affect only certain types of people in their areas, and some projects (education) do not affect people within distinguishable geographic areas. A *project population* would comprise the people, wherever they live, variously affected by a project. A project population would include:

1. *beneficiaries,* who would gain, from the project outcomes;
2. *benefactors,* who would have to pay some of the project costs in taxes, fees, charges and the like;
3. *victims,* who would suffer harm, losses, or dislocation.

The most effective way to identify a project population is to begin with the project design, describe the primary project outcomes, and carefully identify the types of people who would be affected by each of the expected outcomes. Only then would one assess their total numbers. For example, a comprehensive river-basin project might include the following primary outcomes: *hydroelectricity*—affecting people in cities or towns large enough to provide economic markets (and those in subsidized village markets); *water impoundment*—flooding out those below the water line, providing fishing to those able to take it up, new water transport to those living up-stream, water sports to those (mainly townspeople) able to afford it, and water access to the hills and forests of the upper watershed to those able to take advantage of it; *irrigated agriculture*—providing greater water control (against floods and droughts) to those with land in the command area or with funds to pump water outside it; perhaps *year-round river transportation* to those (especially boat owners) living downstream; and perhaps *long-term risks* of reservoir silting, aquatic weeds, and river-borne diseases to those living in the command area and flood plain downstream. When appropriate, the primary outcomes of project *construction*—and their respective populations—should be covered in the same way that project *operations* were treated in the above example. Even in small, simple projects, it is essential to identify the types of people to be affected. In a project in Cameroon to improve communal wells, social analysis revealed the need for more discriminating planning: some of the wells chosen for upgrading were private and would benefit only family owners, rather than entire communities, as intended.

Sociocultural Characteristics of the Population. The following are the characteristics to be identified:

1. Main occupations
2. Socio-economic status
3. Ethnic, tribal, regional, religious identities
4. Urban-rural distribution
5. Patterns of social mobility
6. Experience with previous development projects
7. Current reactions to potential project outcomes

Given their central preoccupation with the project, project designers often ignore the historical experience of the project population with previous development projects. This shallow focus reduces the chances of project success by failing to consider people's current positive and negative incentives for participating in a new project, as well as the ways in which it could be related to other current development projects affecting the same people.

Demographic Characteristics of the Population. Demographic characteristics to be identified are as follows:

1. Size of communities—average and range of sizes
2. Estimated number of people by each major type of project outcome
3. Density of people in their settlements
4. Age distribution
5. Sex distribution
6. Population growth trends
7. Migration trends
8. Education level

The numbers of each type of people in the project population should be aggregated as appropriate for the social implications of the project. For example, the total numbers of project beneficiaries, benefactors, and victims should be ascertained. If project victims tend to be of one age, sex, or ethnic group, this point should be made clear. These total figures, depending on the type of project, will be essential for computing project costs and benefits.

For major projects, involving heavy investment and extensive project studies, general or sample survey studies of the types of project population may be necessary—for economic as well as social planning and appraisal. For smaller projects with lower budgets, however, demographic analyses and estimates may have to be based on available census and other government statistics. These sources can provide useful estimates and comparative orders of magnitude, especially after project analysts have made allowances for known biases or errors (such as farmers' fear of reporting income or surveyors' reluctance to cover remote villages or households). Census data or government statistics are less useful, however, for projects located in particular ecosystems, such as river basins, uplands, or coasts. These natural areas usually do not correspond with government boundaries, within which government statistics are organized. Even small river basins may occupy parts of several districts in two or three provinces, making use of government statistics very difficult for project planning and appraisal. Such projects, even when not very large, may require more extensive demographic project studies.

A demographic profile should provide a working understanding of the major types of people in the project populations and their numbers. The most useful guidance for project implementation, however, is not so much quantitative precision (which can be very expensive) as a clear picture of how things are working for a given population and how project investments might improve the situation. It is essential to have reasonable estimates of the number of people involved but even more important to have good descriptions of foreseeable project impacts on different groups of the project population.

Social Organization of Productive Activities

The following are the main questions to be asked:

1. What are the most important local institutions in which people carry out the production and distribution of their goods and services (house-holds, family groups, mutual help groups, farmers' associations, coops, markets, water and land tenure patterns, plantations, local and outside employers . . .)? a. How do people work individually and collectively in their local institutions in carrying out productive activities? b. How do these institutions serve as practical resources for, and constraints to, people's capacity for development (particularly in kinship relations, division of labor by sex, and control over, or access to, land and other productive resources)? c. How do these local institutions relate to higher-level counterparts in the larger society? How do these hierarchical relationships affect the adequacy of local institutions to support development?
2. Do small producers or poorer residents have reasonable access to, or information about, wider markets and regional economic opportunities? Putting it differently, is the outreach capacity of the concerned government agencies adequate for the proposed project activities?
3. Is access to credit or indebtedness a significant constraint to the people's capacity for development?
4. What alternatives do households have among wage income, cash crops, sale of agricultural surplus, and subsistence activities? Do off-farm income opportunities exist for rural households, and who benefits from these opportunities?
5. How do local people think about their current production choices, costs, and risks compared to those associated with the project?

This section is designed to give a working description of the project population's way of organizing and carrying out its productive activities. The point in this section is to select those institutional relations and values that bear directly on organized productive activities, in order to assess the existing social setting in which the people make their living.

Cultural Acceptability of the Project

The next task is to determine the mutual fit, or lack of it, between the people's current life and the project design. The main questions are:

1. Can the main features of the project design and of the people's way of life be adapted to each other?
2. Can the people see project outcomes as rewards to them in their own terms, giving them real incentives to organize themselves and learn new practices in order to take advantage of the perceived benefits?
3. Do the people understand the project and agree with it? What training, information program, or changes in the project design would improve such understanding and agreement?
4. What changes in behavior or practices of the people are implied in the project design? What incentives would the people have to make such changes. Can the project provide needed incentives?
5. What gaps or discrepancies remain between project means and ends and the people's practices, resources, values, and felt needs? What would be required to narrow or remove these discrepancies?

The significant point here is that both projects and people's way of life are dynamic and tend to adapt to changing external and internal conditions. Projects and people both change in response to each other during implementation in really successful cases. Thus, a project is "culturally acceptable" if it is well-enough suited to people's conditions that they can see the advantages of adapting their lives to the project, modifying some of their practices to attain new benefits. A technical education project in Indonesia, for example, achieved enough improvement in training and employability of students to raise the prestige of technical education in the minds of parents who had previously favored professional education for their children. The project acquired enough cultural acceptability to influence a cultural change among the people. The purpose of this section is to fit the project design with the cultural characteristics of the people. The task here is to examine the mutual adaptability between them, in order to plan the strategy of the project, as described in the next section.

Social Strategy of the Project

Building on the foundations of cultural acceptability, a project may be judged socially sound if it contains specific strategies to manage project resources in ways which would: (1) encourage the commitment and active participation of the people; (2) maximize the equitable distribution of project benefits and burdens among the project population; (3) ensure the diffusion and durability of project benefits; and (4) anticipate the significant longer term impacts—direct and indirect as well as positive and adverse. The following points should be considered in assessing the strategy of a proposed project.

Commitment and Participation. Several questions can be asked to determine the extent of commitment.

1. In what ways would the project strengthen the commitment and participation of the project population?
2. In what ways were they involved in project identification?
3. In what ways are they to be involved in project implementation, monitoring, and evaluation; such as deciding project goals and methods, carrying out project activities, and acquiring project benefits?
4. What types of training or assistance would they need to participate effectively?
5. How and how well do they currently understand and appreciate the proposed project? a. Do they want it enough to work at it, to invest in it? (knowledge, resources, labor, time . . .) b. Can they turn intended project benefits into their own incentives and rewards? c. In what specific ways would the project help them improve their own abilities to support themselves or to sustain some aspect of their well-being?
6. Does the project design encourage mutual learning and adjustment by the people along with the project staff?

Despite the very wide agreement on the need for popular participation in development projects if they are to succeed, most projects are still not planned from the beginning with a strong participatory approach. The appraisal stage is too late to begin this approach; it should begin in the identification stage, as an active collaboration between project officials and the local people. Many governments have been unwilling to adopt a full participatory approach, fearing that local organizations or leaders could become too strong, or that they could be exploited by political dissidents (Ingersoll and Ingersoll, 1985:481). The resulting widespread paternalistic approach only ensures a continuing dependent, rather than self-reliant, response from people; they continue to expect government initiatives and resources rather than rely on their own (Uphoff, 1985:387).

Equity. The following questions are useful in assessing equity issues.

1. In what ways would the project encourage the equitable distribution of project benefits and costs among the project population?
2. If people's productive capacities are currently inhibited by inequality or exploitation, how would the project particularly help disadvantaged people (such as landless, women, minorities . . .) to participate? a. What local circumstances currently impede women or disadvantaged minorities? b. What project design changes would such people find particularly beneficial, and particularly adverse? c. What special contributions could such people make to the achievement of project objectives? d. How could project monitoring help with these issues?
3. What forms of help or compensation would the project provide for project victims to mitigate their losses?
4. What means would the project use to ensure the widest distribution of project outputs among beneficiaries?

A socially well-conceived project would include specific strategies and incentives to encourage participation of disadvantaged people and to avoid excluding them. The project should plan for their physical and financial *access* to project resources and for their continued *use* of such resources (Perrett and Lethem, 1980:2).

Diffusion and Sustainability. A checklist for ensuring diffusion might include the following points.

1. In what ways would the project ensure the diffusion and durability of project benefits?
2. What important changes would have to be made by the beneficiaries—such as productive practices, control over resources, operation of their institutions, relations with the larger society—in order to achieve the intended project benefits? a. What project resources and mechanisms can be used to support these changes and to sustain them later? b. Does the project have realistic plans and means to reach all the beneficiaries, initially or in phases? c. Are project (or other) information services for the beneficiaries adequate to support their continued learning and change?
3. Does a wider group of potential beneficiaries exist who might be reached at a later stage?
4. Does the project design take advantage of, and build on, development projects or programs which address similar development problems or relate to comparable project populations?
5. When the project ends would the beneficiaries be able to act so as to continue to receive benefits and achieve project goals?

Long-term Effects. Three questions will serve to evaluate long-term impact.

1. What are the likely long-term project impacts—direct and indirect as well as positive and adverse?
2. Do any features of the project (hazards, risks, uncertainties, or unknowns) make it seem less socially feasible?
3. Does the project budget or the project authority include adequate resources to handle anticipated social costs?

Project effects flow through local, regional, and national systems which are formed by various combinations of natural, technological, economic, political, and sociocultural forces. Project impacts, therefore, are not simple cause-and-effect events. The social strategy, therefore, should include at least the three following steps. One, project designers should take advantage of experience gathered from previous, similar projects. Two, given that development projects must contend with the forces of the status quo, project designers should take appropriate precautions against project benefits being diverted sooner or later from poorer, less well organized beneficiaries. Third, given the complex systems in which people live and projects operate, designers should build on these two previous steps and try to make provision for the necessary resources and actions to avoid or reduce risks and social costs likely to arise as indirect project impacts. Planners of a cattle project in Indonesia ignored all of these points. Failing to inquire into the annual round of farming activities, the planners sought to raise local incomes by introducing 2,500 cattle in hills which they assumed to be unoccupied. But farmers had long grazed their cattle (about 5,000) in these 'unoccupied' hills during the rice growing season and on the plains during the rest of the year. The project was a loss to both farmers and the government.

Special or Sensitive Project Populations

Development programs have been reaching out to more isolated populations, including tribal minority groups in mountains and in jungles, affecting some of them directly and others indirectly. Infrastructure projects have also impinged on other marginal groups, forcing them to move out of the path of a reservoir, highway, mine, oil field, and the like. Project design and appraisal affecting such people include many of the points discussed above, but also require additional points for these special, sensitive human groups.

Tribal Minority Groups. Given the special circumstances of tribal people, usually marginal to the main stream of society, project designs impinging on them usually need particularly intensive pre-preparation study of local social conditions. Appraisal must then review the adequacy of arrangements to preserve tribal interests in the development process, including such issues as the following:

1. Does the design have provisions to recognize, delimit, and protect tribal areas containing the resources they need to sustain the traditional means of livelihood?
2. Would social services, appropriate to the current (and continuing) level of tribal acculturation, be available—especially protection against diseases (including new ones) and health maintenance?
3. Have provisions been made, acceptable to the people, for maintaining tribal cultural integrity, including any of its physical embodiments?
4. Would a forum be established in which tribal people could participate in decisions affecting them, handle legal questions, and redress grievances?
5. Since acculturation changes are gradual and may take longer than Bank participation in the project, has agreement been reached that the above commitment would be continued beyond the time of Bank participation?

Involuntary Settlement. Among the issues for appraising projects involving forced resettlement are the following:

1. Does the resettlement plan include adequate compensation for their losses, relocation services, establishment in the new settlement and integration with existing host communities?
2. Would the resettlers be able to regain a standard of living comparable to their previous one?
3. Would their skills be readily usable in the new area(s)?
4. Would their access to land, markets, employment, and needed services be adequate?
5. Has adequate preparatory work been done with both resettlers and the new host communities?
6. Has preparation involved active support for, and use of, resettlers' own institutions as a basis for encouraging their own initiative and self-help efforts?
7. Do resettlers have alternatives for rebuilding their lives that offer incentives for using their own efforts?

Summary

In sum, these AID and World Bank guidelines suggest alternative approaches to analyzing the social impacts of development projects and to improving their social compatibility at all phases: identification, design, assessment, and implementation. These guidelines are broad enough to cover the range of social issues that might emerge in any project. The value of such wide-ranging frameworks is that they provide social analysts opportunities to be selective in adapting them to assessment of individual projects. By extension, social analysts can simplify either of these guidelines and adapt them to very modest, low-cost development projects.

It is of special significance that both sets of guidelines—despite the 'establishment' nature of AID and the World Bank—suggest questions which could raise critical political issues of injustice or exploitation by local elites or by government. These issues are of crucial importance to realistic human prospects for proposed projects. Drawing on these guidelines, social analysts in all countries can conduct SIA that would probe well beneath the surface of most official, technocratic, centralized project planning.

Such probing assessments may appear threatening or destructive to defensive official planning agencies, but ignoring social problems does not solve them:

> Not only does a failure to consider the social and cultural context of a project invite inappropriate design at best (and user hostility at worst), but . . . it usually leads to projects that are ultimately ineffective, wanted neither by their supposed beneficiaries nor by the investing public agencies (Cernea, 1985:323).

Experience has shown that critical analysis of social implications of projects—even if sometimes initially embarrassing—pays off in the long run. Kottak examined sixty-eight ex post evaluations of World Bank funded projects. He found that thirty-six projects deemed socioculturally compatible with the project population had an economic rate of return (economic profitability) more than *twice as high* as thirty-two projects found deficient in sociocultural compatibility (Kottak, 1985:350). Projects that are socially sound are usually economically profitable.

Finally, development projects are vertical links between national and local interests. On the one hand, governments pursue very general policies: higher employment, national growth, industrialization, food self-sufficiency, better health care, national security, and the like. On the other hand, people in their own communities struggle to survive, make use of local opportunities, live within local material and power constraints, seek some enjoyment in life, and even hope for a little improvement in the future. Development projects are investments in the future, poised uneasily between these very different national and local levels. Governments pursue their broad national goals on the very fragmented foundation of individual, diverse, often uncoordinated projects. Successful development projects are thus limited links between government policies and investments and people's local interests, needs, and resources.

The wider task of social analysis of projects is thus building bridges between bottom-up initiative and investment by local people and top-down organization and investment by governments (Uphoff, 1985:389). The two processes of investment are somewhat contradictory in intent and often unconnected in operation, but they meet and merge in successful development programs. In the case of communal irrigation in the Philippines, for example, social analysis and planning built firm bridges between people's lives, project design, and government policy (Bagadion and Korten, 1985). In such cases social analysis can make its essential contribution, as Mabub ul Haq has eloquently stated, to "building development around people rather than people around development" (Seligson, 1984:12).

References

Bagadion, Benjamin U. and Korten, Frances F. "Developing Irrigators' Organizations: a Learning Process Approach." In *Putting People First: Sociological Variables in Rural Development.* Edited by Michael M. Cernea. New York: Oxford University Press, 1985.

Cernea, Michael M. (ed.). *Putting People First: Sociological Variables in Rural Devleopment.* New York: Oxford University Press, 1985.

Cook, Cynthia. "Social Analysis in Rural Road Projects." In *Putting People First: Sociological Variables in Rural Development.* Edited by Michael M. Cernea. New York: Oxford University Press, 1985.

Kottak, Conrad Phillip. "When People Don't Come First: Some Sociological Lessons from Completed Projects." In *Putting People First: Sociological Variables in Rural Development.* Edited by Michael M. Cernea. New York: Oxford University Press, 1985.

Ingersoll, Jasper and Ingersoll, Fern. "Social Analysis." In *Investing in Development: Lessons of World Bank Experience.* Edited by Warren C. Baum and Stokes M. Tolbert. New York, Oxford University Press, 1985.

Perrett, Heli and Lethem, Francis J. *Human Factors in Project Work: Staff Working Paper No. 397.* Washington, D.C.: World Bank, 1980.

Seligson, Mitchell. *The Gap Between Rich and Poor: Contending Perspectives on the Political Economy of Development.* Boulder, Colo. and London: Westview Press, 1984.

Uphoff, Norman. "Fitting Projects to People." In *Putting People First: Sociological Variables in Rural Development.* Edited by Michael M. Cernea. New York: Oxford University Press. 1985.

2
A New Zealand
Issues-Oriented Approach
to Social Impact Assessment

C. Nicholas Taylor and C. Hobson Bryan

Introduction

This chapter contains a description of an issues-oriented approach to social impact assessment (SIA) developed in New Zealand. The emphasis is on a process for managing social change from the inception of a policy or project through the main periods of change. The approach has evolved through its application in the planning and construction of major energy projects, management of plant closures, implementation of large administrative re-structuring of government agencies with associated unemployment, and a variety of rural projects including irrigation schemes, horticultural development, and land development.

The first section provides an overview of the New Zealand experience with SIA and some of the procedural and methodological questions that have emerged, especially during the "think big" era of resource development. We provide a summary of the common problems that have been faced and suggest solutions in the form of an issues-oriented approach. Included are details of the approach, description of some of the specific methods, and general conclusions.

Origins of a New Zealand Issues-Oriented Approach

The Development Context

To understand the origins of a New Zealand approach to SIA this small island country in the South Pacific of just over 3 million people must be placed into its context in the world economy. In the past 20 years, New Zealand has faced great social change. Although the society is now highly urbanized, primary production remains vital. The trend has been change from a neo-colonial economy supplying staples to a guaranteed market, to a more complex position, but one still very dependent internationally. Its economy is characterized by a reliance on external capital, technology, and expertise; high overseas debt and inflation; continuing dependence on the export of primary produce; and problems with trade deficits.

Planners and politicians in the 1970s saw energy self-sufficiency as the path to national economic development. Construction of several major oil and gas, coal, and hydro-electric projects resulted. Pastoral farming remains important, but the rural economy is being rapidly restructured with increased corporate investment. Family farms in rural communities are struggling to remain viable. There is some diversification into new land and resource uses such as horticulture and tourism. Sectors of the population in peripheral regions suffer from social and economic underdevelopment. This is especially the case for a large portion of the indigenous Maori population in both urban and rural locations.

New Zealand has a strong historical tradition of environmentalism and social planning. Formal environmental procedures were initiated in 1973. No legislative basis existed for these procedures, however, despite the parallels to the establishment of environmental legislation in the United States (Gilbert, 1986). In addition to the procedures, legislation for local government and town and country planning has provided a formal institutional basis for social planning. The Town and Country Planning Directorate of the Ministry of Works and Development was responsible for local, regional, and public work planning. In the late 1970s, it became the key agency for developing SIA. A social planning group in this agency was active in coordinating national effort to improve SIA policy and approaches in conjunction with the few government and university social scientists who showed an interest in SIA and related social research (Taylor and Bryan, 1987).

Original SIA work under the Environmental Procedures was very limited in scope. Elementary projections of social impacts were made in Environmental Impact Reports, usually around such readily quantifiable variables as work force or housing demands. Although the approach was basically technical in nature, some public participation occurred in the official audit procedures by the Commission for the Environment through submissions by interest groups and communities likely to experience impacts. These submissions were usually qualitative and narrative in form, but were important in identifying social issues otherwise neglected in the development process.

Considerable impetus for an increased and improved effort at SIA came from the "think big" strategy of energy-based industrialization in the late 1970s and early 1980s. The projects were based on a philosophy of direct state involvement in economic development to provide for greatly increased self sufficiency in energy. Officials took advantage of new "fast track" environmental legislation to speed up planning procedures and thwart opposition to the projects.

There was also an incentive for local and regional government to be involved in SIA, through Development Levy and Amenity Grant legislation. Under this legislation, developers were required to pay up to 0.5 percent of the capital cost of their project to local and regional government to assist with the mitigation and management of impacts. The guidelines for allocating funds were in some cases very narrowly defined. This proved to be very disadvantageous to some groups, such as Maori people (Lynn, 1987). Agencies and community groups responsible for provision of social services and welfare and community development had to have clear information on community needs to make a case for part of this funding. This requirement for practical information linked to social development was an important factor in shaping the emerging approach to SIA.

The Huntly Power Project

One major SIA research project stood out in the late 1970s, a study of the construction of a large thermal power station at Huntly, on the North Island's Waikato River. The Huntly Monitoring Project, as it was called, was largely academic in orientation, being based at nearby Waikato University—in spite of its primary funding by government agencies. The main research approach has been described as an "information sponge" method. In other words, as much data were collected as possible for analysis. The result was a study which included intensive data collection around 41 separate variables on such topics as demography, work force, social services and economy, etc. (Fookes, 1981). But confusion existed over the goals for collecting these data. Their use was described in the concluding reports as "a sequel to the monitoring process" (Fookes, 1981:1). In contrast, the original objectives were short-term management of social effects, application to planning and the provision of a basis for comparative research.

Although the monitoring data were reported publicly, including via a community forum, they were largely confined to reproduction in university reports and papers. The approach therefore did not emphasize public participation. And the community and agencies that were the object of the research were not directly involved in the ongoing collection and use of the data. Problems arose in gaining cooperation in the collection of data. The project was not useful to short-term management. It was also of limited use in its application to planning and comparative research.

The most serious flaw of the original SIA work on the Huntly project, especially the assessment for the EIA, was its limited assessment of impacts on the Maori people. As Lynn (1987) notes, the project was in the center of three Maori communities and on the culturally important Waikato River. There were considerable social, spiritual, and economic impacts on these communities. As these impacts unfolded, serious questions were raised about the Euro-centric orientation of planning and impact assessment.

Energy Projects in Taranaki and Northland

Despite the limitations of SIA work at Huntly, many lessons were learned (Krawetz, 1981) and applied to the large-scale energy-resource projects to follow elsewhere in New Zealand. In Taranaki, for example, government audits of the Environmental Impact Reports for the large natural gas projects, such as the synthetic petrol plant at Motunui, recommended ongoing monitoring of social effects. This resulted from public submissions and a preliminary identification of issues for monitoring (Landon, 1982). Consequently, a regional social needs committee was established, and the Regional Planning Authority began to monitor social impacts. Similarly, as construction began on the large oil refinery expansion at Marsden Point in Northland, social issues soon emerged as the construction work force moved in. A community group set up a social needs committee, and the Marsden Point Social Impact Monitoring work was initiated. These social needs groups were useful in identifying issues and also in setting priorities for mitigation in association with SIA work.

The two social monitoring projects in Northland and Taranaki were different from the Huntly project because they were able to operate within the emerging framework of regional planning; They each had an action component linking the projects' results to specific social development goals (e.g., minimizing disruption of the communities' infrastructures, enhancement of community services). Yet the styles of data gathering and the application of resulting knowledge were different for the respective projects. The Marsden Point project emphasized qualitative methods, issues identification, and networking in the community as integral to the process (McPherson, 1982–1984). In the Taranaki project investigators used the "information sponge" approach mentioned earlier, setting out to collect as much data as possible. Both approaches were much more participatory than at Huntly. "Social needs committees" were employed, as well as other community liaison techniques, to represent the perspectives of different stake holders such as developers, government agencies, unions, and other interest groups. The Marsden Point project was distinguished by its excellent use of timely, readable, and issues-oriented reports.

Maori Concerns

Perhaps the most significant new factor that arose during the major energy projects was the issue of Maori cultural concerns. These emerged for the Huntly project as noted above and then were reinforced by experiences at Taranaki and Northland (Lynn, 1987). The projects directly affected Maori cultural resources connected with waterways and coastlines through water abstraction and effluent disposal, as well as burial grounds and other sacred sites. The projects also affected local Maori groups as they participated in the construction work forces. It became apparent that the Maori people were not receiving fair compensation from litigation measures. For example, of $5 million paid in development levies for Northland only 4.5 percent went to Maori interests. Yet around 25 percent of the project work force and the regional population were Maori (Lynn, 1987:9).

These impacts emerged at a time when the Maori people were raising many concerns about their part in New Zealand society, including issues of land rights, language and customs, and social development. New legislation in 1975 regarding the original treaty of Waitangi (signed in 1840) allowed Maori to make claims to a Tribunal regarding impacts of development (Gilbert, 1986). Maori social researchers in the Waikato, recognizing their lack of involvement in the previous Huntly Monitoring Project were successful in obtaining direct funding for their own SIA work on future energy developments (Centre for Maori Studies and Research, 1984).

A distinct Maori perspective regards development which includes historical, cultural, and spiritual dimensions. The Maori have argued that their values should not be seen as a hindrance to development. But these values should be given prominence in development planning, including original decisions on resource policy and use, and with a clearly stated aim for advancing Maori social development. This approach was built on the experience of North American native people to raise critical questions relevant to all SIA work (as discussed by Nottingham, 1986). The thrust of this approach was a critical, political-economy perspective. Additionally, it became clear that data on Maori issues must be obtained without violating the Maori cultural context, with its emphasis on traditional customs of oratory, the use of narrative data and rights to knowledge. Otherwise, many of the Maori people would continue to be alienated from the social research process. The Maori case certainly illustrates that some cultural groups will require their own funding for SIA work, that there be flexibility in the interplay of research and social action.

Innovations Using Adaptive Assessment

Other innovative efforts at SIA were also developing around this time. These included participatory approaches to the early assessment of issues arising from large-scale lignite mining and liquefaction proposed in the South Island (Joint Centre for Environmental Sciences, 1982). The Joint Centre working on contract to the Liquid Fuels Trust Board (an agency responsible for long-term energy planning), utilized a modified system of adaptive environmental assessment (after Hollins, 1978).

Emphasis was placed initially in the assessment on developing a conceptual framework for an interdisciplinary team approach. A wide-ranging literature search was undertaken simultaneously with a series of field activities. The latter included networking, identification of interest groups, semi-structured interviewing, meetings with local communities and regional forums. Emphases were placed on participatory techniques and information exchange at an early stage of the work. The idea was to disseminate information generated by the initial conceptual and literature work to the study populations. In turn, public responses helped to identify and clarify issues for further research and eventually to refine and improve the framework. After this first phase of work, however, the Trust Board tended to revert to more standard methods of consultant research with limited information exchange with the study populations.

Philosophy of the New Issues-Oriented Approach

An ideal-type of SIA process began to emerge out of all these projects for managing the social change from large-scale developments having significant local and regional impacts. The process integrates social assessment, social planning and social development, and attempts to balance the needs for both research and action in SIA. The new approach also emphasizes public participation more than the traditional and centralized approaches.

The assessment, planning, development integration and public participation emphases are the result of reconciling several conflicting tendencies in the SIA process. Is the practice of SIA a research process or more a social action process where research may still play an important but secondary role? We suggest that there is a continual interplay among research, the projection of effects, people's reactions to the proposed effects, and subsequent social action. Can social futures be predicted, planned for, and controlled (largely with primary use of economic analysis) as part of a centralized orientation to social planning and management? We believe that the process has to be less "technocratic," that the process should involve participation by individuals and groups who have a right to help shape their own future in their own terms. The work of Forester (1980) on communication theory and "enabling" planning practices is of considerable interest in this regard (Goodrich and Taylor, 1985).

What has been particularly significant about the New Zealand experience with SIA in our view is that the most effective practitioners of SIA have been those who have moved away from established work environments to undertake their work—independent of the strictures of emphasis on technocratic, participatory, academic, or applied approaches (Taylor and Bryan, 1987). Emphasis shifted from "top-down" decision-making, centralized planning and management to allow for a "bottom-up" information and decision flow. For example, workers on the ground in monitoring and mitigating impacts of large construction projects were active in meeting with both low central government social planners and university researchers. Together they produced new policy and approaches (Conland, 1985) and worked to lobby for improved legislation, better funding for SIA, and agency reorganization.

The Issues-Oriented Approach

The new approach is an issues-oriented approach which provides an ongoing process of impact assessment and management. The focus is on the projection of impacts that might occur and the monitoring of impacts that do occur. The key phases are:

- Scoping—preliminary identification of issues and selection of social variables, impact areas and subareas, usually through networking and consultation strategies;
- Profiling—analysis of the current situation; development of a social overview, including historical trends; identification of key gaps in information;
- Formulation of alternatives—initial comparison and review of changes likely to arise from different sets of actions or proposals, including the status quo;
- Projection/estimation of effects—projection of likely changes arising from alternatives; determine scale, intensity and duration of effects; prepare contributions to formal environmental impact assessment;

- Monitoring, mitigation, and management of impacts—ongoing identification of actual changes caused by the project, implementation of strategies to reduce negative effects and maximize benefits;
- Evaluation of effects—ex post facto examination of effects of the project, including critical review of SIA work, establishment of data-bases for comparative purposes or use in later phases of SIA.

The issues-oriented approach can be used in making basic decisions on policy and options for resource use. The approach is also used for siting and design work and for managing processes of social change through different stages of the process. Thus:

1. The approach is anticipatory. The idea is to identify issues for development at an early stage so that conflict resolution can be attempted. Resolution may take place either within existing institutions or in new institutional arrangements if necessary.
2. The approach is adaptive and eclectic. It is flexible in terms of the analytical framework to be used and the concepts developed within it. The conceptual framework guides the SIA work. But the concepts used can be broadened, narrowed, or adapted according to issues arising from the study process or from changes in the proponent's scheme for change. Fieldwork should actually include both qualitative and quantitative methods in order to establish the validity of any issue.
3. The approach is interdisciplinary. It can be attempted by a practitioner with any disciplinary background, including a "layman." All issues are therefore assumed to be as social in nature as they are ecological or economic. In most cases the approach is best implemented by a study team, allowing individuals without strong social science backgrounds to take an active part. The team approach also enables concentrated work when there are severe time restrictions and allows a range of social-science techniques to be applied, from quantitative surveys to qualitative field interviews and observations.
4. The approach assumes that participation by affected community and interest groups is at least as important as either academic or technical input. Particular emphasis is placed on facilitating the flow of information among the participant groups.
5. The approach is responsive. At any stage of the study information can be disseminated for a particular need. The proponent may require information in order to modify the planned change. An interest group may require information to mitigate the effects of

change. A local authority may use information to establish new
public services necessary as a result of social change.
6. The approach is cost effective. By concentrating on issues and
conflicts likely to be costly to project or policy implementation,
unnecessary data gathering is avoided. At the same time, social
and economic costs are reduced over the life of the planned
change, and benefits are enhanced for both the developer or agent
of change and the affected groups.
7. The approach is relatively unbiased, as SIA practitioners assume
an independent role, as little tied to vested interests as possible.
An effective process for managing social change is advocated,
rather than the pursuit of particular sets of interests. This neu-
trality does not exclude, however, the possibility of affirmative
action regarding participation in the approach by disadvantaged
groups, as shown by the experience of Maori people in the
assessment process.

Important components of the approach are described in more detail
as follows.

Analytic Induction

A fit between concepts and data is achieved by using the process of
analytic induction (Bryan, 1985). This technique is not new to the
social sciences. But it has been largely overtaken by an emphasis on
deductive, hypothesis-testing approaches. Projections of social change
without guiding concepts are difficult, especially with reliance on frag-
mentary sources of data which may be secondary or qualitative in
nature. The analytic induction process allows the study team to establish
a conceptual framework and then continually revise it in the light of
data generated by the study. No single analytical tool or model is used
uncritically. The iterative process involved enables the study team to
focus on key issues, inconsistencies, and important gaps in their data.
At the same time the validity of conclusions drawn can be assessed by
analyzing the directions of evidence. The technique allows assembling
of both qualitative and quantitative information to provide consistent,
practical interpretations.

A Conceptual Framework for the Assessment

A framework of concepts relevant to the change in question is vital
to the assessment process. Often, unfortunately, basic concepts are not
well defined or organized, or are left as implicit assumptions. In these
cases the assessment suffers as the analytic-inductive technique cannot

provide the advantage of continual refinement of concepts. In essence, there is no explicit model or concept to refine. The analysis may be so unfocused that the right questions are not posed. And valuable research effort can be wasted by "laundry-list" approaches where endless data are accumulated.

A conceptual framework, therefore, provides an analytical basis for the assessment. Theoretical concepts are used to direct the gathering and analysis of data, to ensure this work is comprehensive, cost effective, and properly focused. The concepts often reflect a synthesis of perspectives from team members of varying backgrounds. Initially, the framework will be developed around information about the planned change and literature and experience of similar changes elsewhere.

The most common framework used in SIA in New Zealand is a model of base-line social conditions prior to change and a model of the character of planned change (e.g., a new industry, work force redundancies, or land-use changes) as a basis for projecting impacts. But there is often a paucity of either descriptive or analytical material on existing change in the target community, or on comparative communities not experiencing the impacts in question. In most rural areas, for instance, much general change is taking place in the course of agricultural and rural restructuring without the specific impacts of a major plant construction or closedown.

Experience indicates that the critical stage for establishing the conceptual framework is during preliminary investigations and the scoping of issues. Scoping exercises which place specific changes into a wider social-environmental context are more effective than describing baseline conditions in endless detail (Taylor and McClintock, 1984, Goodrich and Taylor, 1985). Second, concepts about the workings of change taking place (e.g., "boomtowns") have not always been used critically or comprehensively. Focus is frequently on such limited aspects as demographic change and provision of social services. A more comprehensive analysis based on comparative analysis of change in technology and resource use should be undertaken. This allows the assessment of impacts on different social groups, social organizations, and community dynamics (Taylor and Fitzgerald, 1988).

The scoping exercise allows the assessment to distinguish key issues, social variables for describing changing conditions, and boundaries for study areas. Activities at this stage may include literature review, initial gathering of secondary data, media monitoring, networking, and interviews and meetings with key people and groups. Issues are described, categorized, and ranked where possible.

A practical perspective should guide this activity. Useful categories by which a social profile can be compiled were originally suggested by

Bryan and Hendee (1983) for the United States Forest Service and Conland (1985) for New Zealand. They include:

1. Population and land use—including specific demographic trends, residential, agricultural and other land and resource uses, and the sustainability or resource dependence of these uses.
2. Lifestyles—including patterns of work and leisure, customs and patterns of social relationships such as family and friends. Maori lifestyles have been distinguished as particularly important in many cases.
3. Attitudes, beliefs, and values—including perceptions of change and orientations to the future; perceptions of external control and decision making by industry; and perceptions of existing community organization, leadership, and government.
4. Social organization—including the main institutions and social structures, economic, infrastructural, political and community, and their rates of change and stability.

From the scoping work a social overview is established and the assessment of likely effects of change can be made. In many cases these effects can be comparatively simple, such as increased demand for housing for reservoir construction communities. Other effects, however, may be complex and unobvious, such as changes in social networks and relationships. For this reason a set of broad variables is useful to the analysis. The categories comprise a checklist of potential areas of investigation. Within each category the investigator may define subsets of variables to explore.

Variables employed in recent work have included length of residence, gender, proximity of settlement, ethnicity, and social class—including patterns of income, status, power, work, and property ownership. In many impact studies these variables will allow a move beyond general descriptions of community by the study team to a more rigorous explanation for social patterns underlying common or different interests within various social groups. In New Zealand hydro-construction towns, for example, the community might appear as a distinct geographical entity committed to a common economic purpose. In reality, there are many interrelated groups of interest and intense areas of difference and conflict that need to be understood (Taylor and Bettesworth, 1983). These communities also need to be understood within a wider historical framework, such as construction work forces and manpower planning, national energy development, and general social change (Taylor and Fitzgerald, 1988).

Initial Collection of Data

An SIA will normally require the collection and analysis of data. Baseline conditions of change are described and, ideally, control cases can be considered within the formation of a comprehensive data base. This social research effort needs to continue through prediction, planning, monitoring, and evaluation. The resulting information must be applied in a decision-making and management context, to plan social services or justify public expenditures in cases of social costs incurred by a minority group. Also, social data can be used as a basis for action at a local level to modify courses of action established by "top-down" planning and mitigate impacts.

Many decision makers, especially those operating from a "top-down" perspective, want quantitative data. Yet SIA practitioners are usually under strict limitations with regard to time, funding, and personnel available. Consequently, practitioners have to rely on secondary data such as census data and other official statistics, and university research. Secondary data can also include historical and personal accounts. These can be very useful, for while decision makers tend to favor "hard" quantitative data, the most crucial elements of social change are often best represented in qualitative terms. For instance, narrative data on critical issues such as Maori cultural change are needed to interpret fully any quantitative data and projections on such topics as demography and social services.

Consultative Field Research

Field research is commonly an integral part of the issues-oriented approach. As issues emerge from a review of the literature and other secondary data, field validation must take place. Field work allows the issues to be corroborated by the study team working with different social groups affected by change. It also facilitates the participatory process.

Methods that are used most frequently are the qualitative techniques of anthropological field work or ethnography. These include networking, interviews—usually in-depth and semi-structured—with key informants and participant observation. These techniques are particularly important in the context of consultative and participatory research. There are additional qualitative research techniques that can be included in an SIA, such as meetings with interest groups or the public. Additional techniques for exchanges of information in an SIA include open houses and regular liaison forums. In general, meetings have provided a useful method for participatory work. They have typically been used to set up a work program, provide an initial identification of issues, facilitate detailed data collection such as household surveys, and report and validate findings through discussion. Meetings can range in type from informal gatherings, focused discussion groups, to more formal task groups. In the best traditions of social field research, good opportunities are provided during these activities for observing how a community responds to change.

A key part of the field research techniques is to ensure validity of data and representative analysis covering all social groups. In networking, emphasis has to be placed on access to a variety of social groups, some of which might be under-represented in usual planning procedures. The conceptual framework should be a guide here. Also, there are emerging institutional procedures in New Zealand in addition to those in environmental administration and planning agencies. The new Ministry of Women's Affairs, for instance, is taking an active interest in women's issues and SIA. There is increased awareness that SIA should not be gender biased. Also Maori groups are active in seeking resources to ensure they have a full involvement in the SIA process (Nottingham, 1986). Where Maori groups are involved it is necessary to follow traditional meeting protocol. Finally, media monitoring is a good source of further documentary data, contacts, and feedback on research activities such as survey work, a public meeting, or the release of an interim report.

Surveys

Systematic survey research has been conducted as part of data gathering for many SIA projects. The results have frequently been poor, however. This is usually because the survey is the primary focus of the SIA, rather than a supplement to the approach as suggested here. Surveys have resulted in outright antagonism towards the SIA work from affected populations. Government officials have sometimes used surveys as gauges to local reaction to a proposal. Survey work can form the methodological essence of a technocratic approach with this "hands off" orientation to the community.

There is, however, increasing recognition in New Zealand of the need for a selective and systematic use of survey work within SIA. Surveys are now commonly used as an important additional tool within the overall analytical framework. They fill information gaps, improve validity of secondary data sets, and aid in the identification of issues. Common foci of surveys in SIAs have included such topics as household characteristics, the nature of existing and incoming work forces, resources and problems of redundant workers, and the description of business sectors.

In our experience surveys conducted as part of an issues-oriented SIA usually have an excellent response rate. Cooperation is sought with local groups. Surveys in the business community, for example, can be organized in collaboration with the business or employers association. Unions are often a source of contact for employees surveys. Personal contact in the administration of questionnaires in coordination with these groups has increased response rates and proven cost effective. Close consultation and discussion with the survey population in the process of developing, testing, administering, and analyzing phases are important. The quality of the data are improved, and the process also provides a parallel set of qualitative information. The process serves a validation function, and entirely new issues can be identified at any stage.

Social Development and the SIA Process

There are many interconnections between an effective SIA process and social development actions. The process has worked to encourage social development, identified issues with social development implications, and substantiated arguments for appropriate social action.

The most obvious applied use for the SIA is for the provision or strengthening of social services. Rapid social change may create problems such as increased mental health case loads, marital problems, or new demands for pre-school education. In these cases the community development worker has been recommended and paid for out of project funds. The community development worker can provide skills in public participation; facilitate new group networks and community action; and encourage flows of information between powerful groups, decision makers, and the general public (Conland, 1985:10).

It has been shown in New Zealand, particularly in the work on energy development projects in Taranaki and Northland, that social development work that is carried out by a community worker within the SIA process requires a good local and regional institutional base. Accordingly, local task groups and technical advisory groups have proven to be very effective. These groups are generally convened by the SIA workers and will include representatives of appropriate local agencies of government, the developer, and that public interest group. Their tasks include information gathering, consultation, evaluation, guidance for researchers, specific monitoring tasks, and coordination of community workers and social services responding to change. These groups are very effective in bridging the gap that often occurs between research and action.

For this type of work to take place at the local level, social planning should be at a regional level. Regional planning plays an important role in mediating the common differences between national and regional goals. This task is particularly important where priorities for development at the regional level may be very different from the priorities for the metropolitan centers. For instance, a regional planning framework can provide a social policy in critical areas, such as employment strategies and local enterprise development for resource-dependent localities facing cycles of boom and bust. A social policy framework could also accommodate different perspectives with regard to natural resource policy issues such as resource sustainability.

In some cases in New Zealand, regional planning organizations have provided the institutional basis for SIA work. They have convened steering groups including relevant members of parliament, senior government officials, and developers. These groups can initiate SIA work, including local task groups, and articulate a balance between regional and national social costs and benefits. They have been involved in the allocation of development levies. Coordination of different SIAs for one region can also be carried out at this level. In the region of Taranaki, for example, simultaneous SIA work has occurred on several energy projects at different phases, on an industry closedown, and on hill country farming areas in financial difficulty.

At the national level there has to be coordination among agencies, an effort to define coherent social policies, and the establishment of a national research strategy and data bases. Where these activities have been carried out effectively, it has largely been due to the efforts of individual SIA practitioners operating through the national SIA working group and network. These practitioners, scattered among agencies, universities, and local groups, have identified a need for better institutional bases of SIA. They have lobbied government to obtain greater funding and legislative backing and argued for a more proactive role for SIA in defining management options and making decisions (Taylor and Bryan, 1987).

Probably the most important recent move regarding national social policy making and social development has been a call for a new central government agency (Renouf and Taylor, 1985; Cronin, 1987). The agency would provide an institutional basis for social policy, SIA, and social development. Its work would include coordination of agency activity, advice to government, and the administration of procedures for social assessment. It would also include the audit and monitoring of projects and policies with social effects.

Conclusions

Social impact assessment is the analysis of how policies and actions affect social well being. Ideally SIA occurs prior to decision making, so that social change can be identified, monitored, and mitigated to enhance social well being. Increasing the overall use of applied social science in a more proactive role in resource management, as opposed to common reactive uses is the direction to pursue (Bryan and Taylor, 1986). But a number of limitations, primarily in approach and methods, have hindered the usefulness of SIA in New Zealand to social policy, decision making, planning and management.

The SIA process now recommended in New Zealand emphasizes the early identification of social issues in change. A sound base of information is sought, and the identification of social issues and accumulation of information continues through monitoring the main period of change. Also recognized is the fact that the process must include adequate institutional arrangements. For example, coordinated efforts at social planning and the provision of social services at central, regional, and local government levels are essential. Local people and representatives of all cultural groups affected must be involved in the identification of issues, decision making and management. The issues-oriented approach to SIA recognizes that institutional needs may require the process to include, even promote, clear actions of social development.

We believe the issues-oriented approach described for the New Zealand context has potential for wide application in social planning and resource management internationally. The approach is sufficiently flexible for applicability to a variety of social-cultural settings. And the approach can be improved and adapted without losing the basic intent of the process. We look forward to its increased use, evaluation, and refinement.

References

Bryan, Hobson, 1985. Collecting, organizing and validating social information. *Social Science Information and Resource Management. Proceedings from an Interagency Symposium*, Environmental Coordination, United States Forest Service, Washington, D.C.

Bryan, Hobson and Hendee, John C., 1983. Social impact analysis in United States Forest Service decisions; background and proposed principles. In Maurice E. Voland and William A. Fleischman (Eds.), *Sociology and Social Impact Analysis in Federal Resource Management Agencies*, United States Department of Agriculture, Forest Service.

Bryan, C. Hobson and Taylor, C. Nicholas, 1986. Proactive social science for resource management. Plenary paper presented to the First National symposium on Social Science in Resource Management, Corvallis, Oregon, 12–16 May.

Centre for Maori Studies and Research, 1984. *The development of coal-fired power stations in the Waikato—a Maori perspective.* University of Waikato.

Conland, Jeanette, Ed. 1985. *Social impact assessment in New Zealand—a practical approach.* Town and Country Planning Directorate, Ministry of Works and Development.

Cronin, Karen, 1987. Social impact assessment and social policy—an overview. Paper presented to the ANZAAS Congress, Palmerston North, New Zealand, 26–30 January.

Fookes, T. W., 1981. Intentions and practice of the monitoring project. Monitoring Social and economic impact, Huntly case study. *Final Report Series,* 9, University of Waikato, Hamilton.

Forester, J., 1980. Critical theory and planning practice. *American Planning Association Journal,* 46:275–86.

Gilbert, John, 1986. Environmental assessment in New Zealand. *Northwest Environmental Journal* 2(2):5–105.

Goodrich, Colin C., and Taylor, C. Nick. 1985. The new environmental paradigm and critical theory: base assumptions for the practice of social impact assessment. Paper presented at the New Zealand Sociological Association Annual Conference, Hamilton, 2–4 December.

Hollins, C. S. (Ed.), 1978. *Adaptive Environmental Assessment and Management.* International Series on Applied Systems Analysis No. 3.

Joint Centre for Environmental Sciences, 1982. Implications of coal recovery and liquefaction of South Island lignites. *Liquid Fuels Trust Board Report, No. LF2024,* Wellington.

Krawetz, N. M., 1981. Intentions and practice reviewed with reference to monitoring prototypes. Monitoring Social and Economic Impact, Huntly Case Study. *Final Report Series,* 10, University of Waikato, Hamilton.

Landon, Y., 1982. A report on the social effects of energy development in North Taranaki: community concerns. *Summary Report, Taranaki Community Monitoring Project.* New Plymouth.

Lynn, Ann, 1987. Energy projects and social impact assessment: implications for the Maori people. Paper presented to a conference on Maori Studies and Research, University of the Waikato, Hamilton.

McPherson, Jill, 1982–1984. Social impact survey: Marsden Point refinery expansion. *Progress Reports No. 1–6.*

Nottingham, Isla, 1986. Social impact reporting in a bicultural state. Paper presented to the Annual Conference of the New Zealand Sociological Association, University of Canterbury, Christchurch, 1–3 December.

Renouf, Jacky and Taylor, Nick, 1985. Economic restructuring: the role and responsibility of social impact assessment. Paper presented to the ASSR/NZSA Social Policy Conference, 31 October–2 November.

Taylor, C. N. and Bettesworth, C. M., 1983. Social Characteristics of New Zealand hydro-towns: a case study. *Information Paper No. 1,* Centre for Resource Management, University of Canterbury and Lincoln College.

Taylor, C. Nick and Bryan, C. Hobson, 1987. Social Impact Assessment in New Zealand Resource Management. In Marc L. Miller, Richard Dale and Terry Brown (eds.), *Social Science in Natural Resource Management Systems*, Westview Press, Boulder.

Taylor, C. Nicholas and Fitzgerald, Gerard, 1988. New Zealand resource communities: impact assessment and management in response to rapid economic change. *Impact Assessment Bulletin*, 6, 2:55–70.

Taylor, C. N. and McClintock, W. L., 1984. Major resource development projects in a regional context: a framework for a New Zealand analysis. *Journal of Sociology*, 20, 3:392.

3
The Development Anthropology Approach

Kurt Finsterbusch and William L. Partridge

Development anthropology is scientific research on the social setting of development projects. "Its objective is to enhance benefits and mitigate negative consequences for the human communities involved in and affected by development efforts" (Partridge and Warren, 1984:1). Beyond these general statements there is no consensus among anthropologists about the definition of the development anthropology approach. Nevertheless, in this chapter we attempt to present an approach to social impact assessment for Third World development projects that is representative of the thinking of the majority of development anthropologists. We draw heavily upon Partridge (1984a) for the first section.

The project cycle involves three stages: design, implementation, and completion. It is true that some designing (mainly in the sense of redesigning) occurs in the implementation stage, but these three stages are useful for organizing our discussion of the development anthropology approach.

The Design Stage

The design stage includes both origin and design phases and our discussion centers on the latter. The origin phase is highly variable from project to project. The idea of the project might arise in the host government, a donor organization, or even occasionally in a community. If a donor organization is to be involved, it must at some point prepare "identification" papers which lay out the basic project idea and some of its parameters. Identification papers specify the project sufficiently to enter it into the bureaucratic decision-making process. The donor organization can put them out for bids, call for further research into project feasibility and soundness, or append the project onto an existing project. Important course-setting decisions are made in this phase, so it is important that development anthropologists are able from the beginning to input their perspective into the decision-making process. Two decades ago technical experts such as agronomists and engineers made these decisions in collaboration with economists and fiscal experts. It is now more widely recognized that the expertise of agronomists and engineers does not extend to the social milieu of the project and that the expertise of the development anthropologist should be added informally if not formally.

In the design phase the development anthropologist should bring human factors into the planning of the project. He does this by estimating the impacts on people of design alternatives and championing the consideration of these impacts in the decision-making process. The development anthropologist not only considers the community contexts and project outputs in estimating social impacts but also considers the administrative arrangements, financial operations, characteristics of project staff, and political influence. He champions social factors in design decisions and project plans not only by reporting his social analysis but also by arguing that social factors influence the effectiveness of projects and by negotiating with other professionals on the project design.

The development anthropologist engages in three major sets of activities in bringing the human factors into project design:

1. Assembling background data
2. Field Research
3. Report production

The following sections are organized around these activities.

Assembling Background Data

In assembling background data the anthropologist describes the local environmental and cultural characteristics of communities likely to be affected. Ideally the anthropologist has first-hand knowledge of the people and activities of the area to build upon. He or she also utilizes the network of anthropologists and other professionals who have worked in the area as well as available residents from the area to supplement his/her knowledge base and to activate the network as a future resource for all phases of the project. The network is also important for obtaining a variety of viewpoints. We cannot emphasize enough the importance of obtaining several viewpoints on social conditions and predicted social impacts. This is a basic principle of field work but also should guide the gathering of baseline data.

If there are previous sociocultural studies of the project area, they should be consulted along with the full range of available secondary data such as censuses, newspapers, and international and national agency reports. Furthermore, national ministries or departments such as agriculture, education, health, industry/commerce or planning should have useful data for compiling a baseline description of the area and identifying potentially impacted categories of people. A major problem with all of these sources is that they are out of date, so one objective of the field research is to gauge how much the sociocultural conditions have changed since these reports. Even before the field research, however, the anthropologist should consult with knowledgeable people about the current accuracy of the reports.

The background information on the project area and its people should include demographic characteristics, socioeconomic factors, and subsistence systems. Sometimes social analysis presents a lot of data in certain of these categories just because it is readily available but makes little or no connection between the data and expected impacts. Obviously this is to be avoided if the social analysis is to be taken seriously and guide decision making. With this warning we provide a list of factors in Table 3.1 that should be qualitatively and/or quantitatively described for the project area if they are relevant to understanding the project area and/or for anticipating possible projects effects.

Several comments on Table 3.1 are in order. First, the demographic factors are standard factors for demographically describing a population except income, educational, and occupational distributions are often included in demographic descriptions but here are included under socioeconomic factors. Second, the demographic factors are to be quantitatively described. Third, the socioeconomic factors are mainly to be qualitatively described in terms of dominant patterns, but the degree of convergence on that pattern and the divergence should also be discussed. Fourth, the politically significant actions of people are usually taken in organized groups, so the project design should not deal simply with individuals but even more with groups, associations, organizations and systems. Development anthropology focuses on people in groups and organizations and not on isolated individuals.

The importance of groups for social analysis is clearly seen in the political sphere where groups, not individuals, count politically. Social feasibility is an AID term for determining that the project does not run into significant opposition from political jurisdictions and structures; the stratification system; important racial, ethnic, linguistic, and religious groups; business groups or organizations; unions; cooperatives;

TABLE 3.1
Project Area Background Information Factor List
(factors to be selected from list for quantitative and/or qualitative description
as appropriate for a specific project)

Demographic Factors

1. Total population
2. Population by age and sex categories
3. Birth rate
4. Fertility rate

5. Mortality rate, infant mortality
6. Immigration, outmigration and net migration rates
7. Number of households and household composition by age and sex

Socio-Economic Factors

1. Political jurisdictions and structures
2. Local political structures
3. Local stratification system and relationships
4. Racial, ethnic and linguistic groups and relationships
5. Religious groups and their organization
6. Occupational groups and their numbers
7. Principal businesses and their organization
8. Family and kinship systems
9. Organization of household
10. Land ownership and use
11. Resource ownership, use and systems
12. Organization of markets

13. Cooperatives, unions, and economic associations
14. Neighborhood or area organizations and associations
15. Other voluntary associations
16. Social classes
17. Educational attainment levels
18. Income categories
19. Transportation systems and accessibility
20. Education systems
21. Law enforcement systems
22. Health systems
23. Credit systems
24. Workforce participation and unemployment
25. Levels of social and political conflict

Subsistence Systems

1. Farming systems including crops, vegetable garden, livestock, land tenure, technology, markets, supplies, credit, farmer associations, off farm income and storage.
2. Pastoral systems including pasture, fodder production technology, livestock, processing, markets, land tenure, migrating patterns, veterinary, and ancillary activities.

3. Gathering systems (fishing, hunting, and plant collecting) including resource use rights, technology, processing, markets, and migration patterns.
4. Manufacturing systems including supplies, organization, technology credit, labor force, markets, and regulations.

kinship groups; and other associations. Individuals' responses to the project are likely to be mobilized and directed through these groups. Even participation in the project is enhanced if participants are organized (Finsterbusch and Van Wicklin, 1987, 1989; Esman and Uphoff, 1984). Social life involves social interaction in groups where individuals support each other, become committed to each other, share common goals, respond to leaders who in turn are responsive to them, and in the process channel their energies collectively so that they have corporate impact.

The final section in Table 3.1 presents the four major types of subsistence systems. Each involves very different man/environment relationships and there is considerable variation within each type. Each subsistence system involves many activities and the complex social arrangements that are responsible for them. Again the development anthropology approach examines the connections between people and between people and the environment. Too often project designs ignore the systems in which beneficiaries are involved so the project changes one feature of their lives without understanding the effect of that change on these systems.

We realize that seldom can secondary sources provide in-depth information on most of the factors in Table 3.1, even on the smaller set of factors that are germane to the project and its impacts. We also call attention to the problem of the accuracy of secondary sources. Most secondary data are not gathered by social scientists. Even census or public health personnel may be poorly trained in reliable data gathering techniques. Furthermore, interviewers and respondents often have very different backgrounds that lead to misunderstandings or non-candid responses. In fact, they may not even be able to convince the local people to cooperate (Stykos, 1960). The information gatherer is likely to be viewed as a representative of the urban, educated elite, and therefore not taken into confidence. Secondary data should always be taken as somewhat unreliable so any analysis that is based on them has an extra degree of uncertainty. This observation means that secondary data should be verified in the field.

Another valuable source of background information are the reports of similar projects in other places. The best guide to the future is the past. Past experience provides lessons on problems that projects are likely to produce. Every project, however, is likely to be unique. Past cases are valuable guides to expected impacts, but the new project will always deviate in some ways from identified general patterns. Field research therefore is needed to identify how the new project will deviate from the general patterns.

Increasingly development agencies are evaluating past projects in order to learn how to design and implement projects better, and some of these reports are publicly available. For example, AID has a growing list of past *Project Impact Evaluation Reports* and summary volumes on specific types of projects which can be useful for anticipating problems and outcomes for new projects. Another source for previous cases are interviews with knowledgeable people including agency staff, contractors, local leaders and experts.

The development anthropologist should synthesize all of the background information that he/she has collected orally and in reports and produce a description of the typical project of the relevant type. Then he/she and consulted experts should estimate the likelihood that the typical pattern will occur in the new case and why not if not. Later he/she will check out these judgments during the field research.

Field Research

Secondary data and the judgments of experts always should be "ground tested" to verify their accuracy for the current situation and to obtain the viewpoints of area residents. Furthermore, the statistics and reports provide general pictures but lack much of the micro-level details that are needed for anticipating reactions and results. Experts can be badly mistaken so field verification is needed to lower the risks. The consulted experts may also have specialized knowledge and lack specific knowledge of characteristics of individuals and communities that are essential to project success. Finally, field research is necessary to insure that target populations have some input into project design. The amount and breadth of consultation with the affected residents may necessarily be small but even a little is much better than none.

The field research for the design phase is not extensive ethnography but a short term study to verify and update information, collect missing data, canvass local attitudes, check interpretations, evaluate and revise predictions, and test the viability of plans. Rapid rural appraisal techniques, discussed in Chapter 8, are usually employed. A one to several month visit by a multidisciplinary team of experts including one anthropologist is needed for reasonably accurate assessments of local conditions and estimates of expected outcomes of the project.

The field research will cover the factors in Table 3.1 but will focus on the social processes that are crucial to survival and to community life. For the factors in Table 3.1 the field research will indicate what characteristics are changing significantly and why. It will explain unusual characteristics such as extremely high infant mortality rates or unusual land use patterns. Finally it will correct, update, and amplify the description of many factors:

The basic social processes that the field research reports include:

1. How groups are biologically and socially reproduced, including how the young are nurtured and incorporated into adult status and how adults progress through their various social careers into the status of elder.

2. How people are recruited into the task or activity groups and organizations (e.g., work groups, religious brotherhoods, political-action associations) and how leaders of such organizations are chosen by followers (e.g., seniority in kin or nonkin group, accumulated wealth, formal education, role in production process).
3. How value priorities are given expression and made compelling for members of groups, such as ritual cycles involving priests and their publics or shamans and their clients, community festivals, political rites, marriage ceremonies, initiations, and funerals (Partridge 1984a:26).

Understanding these processes is essential to estimating project impacts. They should be described both qualitatively and quantitatively. Knowledge of the size of groups and the number of people with specified experiences is necessary for estimating the magnitude of project effects on various categories of people and the magnitude of their responses. In fact, quantification greatly increases the weight social factors have in decision making so numerical estimates are to be preferred to the crude terms for defining quantities such as a few, many, and most. We have noticed also that the social impact of projects can be greatly improved when impact magnitudes can be quantified.

The field research should be interactive with the project design. The first determinations of the dimensions of the project precedes field work which then estimates the population placed at risk, the beneficiaries, the project induced migrants, and the likely responses to the project. The field research might estimate that the project should be abandoned or that it should be modified to minimize the negative social impacts and maximize the benefits. The development anthropologist might recommend changes in the project's size, schedule, location, structure, methods, or outputs to better fit the social context. He/she will particularly explore the issue of beneficiary participation in design, redesign, implementation, maintenance/operation and evaluation. Only field research can determine the possible roles of the affected population in the project and how participation should be instituted and organized. So field work feeds back into project redesign in both a formal and informal negotiation process. After a redesign is worked out its new elements should be tested and explored in further field research.

Another local issue for the development anthropologist is migration. Development activities usually require some skills or personpower that are not locally available so the number of immigrants and their impacts need to be estimated. On the other hand some development activities displace local residents so resettlement becomes a major concern. Recognizing this, the World Bank has sponsored some important research

on resettlement to guide development anthropologists studying resettlement issues (Cernea, 1988; Hansen and Oliver-Smith, 1982; Schuh et
al. 1987).

Another goal of field research is to establish working relationships
with local, county, and area anthropologists, scientists, professionals,
and community leaders. Every opportunity should be taken to involve
them and/or contract for their services in the research process and in
the project design, implementation, and evaluation. They will strengthen
the projects and better integrate the project into the local settings. Of
course they should be extended the courtesy of generous formal ac-
knowledgement of their contributions and where possible given co-
authorship. If they are well trained and have field experience in the
project area they can carry the research load while the anthropologist
on the planning team simply makes short trips to the area and advises
and assists them in the social analysis. Developing local research
capacity is another aspect of achieving sustainable project benefits.

Report Production

All preceding activities are directed toward the preparation of a
report. The anthropologist makes many informal contributions to the
shaping and design of the project and the report is his formal contribution. The report also brings the political issues of the participation
of the anthropologist in the project to a head. He/she may be expected
to write a report that justifies or supports a project that he believes is
socially unacceptable. He/she might choose to write a negative or no
report in such cases. If design decisions are still open to change he/
she needs to write his/her report for maximum effect so it should focus
on the three broad categories of project design: financial arrangements,
personnel, and administrative arrangements. An insightful narrative on
local conditions, practices, and cultures will have little policy impact
and should be made an appendix or published separately if drafted at
all. The body of the report must discuss the features of the project and
the way it will articulate with communities. It then recommends ways
for improving project impacts that derive from the analysis and are
stated in terms of budget, personnel and administrative recommendations.

The report should evaluate how project monies are allocated and
recommend changes in these allocations. For example, the anthropologist might criticize a potable water project that allocates 90% of its
funds to a central ministry that will build the potable water systems
and only 10% to local maintenance of the systems. He/she might
recommend an additional 10% of the funds for maintenance if villagers

have no slack resources for this purpose. (He/she might also recommend in the personnel sector using local labor to construct the system.) The anthropologists looks at every line in the budget with his concerns for human factors in mind. If the budget has no funds for resettling displaced residents, he/she recommends an appropriate amount. If the budget has no funds for other needed mitigation measures he recommends them. If all funds address male production activities and ignore or possibly create difficulties for female production activities, the anthropologist recommends reallocations to fund female production activities. He/she questions why most funds are spent on urban bureaucracies and not in local communities. He/she objects to money spent for expensive American pumps for which spare parts will not be available in country. He/she criticizes that large amounts of money go to American experts, when local experts could be used at a quarter of the cost and with better integration of the project into its human setting. Finally, he/she strongly objects to the budget's reflection of a short-range perspective. He/she will recommend that long-range fiscal costs of the project (that is, recurrent costs including maintenance) are taken into account in the budget. He/she might recommend that the project be redesigned in such a way that the recurrent costs, when funding ceases, will be at the lowest possible levels so they can readily be absorbed by the government or local associations.

The anthropologist also reviews the personnel specifications for the project. He/she is likely to identify additional personnel requirements such as language skills, ethnic background, sex, and status characteristics that are needed for effective communication with the villagers. We find that urban professionals with no experience in the area are sometimes worse than foreigners who are more aware of their ignorance of local customs and more ready to listen.

The anthropologist is aware of the range of expected social impacts, and therefore, identifies personnel that are needed to address these impacts. If migration is involved he/she recommends a specialist in resettlement. For the mitigation of other negative impacts he/she might recommend a health worker, skill instructor, nutrition expert or community organizer. Unfortunately he/she usually must also identify personnel that would be dropped to make room for the recommended workers. Bureaucratic politics will be involved.

Finally, the anthropologist reviews the administrative arrangements and recommends changes. His/her field research should have determined the capacity of the relevant existing administrations. Can these handle additional tasks? Are they already extended beyond their resources? Do they have a record of effective performance in the required areas? It is common for the answers to be no but the project simply plugs in a technical assistance training component in the hope that this will solve the problem. Post project evaluations, however, repeatedly show that inadequate institutional capacity is a major cause of projects being unsustainable (Finsterbusch and Van Wicklin, 1988). The anthropologist has the unpleasant task of making the project designers face this reality squarely and deal with it realistically.

The Implementation Stage

On the whole development projects are initiated to provide badly needed infrastructure, training, technology, or services in the hopes of improving the productivity and well being of poor peoples. Traditionally they have been designed by the appropriate technical experts and evaluated on economic criteria. Over time unexpectedly high failure rates led to the recognition that the social context had to be assessed for its social feasibility, a design criteria that was to take its place beside technical feasibility and economic rate of return. Social feasibility, however, continues to be treated as a second class citizen in project design. Its status is demoted even further in project implementation. Cost overruns are commonplace (see Finsterbusch and Van Wicklin, 1988) so items must be cut from the budget. Social components are often the first to go, especially a social research component that is easily viewed as non-essential. Nevertheless, we will describe the role of development anthropologists in evaluating and monitoring project implementation when they get the opportunity. Development anthropologists are also called upon as managers and specialists to actually implement projects but we do not discuss these roles for development anthropologists because they are not mainly social research roles or they are highly specialized. Case studies for these roles can be found in Partridge (1984b) and Green (1986). For a more extensive discussion of the role of the development anthropologist in evaluation and monitoring see Epstein and Ahmed (1984) and Pillsbury (1984).

Ideally evaluation and monitoring provide feedback to managers that lead to project improvements. Many managers, however, are threatened by evaluation, especially by outsiders, because it may reveal their weaknesses, so they are often somewhat hostile to it. An anthropologist involved in evaluation, therefore, must proceed with political astuteness. Land mines are everywhere.

Monitoring usually involves an institutionalized regular ongoing data gathering and review system which provides managers with the information they need to direct their staff and manage resources to meet current demands. Evaluation occurs infrequently and usually is conducted by evaluators who are external to the implementing organization.

Occasionally anthropologists are on the implementing agencies' staff and participate in project monitoring. More frequently anthropologists participate in evaluations. Since managers generally create and control monitoring systems and anthropologists have less discretion when they monitor than when they evaluate, we concentrate our discussion on evaluation.

There are two major types of evaluations during implementation: process and impact evaluations. These are described by Pillsbury (1984:51) as follows:

> *Process evaluation* may be defined as evaluation that attempts to assess progress being made in implementing the project in accord with project design, to understand those characteristics of the environment in which the project is being implemented that may be impeding its progress, and to make recommendations for its future. These recommendations may be for early or even immediate termination of the project (very rare), major redesign of the project (quite unusual), or improvements in numerous aspects of the implementation process (the case in most process evaluations).
>
> In contrast, *impact evaluation* may be defined as an evaluation that attempts to assess whether or not the project is producing its intended effects (impacts) on the intended beneficiaries, to assess unintended impacts (beneficial and negative), and to present "lessons learned" and make recommendations applicable either to the project itself or at a higher program or policy level. A process evaluation may be carried out at any time during implementation. An impact evaluation, however, can be undertaken only after the project has been under way long enough to have begun producing an impact (usually at least two or three years).

The process evaluation looks at whether planned and contracted tasks are being carried out, supplies and equipment are purchased and put in service, and outputs are being produced as specified in the project plan. The impact evaluation looks at the outputs. Are the new technologies produced by a research center actually being used by farmers and with what concrete result? How heavily is the project road being used and for what purposes? Is a family planning program actually lowering the birth rate?

Both types of evaluation demonstrate success and failure and seek to explain the latter so corrective steps can be taken. The procedures for conducting such evaluations in developing countries has been spelled out by Freeman, Rossi, and Wright (1979). Their description is too idealistic for most concrete project evaluation situations, but it can serve as a useful reference point. Pillsbury (1984) describes how messy actual project evaluations are in the Third World and describes a less ambitious procedure. A multidisciplinary team is assembled, briefed, and sent to the field. Large teams split up and small ones usually do not. After a few weeks they return to project headquarters to write a draft of their report and make recommendations on the basis of their brief study. She emphasizes that the anthropologist is likely to work in a team which might make it difficult for him/her to do true anthropological field work. He/she should be assertive, however, and if necessary ". . . temporarily leave the team and spend several days in one of the project villages, using anthropological methods to gather data about the project from the perspective of rural people who are supposed to benefit from it" (p. 57).

We recommend a tripartite methodology for social analysis for evaluation and monitoring during project implementation, but we recognize that the great variability among project situations will call for great variability in methodological approaches. Our tripartite methodology involves widespread informant interviews with village leaders, a widespread social survey and an in-depth case study. These three methods are selected to balance strengths and weaknesses. The informant interview with village leaders throughout the project area is efficient in providing a vast amount of information on project effects over a wide area but it has an elite bias and lacks depth of understanding of the processes involved. The social survey corrects the elite bias and captures the distribution of benefits and negative impacts but it is somewhat superficial and lacks depth. The in-depth case study corrects the problem of superficiality and explores the intricate processes that underlie the readily observed and reported changes. However, it is time consuming and can only be conducted in one place so it lacks breadth. We also acknowledge that the depth of the in-depth case study, the sampling and administration of the social survey and the procedures of the informant interviews involve short cuts, corner cutting, and flexibility that might not be tolerated in basic anthropological research but often are required in the development context.

Finally we reiterate that the development anthropologist must work with a network of national and local anthropologists, professionals, and villagers in gathering and interpreting information. Multiple informed viewpoints can save us from mistakes, hasty conclusions, and overgeneralized findings. Since development anthropologists must move so rapidly, they need better brakes and seat belts than academic anthropologists.

The Project Completion Stage

Anthropologists are sometimes involved in project evaluations at the end of project (part of a wrap-up report) or several years after project completion. The purpose is to learn lessons that can improve future projects and influence development policy. The end-of-project evaluation compiles a record of what was done and what resulted. These are usually minimal effort studies unless they are justifying follow-on projects or investigating why a project failed. The ex-post evaluation not only describes what was done but also examines the impacts of the project several years later. Are roads, irrigation systems, new technologies, and new institutions still in use and effective? Ex-post evaluations can be relatively thorough studies that can call upon the full range of the anthropologist's skills and methods. More often they will depend largely on the rapid appraisal techniques that are the bread and butter of the development anthropologist. Increasingly, however, project monitoring and evaluation during implementation by independent social research organizations in the host country are built into project designs. The results of these concurrent studies by host-country professionals assist us in formulating project completion analyses and deriving lessons from prior experience which hold the potential for improving performance in the future.

References

Cernea, Michael M. *Involuntary Resettlement in Development Projects: Policy Guidelines in World Bank-Financial Projects,* World Bank Technical Paper No. 80, Washington, D.C.: The World Bank, 1988.

Epstein, T. Scarlett, and Ahmed, Akbar. "Development Anthropology in Project Implementation," in *Training Manual in Development Anthropology.* Washington, D.C.: American Anthropological Association, pp. 31–41, 1984.

Esman, Milton, and Uphoff, Norman T. *Local Development Association: Intermediaries in Rural Development.* Ithaca: Cornell University Press, 1984.

Finsterbusch, Kurt, and Van Wicklin, III, Warren. "The Contribution of Beneficiary Participation to Development Project Effectiveness," *Public Administration and Development,* 7, 1, pp. 1–23, 1987.

_____ . "Unanticipated Consequences of AID Projects: Lessons from Impact Assessment for Project Planning," *Policy Studies Review,* 8 (Autumn), 1988.

_____ . "Beneficiary Participation in Development Projects: Empirical Tests of Popular Theories," *Economic Development and Cultural Change,* 37, 3 (April), 1989.

Freeman, Howard, Rossi, Peter, and Wright, Sonia. *Evaluating Social Projects in Developing Countries.* Paris: Development Centre of the Organization of Economic Cooperation and Development, 1979.

Green, Edward C. (ed.). *Practicing Development Anthropology.* Boulder: Westview, 1986.

Hansen, Art, and Oliver-Smith, A. (eds.). *Involuntary Migration and Resettlement.* Boulder: Westview, 1982.

Partridge, William L. "Planning and Design Stage," in *Training Manual in Development Anthropology*, edited by William L. Partridge. Washington, D.C.: American Anthropological Association, pp. 18–30, 1984a.

Partridge, William (ed.). *Training Manual in Development Anthropology*. Washington, D.C.: American Anthropological Association, 1984b.

Partridge, William L., and Warren, Dennis M. "Introduction: Development Anthropology and the Life Cycle of Development Projects," in *Training Manual in Development Anthropology*. Washington, D.C.: American Anthropological Association, pp. 1–8, 1984.

Pillsbury, Barbara L. K. "Evaluation and Monitoring" in *Training Manual in Development Anthropology*. Washington, D.C.: American Anthropological Association, pp. 42–63, 1984.

Schuh, G. E. et al. *Social and Environmental Impacts of Dams: The World Bank Experience*. Washington, D.C.: The World Bank, 1987.

Stykes, J. M. "Sample Surveys for Social Science in Underdeveloped Areas," in *Human Organization Research*, edited by R. M. Adams and J. J. Preiss. Homewood, IL: Dorsey Press, pp. 375–388, 1960.

Part 2

Basic Methods

4
Surveys: Avoiding the Common Problems

Shirley Buzzard

Carrying out surveys in developing countries is both different and more difficult than conducting surveys in a developed country. At the same time, survey research is sometimes required for social impact assessment, baseline studies, or evaluation. The objective of this chapter is to offer some guidelines on planning, conducting, and analyzing survey data that will help avoid some of the most common problems.

The problems of collecting information may be both in logistics and in cultural differences. Logistic problems may include:

- Transportation problems such as a shortage of vehicles, difficult or impassable roads, or long distances between homes.
- There may be a shortage of skilled staff to help the survey.
- There may be language problems. People may only be fluent in a local dialect so that questions must be asked in more than one language. Translation into a national language or English can take time and introduce error.
- There may be no dependable facilities for computer analysis of data.

Cultural problems may include:

- People may be suspicious and uncooperative.
- People may not be sophisticated in answering questions so that interviews take a long time.
- Local customs or rules of courtesy preclude this type of research or make it unlikely that the data will be reliable.

After the data are collected, other problems can occur in the analysis and use of the information. Computers that were thought to be accessible and dependable are not. Many surveys carried out in developing countries are never analyzed. This is often because planned data analysis cannot take place. For example, universities may close for strikes or be closed when there is political unrest. Hardware may break down and there may be no replacement parts. In one case analysis of government census data took priority in the use of facilities. All too often, the time allowed for survey analyses is severely underestimated and results are only available months or years after they were needed.

Another common problem is the over analysis of the data so that those who need to use the information cannot understand the results. Complex statistical programs are run when mean, median, mode, and percentages or other simple descriptive statistics would have been adequate and much more understandable. It is also often the case that no summary of the data is written for laymen or project staff to explain how the results can be translated into action.

In carrying out a survey, many of these problems can be overcome with proper planning. The remainder of this chapter presents twelve suggestions which may help.

Be Sure a Survey Is the Proper Tool
for the Task

Research methods should be viewed as a tool kit. Choosing the correct one for the task is half the job. Surveys, or questionnaires, are very useful in collecting some types of information but they are expensive and time consuming to administer and analyze. Sometimes other tools are simpler, faster, easier, or more accurate. Surveys are appropriate for the following purposes:

- for a demographic profile of the community. For example, in a health program, it may be important to know the number of women of child bearing age or the number of children under five. If the project is expected to have some impact on migration patterns or male out-migration, then a statistical profile of the community is needed.
- for a broad look at people's opinions about a program. For example, it may be important to know men's attitudes toward agricultural training for women or to know women's attitudes towards the introduction of cash crops. People's opinions must be taken into account for widening roads, relocating markets, and many other proposed "improvements."
- to find out "what if" a project were implemented. For example, if a dam flooded an area and required relocation, where would

people prefer to move. Or, would people be willing to pay for the maintenance of a water system if the government were to install it.
* to confirm the validity or reliability of existing data. Some countries, such as Kenya and Indonesia, have fairly sophisticated routine census collection. A mini-survey can help determine whether existing information is reliable or whether new data should be collected.
* and always, when the time as well as human and financial resources allow for the proper gathering and analysis of the information.

Surveys may not be appropriate when:

* gathering information on income. Because income varies seasonally or is paid daily (and irregularly), people in developing countries sometimes do not know their annual or monthly income. In rural areas income is often "in kind" exchanges of produce, labor, or family sharing. Even when income is known, people may be unwilling to report it accurately for fear of taxation or that extended family members may find out.
* gathering information on personal behavior such as sexual activity, contraceptives, family interactions, political views. Also subjects which may be embarrassing such as certain health problems, illiteracy, or family problems are not amenable to survey research.
* a fast turnaround of information is required.

Before a survey questionnaire is chosen as the research method, consider some alternative methods and see if they might be more appropriate. The Bureau of the Census report (1985) for AID discusses alternative types of data collection and some of the practical considerations in choosing one. Alternative, or supplementary methods, might include:

* unstructured interviews with small groups of people (Kumar 1987).
* using existing information. In many developing countries local chiefs, district officers, or head men have very accurate records of the number of families, their age and sex composition, and other information (cf. Kiecolt and Nathan 1987).
* observations of behavior. Systematic observations of behavior, even limited in time or scope, are more accurate than asking people what they do. For example, an Indonesian survey indicated that people were aware of the importance of vitamin A in the diet and were eating more of it. Yet observations in three communities

during the evening meal indicated that very few families were eating food rich in vitamin A. Similarly, in Belize, when household heads were asked who carried household water, a very high percent of the men said they carried household water. Observations indicated that was not at all the case. Almost all water was carried by women and children.

• interviewing community leaders such as school teachers, business people, government officials, or elders. Leaders often have a very good sense of community sentiment on certain issues. In any event, the views of leaders are critical to the success of the project.

• case studies. These have become increasingly popular as a research method because they describe the cultural, political and economic context within which the project will operate.

Take Cultural Sensitivities into Account

There is no way to describe here all the possible things which people may find offensive or amusing. When deciding whether or not to do the survey, it is advisable to talk with some local social scientists, community leaders, and others to find out what research styles are most suitable to the situation and what subjects are best avoided.

In Asia, people's eagerness to be polite may mean that they say what they think you want to hear rather than what they really do or think. Jones (1963) calls this the "courtesy bias." In communities where a number of development projects have already been done, such as Haiti, people may respond with what might be called the "oh, woe is me" bias. Realizing that most programs target the poor, respondents present themselves in the worst possible light in order to benefit from any programs which may be forthcoming.

In Moslem countries, women may be uncomfortable with interviews even with women researchers and it may be necessary to obtain their husband's permission to do the interview. Or the husband may insist on being present during the interview making the woman less than candid.

In some parts of Africa it is considered impertinent to ask how many children a family has since counting children likens them to animals. In very traditional communities any visitor is expected to visit, eat, and stay a while. Overlooking conventions of courtesy and getting right to the interview and leaving is considered brusque and offensive. However, under these circumstances a "short" interview can take two hours.

In one study of women in a part of Kenya people are called by their children's names, a practice anthropologists call teknonomy. It is much like American's referring to their neighbors as "Suzy's Mom" or "Tommy's Dad." In this case, women sometimes used their husband's names (for contact with Europeans and some government records) and sometimes their father's last name. They also had nicknames. The confusion was compounded by the feeling that it was rude to ask how to spell a name (it is considered ignorant for the researcher not to know how to spell and it may embarrass a non-literate woman to ask her to spell her name). Each woman, then, had used up to four different names, all written by researchers in their best estimation of what they heard. It was very difficult to determine who had been interviewed, who was related to whom, and how to compare information collected from other research methods.

On the other hand, some topics that might be expected to be sensitive may not be. In Indonesia, family planning researchers have made such a nuisance of themselves that many families have posted their name, number and sex of children, and family planning method on a sign in their front yard. Sometimes so many researchers have been around asking questions people become very savvy. Rely on the advice of local researchers, community leaders and pre-tests to find out what is and is not acceptable.

Get Support from Local Officials and Announce the Dates and Purpose of the Survey

People are much more apt to be cooperative in data collection if they have been informed that such a survey will be done, what its purpose is, and that the researchers are legitimate. Gaining the permission and support of local government officials may be both a courtesy as well as a legal requirement.

Before starting the survey, visit district and local officials and explain the purpose of the survey and provide any information they need on how it will be carried out and used. Show them a copy of the intended data collection form. Ask for advice on the wording of the questionnaire, logistic arrangements, and cultural factors. Ask them to lend their support and announce the survey. Announcements at community meetings, posters on trees or at the market, or announcements on the local radio station will help people prepare for the inverviewers' visit and it will save time if they know, generally, what will be asked, how the information will be used, and that the research is sanctioned by local officials.

Keep It Short

At the beginning, decide exactly what information is needed and try to get that information with as few questions as possible. Define very clearly the goals of the research and keep the information collection focused on those objectives.

In developing countries, it is almost always necessary to have interviewers do the actual data collection. Methods used in industrialized countries, such as mail-in forms and telephone interviews, are almost never used. If it is necessary to hand tabulate the results of more than 500 interviews, then the form should be no longer than one page. Hand tabulation is not only time consuming, errors are more common than with computers.

Resist the temptation to "add on" questions because the answers would be interesting or because of preconceived ideas about what should be on a questionnaire. All too often, questionnaires ask too many questions about too many subjects. This shotgun approach only adds work and increases the amount of time it will take to administer and analyze the information (Buzzard 1984:275).

Take care that data collection forms are laid out in a simple, readable style and that responses can be recorded quickly and accurately. If data will be analyzed by computer, pre-code the answers so results may be entered directly into the computer without having to code data. Look at each question critically and ask whether that information is really needed and how the answer will be used in the analysis. If there is no clear reason for asking the question, leave it out.

Pre-test the Questionnaire Carefully

Pre-testing means trying out the questionnaire on a few people before the survey begins. After the questionnaire has been designed, discussed with local officials, and reviewed for cultural sensitivities, the next step is to train those who will administer it. The pre-test has the dual purpose of refining the questionnaire and training the research assistants who will administer it.

Attendance at the training session must be required of all those involved in the survey. Review the purpose of the survey, its objectives, and be sure that all the interviewers know enough about the sponsoring organization and reasons for doing the survey to be able to answer any questions respondents may have. Go over the form question by question to be sure that everyone has the same understanding of the meaning, alternative responses, and how to mark answers.

Ask each interviewer to try out the form on five or ten people (who are not included in the sample) and then meet again. Discuss each question and identify those in need of re-writing, revision, or omission. At the follow-up meeting, discuss whether

- people understood the questions.
- anything could be phrased more simply.
- anything was redundant, offensive, or inappropriate.
- answers were recorded as clearly and simply as possible.

After the pre-test, make all suitable revisions of the questionnaire. Check to see that each interviewer marked it correctly, clearly, and in the same way as other interviewers. Some interviewers may need a special review session to understand the requirements of the job.

If everyone gives the same answer to a question, either rephrase the question to spread the responses out or omit the question. If there is a strong consensus in the community on an issue then the survey is probably the wrong research method. Unstructured interviews would give more dimensions of the issue.

In gathering opinions, take care that questions are worded so that they are neutral and do not lead the respondent to a particular answer.

Choosing a language to use for the survey can be a problem in itself. If the survey covers a large rural area or an urban slum, very different dialects or languages may be represented. Men are sometimes insulted when addressed in a local dialect because it implies they are not fluent in the national language. Sometimes a national language is associated with a particular ethnic group and rival groups are offended by it. At the same time, people in rural areas and women may not be fluent in the national language.

Print the questionnaire in the language that will actually be used in interviews and record answers in the same language. Do not expect interviewers to translate questions or answers at the time of the interview as this introduces error. Translations, if needed, should be done after the information is collected and by a few people working together to be sure all terms are translated in the same way.

Sometimes questionnaires are printed in two languages. If this is done, double check whether the question is understood the same in both languages. Sometimes an English translation is printed under each question so that analysis can proceed on the basis of the English even though the questions were asked in another language.

Choose the Sample Carefully

When it has been decided that a questionnaire is the correct research method, when the community is willing to cooperate with the survey, and when a good, tight questionnaire or interview form has been developed, the survey can begin.

Only very rarely is it necessary to interview every individual or family in a community. Rather, a sample is drawn from the target population. The target population is all those people who are likely to be affected by the project. Choosing the sample is difficult but important. The sample must be large enough to accurately represent the population from which it is drawn but as small as possible in order to save time and money.

If the target population is relatively homogeneous and simple descriptive statistics will be used, a sample size of 100 may be adequate. If the target population is heterogeneous or if multivariate analysis is planned, then 300 to 500 respondents may be needed. Even samples of 40, however, can be useful if time and money are not available for larger samples (cf. Finsterbusch 1977a and 1977b).

A larger sample is not necessarily better than a small sample. It is preferable to choose a small sample and carry out the survey very carefully than to choose a large sample and do it in a sloppy way. One of the most common errors among researchers who are unfamiliar with questionnaires is a sample that is too large or improperly chosen.

The two considerations in choosing the sample to population ratio are the size and heterogeneity of the target population. The smaller the target population, the higher the proportion that must be sampled. If there are only 100 families, for example, you may want as much as a 30 or even 50 percent sample. But, if you are surveying a large area with 10,000 families, then a 1 or 2 percent sample should be adequate.

If people living in the area are relatively similar to each other, that is, of the same religion, ethnicity, birthplace, and language, as they often are in rural areas, then a smaller sample will be adequate. If the population is heterogeneous, as they usually are in urban areas, then a larger sample is required to be sure all groups are adequately represented.

In most surveys connected with development projects, the unit of analysis is the household. Defining a household may be a problem in places where a household is not equivalent to a house. For example, in most parts of Africa a household is a compound of several houses with three generations and as many as a hundred people. Where households are large, complex, or polygynous it may be preferable to define a household as a married woman and all her unmarried children although this is a culturally artificial term.

Most governments have some definition of "household" which is used for census purposes. If possible, use the government definition as it makes the data more comparable with that of other researchers and government statistics.

There are many ways of choosing a sample and it will be very helpful to consult research methods books for detailed descriptions of different types of samples and the strengths and weaknesses of each (cf. Williams 1978, Kalton 1983). For surveys in developing countries, there are two practical types of samples: random and stratified.

A random sample technically is one where each respondent had as much chance of being selected as any other individual in the population. In practice, that means choosing people to interview on the basis of chance rather than because of any quality or attribute they may have. Individuals interviewed may be chosen in any number of ways:

- Assign house numbers to houses (if there are none) and interview the head of each household with a number ending in 5 or 0. Or use a table of random numbers to choose the households.
- Use lists of families or individuals provided by census takers or government offices; choose every fifth or tenth name.
- With a large geographic area, section off a map into one mile squares and interview everyone in those squares which have been chosen at random.

Stratified samples, where the number of respondents in various categories is predetermined, are also useful in developing countries. The researcher might, for example, decide to interview 25 men and 25 women from each of of four districts and from each of five age groups for a total sample of 500 respondents.

In a heterogeneous population where a small sample is necessary, then a stratified sample assures that all the categories of people are represented. If the researcher is not familiar with the population then there is always the danger that some socially or politically important attribute may be overlooked. Also, it is important that those individuals who represent the category are chosen at random. If the sample calls for interviews with 25 women of a particular religion, age, and language, then those women must be selected from the pool of women with those attributes in an unbiased way.

There are other types of samples which are sometimes used because time does not allow a more rigorous sampling frame. These "quick and dirty" samples are used very often in development work, particularly in project evaluation. The "convenience sample" is interviews with everyone it is possible to interview. If the researcher has only a few days in the field, he should try to see as much of the program (or area) as possible and try to ask the same three or four questions of everyone contacted. Naturally the results of a convenience sample are not statistically valid but it may be the best way to use limited time.

The "snowball sample" is one where each person interviewed is asked to introduce the researcher to someone else to interview. A snowball sample may be a reasonable way of choosing informants within the categories of the stratified sample if there is no way of getting a true random selection. Each respondent in a specific category is asked to name another person in that category. Snowball samples, however, tend not to cross certain social boundaries so that people who should be included are left out. It is not an ideal way to collect information but can be used where time is limited and, the fact is, most development research is carried out under less than ideal conditions.

All research should be as valid and reliable as possible. Validity means that the information gathered really measures what it was expected to measure. As long as fairly concrete variables such as family size, crops planted, or years of schooling, are measured, it is likely the data will be fairly valid. In trying to measure more abstract variables such as family cohesion, willingness to pay, or social barriers the validity of the data is more uncertain. If it is necessary to quantify abstract concepts in a questionnaire, then carry out some prior observations and interviews to be sure that the indicator really measures the abstract concept.

Reliability means that if the research were repeated, the results would be the same. Reliability is directly proportional to the rigor of the research design. If the sample is properly chosen, interviews are carried out in the same way by different interviewers, and data are recorded and analyzed carefully, then the research is probably reliable.

If validity and reliability are of concern, there are statistical tests which can help determine the validity and reliability of data. Standard statistics texts should be consulted for a more thorough discussion.

Plan Data Analysis Before
Carrying Out the Survey

All too often, questionnaires are administered with the idea that the analysis of the data is a separate and later task. First gather the data, then figure out what to do with it. The process will proceed much more quickly and smoothly if data analysis is planned from the beginning.

At the time the final questionnaire is constructed, plan the data analysis and perhaps even write the computer programs. Code all the responses so that the results can be entered into the computer as they come in, daily if possible.

Determine which statistical tests will be done on each question and decide how the results will be used in the analysis. If each question has no clear reason for being on the questionnaire, either to gather specific information or to cross check some other question, then leave it out.

Although data analysis in the field is fraught with many possible difficulties, the immediate analysis of information is preferable to bringing data back to the United States and analyzing it. Some statistical results need to be backed up with interviews. For example, one survey in Kenya showed that although most women understood the value of childhood vaccinations, few had their children vaccinated. Follow-up interviews determined that a rumor that vaccinations also contained sterility drugs had kept many women from taking their children for vaccination. Had the data been analyzed later, there would have been no opportunity to clarify this problem.

It cannot be overemphasized that dependable access to computer facilities in developing countries should not be taken for granted. One project which funded fifty research projects in developing countries found that 80 percent did a survey but only 10 percent of those actually got the data analyzed in time to use it.

AID has had a similar experience. In a review of ten complex surveys carried out by AID, it was found that fewer than half were used in project decision making and five of the surveys cost between $300,000 and $1.5 million per survey and none of these were used (Norton and Benoliel, 1987:5,6).

There are many reasons why data analysis may be delayed if a public institution such as the government or a university is expected to handle the actual analysis. Where resources are limited, other work may take priority. Universities may be closed in times of political unrest. Power failure, hardware breakdowns and software bugs can all create very long delays. Private data analysis firms are more dependable but, of course, more costly. The dependability of microcomputers has increased and doing your own analysis is preferred. Even then, electricity can go out, software can melt, or equipment may end up on the other side of the world with the luggage. There are many cases of consultants who have carried a microcomputer and a printer to a research site only to find the plug does not fit, the ribbon on the printer is used up, or they forgot the printer cable.

The moral here is to always plan a backup if field analysis of data is planned. If the analysis depends on a microcomputer, check with a university or a private data analysis firm to see if there will be a backup if something goes wrong. If possible, find out whether supplies and parts for that brand of microcomputer are available in country. Increasingly in capital cities, there are small firms which sell and repair popular microcomputers. If the facilities of a university or a government agency will be used, locate another facility to use in an emergency.

By planning data analysis before data collection turnaround time is reduced, wasted efforts are minimized, and data can be entered and analyzed as it comes in. If there are major problems, they can be identified early, not after the data collection has been done.

Carefully Supervise the Collection of Information

During the actual data collection interviewers need a backup, support, and supervisory team to be sure the data collection goes smoothly. Especially when the questionnaires are being administered during long days over a short period of time, then arrangements must be made for interviewers' food, housing, and transportation. They must be supplied with blank questionnaires, pencils, and other materials. Questionnaires should be collected from interviewers frequently and, after being reviewed for accuracy and consistency, sent immediately for data entry and analysis.

Supervisors should visit interviewers, and perhaps accompany them on a few interviews from time to time, to be sure that all interviews are being conducted in the same way. Supervisors should review all forms as they come in for clarity, completeness, accuracy, and comparability. It is advisable to have a meeting with the interviewers each evening if possible to review the events of the day and plan the next days activities.

Where possible, it is helpful to interviewers to travel in teams of two. This enables them to have some moral support while they work and they have someone with whom to talk over problems. Working alone all day can be boring and may lead to some "shortcuts" on collecting information.

It is very important that the interviewers make it clear that they can not change the interviewee's conditions. Sometimes all "officials" are viewed as having authority over everything. Interviewers may be burdened with complaints about the schools, the water shortage, the lack of jobs, and many other problems. Interviewers must make no promises to those interviewed.

In one case in Kenya the survey was poorly planned and people were not cooperating with the survey. To gain cooperation, one interviewer promised that the development agency would give each family a bed for participating in the interview. It created havoc when people started visiting the agency demanding their bed. In another similar case, women were told they would be given a new dress if they would agree to be interviewed.

Giving gifts or paying people to cooperate most often leads to problems. If small gifts (a pen, a tube of toothpaste, a calendar) are given, they should be given after the interview as a gift and not before as a bribe to cooperate. Be absolutely sure there are enough gifts for all who participate or there will be complaints. In general, it is better not to use gifts or payments unless the interview is particularly long or people have been severely inconvenienced by the research.

Schedule interviews at a time that is convenient to people. Most heads of households are out during the day and may go to bed very early at night. If possible, make an appointment ahead of time and tell the family when the interviewer will visit and approximately how long the interview will take. If appointments are made, be scrupulous in keeping them. Evenings and weekends are often the best times for interviews with men while women are more apt to be available in the afternoons.

Be Sure That Everyone Involved Realizes
How Much Time and Money a Survey Takes

Everyone who has carried out research in a developing country knows that no matter how long you think something will take, it actually will take longer. Sometimes employers or others who are interested in the results of the research do not realize how much time and money are involved in a good survey. They give the researcher three weeks to carry out a major survey as well as do interviews, and collect information on other social, political and economic issues.

Before beginning a survey, clarify with the employer, and appropriate government officials, that a well designed survey of 1,000 households will probably take at least three months and will cost about $10,000 in addition to the researchers salary, transportation, and housing. Planning the survey, pre-testing forms, training interviewers, actual collection of data, and analysis all take time and each phase can easily get bogged down because of a shortage of vehicles, political unrest, an earthquake, or a typhoid epidemic. Costs include salaries for interviewers, drivers, and clerical backup. In planning budgets, remember that inflation rates are very high in some places and costs may go up almost daily. The reproduction of forms and other supplies for the interviewers can be costly. If the survey can be kept short and is hand tabulated, data analysis costs may be less.

Draw up a realistic time schedule and budget, add an additional 25 percent and discuss it with the agency that has requested the survey. If the results are needed more quickly or there is not enough money for a survey, then it is a good idea to use other research methods. Some officials request a survey simply because they do not know there are alternatives. Go to the discussions prepared to describe other methods and estimate the time and costs involved.

Do Not Overanalyze the Data

For most applied research in development projects, social impact assessments, evaluations, or planning research, elaborate statistical analysis is not needed. A few descriptive statistics such as range, mean, and standard deviation are adequate to describe the population. Percentages, chi-squares, correlations, and tests of significance are also useful.

However, where computers are used in analysis, there is a tendency to use sophisticated multiple regressions and to do correlations between each variable and every other variable. This generates stacks of computer printouts that are difficult to sort through, are intimidating, or are often misinterpreted.

Unless the technical expertise is available to use *and interpret* sophisticated statistics, stick to the simpler ones.

Write a Summary of the Results in Layperson's Language

After the data are analyzed, it is important that a narrative be written on the results. The narrative should as simple and clear as possible, giving definitions where technical terms are used. It should be short (under ten pages if possible), contain a methodology section describing how the data were collected and analyzed, and present the five or so major findings of the study.

Tables can be appended to the report but data presented in the body of the report should be in graphs (pie, bar, or line) or in other easily interpreted ways. The data should be presented objectively in one section of the paper and a final section of "analysis" should tell how to interpret the findings and what they mean. Offer alternative interpretations if there is no single one that makes sense of the information.

It is almost always useful to carry out some open-ended interviews with people to help understand any statistical results. Questionnaires tell what people do but, for the most part, not why they do it. If unusual correlations or statistically significant patterns appear, talk with some people and ask about the cultural or social circumstances which may account for the patterns.

Translate Findings into Action Terms

Do not assume that readers of the report will know how to translate findings into action. One of the most common complaints among those who do research relating to development projects is that the research is not used. The shelves of development agencies are lined with dusty volumes of research which is not used because the author failed to help project planners understand how their findings should affect programs.

Depending on the reasons for doing the survey, it is appropriate to suggest program priorities, define target populations, or suggest locations for buildings or roads. When the research arrives at no clear conclusions, that should be stated clearly. Offer several suggestions if possible. There is no guarantee that the research will be taken into consideration but the probability is much higher that it will be used if the funding agency is clear about what the research means in program terms.

A good example is a development organization which carried out an expensive and time consuming study of health conditions and services in a community prior to beginning a community health program. The researcher presented the results of the study to the health technicians who would plan the program mainly as a bound stack of computer printouts with a few numbers circled. Because they could not understand the data or the program implications, the report was ignored.

Had they been given an accompanying narrative report which presented simple statistics on patterns of illnesses and their distribution among different age and sex groups, they could have incorporated it into their planning. The researchers should also have made some suggestions about target groups and program priorities. This step between analyzing the data and translating it into programmatic terms is all too often overlooked.

Conclusion

This chapter has assumed the reader has some familiarity with surveys, sampling, data analysis, and interpretation. There are excellent texts on survey design, questionnaire lay-out, statistics, and research methods in general. The discussion here has focused on some of the problems of carrying out surveys overseas under the realistic conditions found there.

Survey work overseas is apt to be less "scientific" than it might be in a situation where there is more control over data collection, when informants are literate and familiar with the usual research techniques. Survey research is time consuming and costly. It is one of many research tools a development professional should know how to use. It is certainly the most efficient way to gather information on a large population.

However, questionnaires and survey methods were developed by sociologists for use in industrialized, literate societies. They adapt imperfectly to conditions in other cultures and levels of development. By following these twelve suggestions, the problems can be minimized and the value of surveys substantially increased.

References

Agency for International Development. *A.I.D. Evaluation Handbook. AID Program Design and Evaluation Methodology Report No. 7.* Washington: PPC/CDIE, 1987.

Bureau of the Census and Center for Development Information and Evaluation. *Selecting Data Collection Methods and Preparing Contractor Scopes of Work. AID Program Design and Evaluation Method Report No. 3.* Evaluative Studies Branch of International Statistical Programs Center and AID/PPC/CDIE. Washington: AID, 1985.

Buzzard, Shirley. "Appropriate Research for Primary Health Care: An Anthropologist's View." *Social Science and Medicine* 19:273-277, 1984.

Converse, Jean M., and Presser, Stanley. *Handcrafting the Standardized Questionnaire.* Sage University Papers Series Paper No. 63. Newbury Park, CA: Sage, 1987.

Fink, Arlene, and Kosecoff, Jacqueline. *How to Conduct Surveys: A Step by Step Guide.* Newbury Park, CA: Sage, 1985.

Finsterbusch, Kurt. "The Mini-Survey: An Underemployed Research Tool." *Social Science Research,* 5 (1) March, pp. 81-93, 1977a.

———. "Demonstrating the Value of Mini-Surveys in Social Research." *Sociological Methods and Research,* 5 (1) August, pp. 117-136, 1977b.

———. "Survey Research." *Social Impact Assessment Methods.* Kurt Finsterbusch, Lynn Llewellyn, and C. P. Wolf (eds). pp. 75-94. Beverly Hills: Sage, 1983.

Fowler, Floyd J. *Survey Research Methods.* Newbury Park, CA: Sage, 1984.

Grootaert, Christiaan. *Measuring and Analyzing Levels of Living in Developing Countries: An Annotated Questionnaire. Living Standards Measurement Study Working Paper No. 24.* Washington: World Bank, 1986.

Hageboeck, Molly. *Manager's Guide to Data Collection.* AID Program Design and Evaluations Methods. Washington: AID, 1979.

Ingersoll, Jasper, Sullivan, Mark, and Lenkerd, Barbara. "Social Analysis of AID Projects: A Review of the Experience." Mimeograph. Washington: AID (PPC/PDPR/HR), 1981.

Jones, E. G. "The Courtesy Bias in South-East Asian Surveys." *International Social Science Journal* 15:70–76, 1963.

Kalton, Graham. *Introduction to Survey Sampling.* Quantitative Applications in the Social Sciences Paper #35. Newbury Park: Sage, 1983.

Kiecolt, K. Jill, and Nathan, Laura E. *Secondary Analysis of Survey Data.* Sage University Papers Series Paper No. 53. Newbury Park, CA: Sage, 1987.

Kumar, Krishna. *Conducting Group Interviews in Developing Countries.* AID Program Design and Evaluation Methodology Report No. 8. Washington: PPC/CDIE, 1987.

Norton, Maureen, and Benoliel, Sharon Pines. *Guidelines for Data Collection, Monitoring, and Evaluation Plans for AID-Assisted Projects.* AID Program Design and Evaluation Methodology Report No. 9. Washington: PPC/CDIE, 1987.

Smith, Kenneth F. *Design and Evaluation of AID-Assisted Projects.* Office of Personnel Management, Training and Development Division. AID: Washington, D.C., 1980.

White, Louise G. *A Practitioner's Guide to Impact Evaluations.* AID Program Design and Evaluation Methods Report No. 5. Washington: AID, 1985.

Williams, Bill. *A Sampler on Sampling.* New York: John Wiley & Sons, 1978.

World Bank. *Living Standards Measurement Study Series No. 1 through 25.* Washington, D.C.: World Bank, 1985–1987.

5
Demography of the Project Population
Cynthia C. Cook

Demography may be defined as the study of the spatial and temporal distribution of population and of key population characteristics such as age, sex, ethnicity, residence, education, occupation, employment, and income. Development projects take place in a particular demographic context, and such projects may bring about significant demographic change. Thus, the methods of demographic analysis provide one set of tools to help identify and evaluate project social impacts. Demographic data can be used to construct indicators of significant social phenomena, such as fertility and mortality rates, literacy rates, proportions of female-headed households, etc. Trends derived from the analysis of demographic data can be used to forecast future conditions under varying assumptions derived from different development scenarios. The comparison of projected conditions following a proposed development project with projected conditions if the project does not take place (the "do-nothing" case) determines the magnitude of expected social impacts. The valuation of these impacts by relevant actors, including beneficiaries, service providers, planners, public officials and donor agencies, helps to determine the course of action selected.

Before bringing the tools of demography to bear on the social evaluation of projects, however, the analyst is faced with the question of "scoping," or defining the scope of the social phenomena to be considered. "Scoping" may involve defining the boundaries of the project population in time and space, describing the social relations presently existing between subgroups within this population and between it and the outside world, and identifying which of these relations are likely to be sensitive to changes introduced by the proposed project. This definition of the problem determines the types of demographic data which need to be collected, the types of indicators to be constructed, and the social changes to be forecast as a result of the project.

Furthermore, after a demographic analysis has been completed, the analyst still has to determine the values to be attached to the different possible outcomes. Any development project is likely to have both positive and negative social consequences. The socially optimal scenario is the one which generates the greatest social benefits at the least social cost. The analyst may be called on to help determine which consequences are desirable and should be strengthened, and which are undesirable and should be minimized and/or compensated.

Ideally, this determination would be made by the project beneficiaries. In practice, however, it is usually made by the project planners, the donors who support the project, and/or by the service providers who implement the project. Part of the social analyst's responsibility, therefore, is to act as an advocate for the project population in order to enhance positive social impacts and to mitigate negative ones.

Theoretical Background

The practice of social impact assessment as it relates to development projects is rooted in one of two theoretical approaches. The first, finding its sources in structural functionalism, exchange theory, and modernization theory, identifies impacts primarily in terms of behavioral change and institutional responses. The other, rooted in conflict theory, social interactionism, and dependency theory, focuses on impacts at the psychological and societal levels. Both perspectives are important for understanding the full range of consequences that may be associated with development interventions.

Demographic analysis is particularly useful for project assessment within the first perspective. In this approach, development projects may be treated as problems in human ecology. Human ecology has to do with the ways in which people interact with their physical environment in order to improve their quality of life. The concept of community in the social sense is analogous to the concept of community in the biological sense: that is, an association of living things providing each other with mutual support and protection. The distinguishing characteristics of human communities are the specialized roles and relationships set up through social organization, and the conscious use of elements from the physical environment to achieve desired goals.

Within the theoretical perspective of human ecology, the pre-project situation may be described in terms of a given size and distribution of population, a given degree and kind of social organization within that population, a given physical environment, and a given level of technology. In fact, this pre-project situation is not static. Rather, the description should be interpreted as a "snapshot" at one point in time of a system in evolution. An accurate description of the pre-project situation will include information on secular trends that can be used to predict the changes that would take place in the absence of the project. Such a description (including trend data) provides the baseline from which project-induced impacts would be measured.

A development project may change this situation in one or several ways. It may act directly on the project area population, by, for example, reducing infant mortality rates, or by introducing new settlers in the area. It may affect social organization by setting up new institutions, e.g. cooperatives, or by changing the scope of traditional institutions, e.g. land tenure and use rights. It will often affect the physical environment, through the construction of infrastructure and changing patterns of land use. Finally, most development projects include some changes in the technology used by the project population to derive economic benefit from their physical and social resources.

It is the task of the social analyst to identify the specific changes which the project is designed to introduce in the pre-project situation and to trace out their possible consequences, which may or may not have been anticipated by project planners. Specifically, the social analyst looks at the effects which the project will have on the demographic characteristics of the project area population and the changes which will occur in patterns of social interaction. Demography provides some of the methodological tools which can be used in this analysis.

Demographic Data Sources

Census Data. The most commonly considered source of demographic data is the national census. In principle, all countries belonging to the United Nations should conduct a census of population every ten years. Many developing countries did so for the first time in 1960, and even more in 1970. The U.N. Statistical Office provides technical assistance to national agencies responsible for planning and carrying out census activities and producing national statistics. A major aspect of this office's activities is the attempt to define census categories on a comparable basis across countries so that the data may be used in cross-national studies with some degree of validity.

However, there are many problems with census data in developing countries. Complete enumerations are often difficult when parts of the country are inaccessible and/or parts of the population are permanently on the move. The use of sampling to do more detailed studies is hampered by the lack of an adequate sample frame. Data are sometimes collected and stored under primitive conditions that can cause significant loss of information. In addition, some of the early censuses were processed by hand tabulation that proved painfully slow and may have introduced additional errors. Typically, it has taken three or four years before census data are made available to the public. In rapidly changing situations, these data may already be obsolete.

Rapid progress is being made in improving the collection and processing of census data in most countries, and in another ten or twenty years most of the problems should no longer exist. However, they do need to be taken into account when trying to use presently available census data as a basis for demographic analysis related to development projects.

Agency Statistics. Often, government agencies serving a project area collect information for their own use that may also serve the purposes of social analysis. The disadvantage of these data is that they generally describe only the population with which the agencies come into contact. Rarely does a government agency conduct an actual census, although this may happen in special cases. For example, the sample design for a study of the impacts of improved river transport on the remote upper reaches of the Rajang River in Malaysia was created from data collected by medical teams charged with completing the country's smallpox vaccination program. These teams made a special effort to reach the population at risk, including very small communities in virtually inaccessible locations. As a result, their population data for the area were far superior to those available from the national census or other sources.

Inferences can be drawn from agency statistics even if they reflect an incomplete coverage of the population, as long as some thought is given to the biases which may be introduced by considering those who are described by the data as if they were representative of the project population. A case in point comes from a study of a housing project in Morocco. Considerable information could be obtained from the records of credit institutions about the demographic characteristics of applicants for housing loans. While this information did not necessarily describe the total target population, it proved to be helpful in suggesting some of the likely differences between families who would and would not apply for loans and in projecting the probable consequences of the project for the latter group.

Usually, agency data provide a richer variety of measures of social phenomena than can be obtained from national census data. For example, the national census may give an estimate of gross literacy rates, but an education agency may have statistics which can be used to relate aggregate educational performance to a variety of service delivery indicators such as numbers of classrooms, numbers of teachers, numbers of textbooks, teacher qualifications, repeater and dropout rates, etc. Hypotheses drawn from such manipulation of partial data may then form the basis for field work aimed at testing the validity of these relationships in the context of the target group.

Previous Studies. Often, a project area population has been studied before and the data can be used to develop a demographic picture of the population, even if this was not the purpose of the original study. For example, a study of travel and transport in a rural Mexican state generated considerable data on household characteristics, farm size, cropping patterns, types of tenure, use of inputs, and patterns of employment and income. These data later proved useful in evaluating the delivery of agricultural services for this area. Most surveys include a number of demographic variables for the purpose of analyzing results by respondent categories. Use of these data to describe the project area population is, of course, subject to all the limitations of the original study. However, imaginative use of existing data sets is often a cost-effective substitute for the collection of original data on the ground.

Data Generation. Sometimes, after all of the above data sources have been tried, there is still no reliable source of information precisely describing the project area population. Frequently, census data cannot be disaggregated to the specific area of concern. Agency data may appear unreliable or may not cover the items of greatest interest. Perhaps no prior work has been done on the target population, or else the data cannot be accessed. In this situation, particularly if the project is targeted on a relatively small population, some original fieldwork may be necessary and feasible.

Demographic Variables

The interpretation of demographic data from developing countries must be done with caution. Even when the objective measurement of a particular variable is well defined, and the data have been collected according to acceptable procedures, there is always a danger of projecting views derived from the analyst's own experience onto data whose cultural meaning for the subjects is quite different. The danger is particularly great when the analyst has not had the opportunity to visit the project area and talk directly with the beneficiaries. It is also present whenever contacts have to be made through translators. While problems of interpretation vary from country to country, some general comments on specific items may be helpful.

Population Size. Unless recent and complete census data are available, it is often impossible to determine accurately the size of the population living in a particular area. A common estimating technique is to determine average household size from survey data and multiply by some readily measured indicator of the number of households, e.g.

number of farm plots. This approach can be misleading when applied to small area populations. A recent study which adopted this approach in Kenya underestimated the project area population by failing to consider that the average household size in a highly productive area would be much higher than the regional average. One should also make sure that major population groups like landless farmers or seasonal migrants are not missed by this method. If the project area is small and project planning requires fairly accurate estimates, a rapid enumeration on the ground would be the best way to provide reliable population data that can serve as a sound basis for the design of project activities and for future project monitoring and evaluation.

Age/Sex Distribution. Again, in the absence of disaggregated census data, these distributions are often inferred from surveys. Unless particular attention was paid to enumerating all household members, very young children and other individuals of low status ("poor relations") are likely to be missed in such surveys. Respondents may also conceal the presence of household members whose status they know to be irregular in the eyes of officials, e.g. those who have no identity papers or who are employed without authorization. These problems are most likely to result in underreporting of the numbers of women and children.

Most developing countries now register all births that take place with medical assistance. In principle, all births should be reported for the purpose of establishing identity and citizenship. These practices are relatively new, however, and reliable estimates of age can only be counted on for persons under the age of thirty or so. Birth and death statistics will be more recent and less reliable in remote areas where health services are not always available.

Typically, more well-off and established families who have some experience in dealing with the outside world will be represented by the available data, while poor, landless, nomadic and/or female-headed households will be less likely to be represented. The presence of female-headed households may also be obscured by cultural norms requiring men to report all females in their families as being under their care. In general, surveys that rely on men as the main informants should be regarded as unreliable with respect to the data provided on women, and possibly also on children. Data on the relative proportions of men and women in different age groups may suggest some interesting trends, especially taken in conjunction with data on education and employment patterns. A typical finding is that younger men who have had educational opportunities tend to leave the village and seek work in the city. If they are successful, they may establish an urban household as well as a rural one. Women in the same age group may be less mobile and may find themselves with increasing responsibility for farm work in order to feed their children. However, later in life the successful city dweller may return to the village, bringing new knowledge and techniques as well as financial resources that can make farming more productive.

Ethnicity. It is surprising how often this critical variable is misrepresented or ignored in data collection activities related to social impact assessment. Census data, in particular, are notoriously incomplete and unreliable on this matter, since the relative proportions of dominant and subjugated groups in the population may be of great political significance. The social analyst must know something about the principal ethnic groups that will be affected by the project, including minority groups that may be subjected to increasing exploitation or may lose access to critical resources as a result of the project. If existing data sets cannot be disaggregated by ethnic group, or if they fail to represent the full range of groups in the area, it may be necessary to conduct specific, highly focused field research in order to test the responses of all relevant groups to project proposals.

Many potential conflicts between social groups can be anticipated by analyzing the alternative uses of physical esources. For example, the semi-arid lands used for grazing in Botswana also provide a habitat to San hunter-gatherers. Rivers dammed in India to provide power and water for irrigation in the plains may inundate traditional lands belonging to hill tribes. In Brazil, the rain forest offers conflicting opportunities to indigenous peoples, rubber tappers, migrant farmers, and cattle barons. Resolution of these conflicts, difficult in any case, is made more difficult by historical resentments and distrust between different ethnic groups. Special attention may need to be paid in project preparation to the design of mitigating measures that will cushion the negative impacts of the project on particular groups and help to assure an equitable distribution of costs and benefits.

Ethnic differences are particularly important in projects that involve moving people from one place to another. In developing countries, ethnic groups are often identified with particular territories where they feel at home, protected by traditional rights and relationships and by the presence of ancestral spirits. Moving away from this territory is psychologically threatening, even if they are physically able to cope in the new environment. Often, too, such unwilling migrants are not welcomed by the inhabitants of the land they invade, and may face major obstacles and harassment in their new homes. In the Ivory Coast, for example, people living behind the Kossou Dam were reluctant to move out because they believed they would be endangered by the witchcraft of the people into whose lands they were to move. Projects that require resettlement therefore call for special measures to protect the displaced population and to ensure an orderly transition to the new way of life for both newcomers and old-timers.

Rural Versus Urban Residence. Census definitions of "urban" and "rural" vary considerably from country to country. Most developing countries are experiencing a high rate of urbanization. This effect is due to a combination of factors. First, the proportions of actual births which are recorded is probably higher in urban areas, and infant mortality rates may be lower due to better health services. Also, cities often contain a disproportionate share of population in the reproductive years of life, resulting in a higher than average birth rate. Secondly, there is the phenomenon of rural-urban migration. A third factor generating apparent urban growth is the growth of many rural centers to the point (often when they have no more than 5,000 population) where they are reclassified as urban. Research has often shown that a relatively high proportion of "urban" households, especially in smaller centers, are principally engaged in agriculture.

Rural-urban migration may take several forms and may occur in a series of stages, sometimes covering several generations. Only under extreme conditions is it likely that a person or household will move permanently from the country to the city. The more usual pattern involves an individual, perhaps a younger son, leaving the farm to seek education or employment in the city. He returns periodically to his village to visit his family, perhaps to till the land or help bring in the harvest or to pay respects to his ancestors. He may marry and set up a household in the village. If he is successful in finding an urban job, he may also establish a home in the city. Towards the end of his life, however, he may return to his village. Thus, the line between rural and urban residence is blurred both in terms of measurement and in terms of meaning.

Education. Available data on education usually describe formal schooling, either in terms of literacy rates or in terms of numbers of years completed. Often the criterion for literacy is the ability to read a foreign language such as French, Spanish, or English, and not one's native tongue, which may not even be written or taught in the schools. To be meaningful, data on the numbers of years completed should be complemented by indicators of the quality of schooling or by performance measurements. While it does not necessarily have anything to do with actual intelligence or ability to cope, data on formal education can be a useful indicator of exposure to new ideas and ways of doing things and contacts with people from the outside world.

Occupation. The occupational categories used in world census-taking reflect the Western concept of a hierarchy of occupational status, with executives and administrators on the top and unskilled workers on the bottom. These categories are often not very useful to the social analyst considering the potential impact of a development project. More useful may be the data on employment by sector, indicating the proportions engaged primarily in farming, fishing, forestry, herding, mining, manufacture, and so on. However, in many project areas even these data are inadequate to describe the full range of household activities.

Nonfarm occupations are an important source of household income in rural areas, as farming is even in cities. Such nonfarm occupations may include craft production, hunting and fishing, gathering of forest products, petty commerce, and a wide variety of service occupations. Frequently the income generated from such activities, including the value of home consumption and locally bartered goods and services, is not included in estimates of total household income. Rural residents may also work for wages in government agencies or local enterprises, in paraprofessional, skilled or unskilled positions. Income from nonfarm employment is likely to be more regular and to provide a better basis for securing credit than income from farming, which is subject to high seasonal variation and a high degree of risk. Rural residents employed in nonfarm occupations can often be helpful in bridging communications gaps between project planners and beneficiaries.

Some projects, particularly those based on advanced technology, involve the introduction of a significant number of skilled workers or agency staff whose characteristics may be quite different from those of project area residents. The superposition of a "modern" occupational hierarchy on the traditional status system is likely to generate conflicts at the local level. For example, in Benin the recruitment of local labor for road construction drew young men away from their fathers' farms, undermining the strength of traditional work groups and challenging the authority of older family members. Traditional leaders and local decision-makers need to be brought into the planning process for such projects in order to avoid disruptive conflicts and negative indirect impacts that might otherwise come about.

Employment. Data on labor force participation are also biased by Western notions of what constitutes employment. Typically, the participation of women and children in the labor force is underestimated. Production of food crops and care of small livestock for domestic consumption may not be seen as legitimate employment, although abandonment of these activities would jeopardize family survival. The seasonality of employment is another important factor in many developing countries that is not usually apparent from secondary data. A sympathetic understanding of the reality behind the numbers is necessary when projects are designed, as many are, to mobilize "under-utilized" human resources.

In some developing countries, there are significant annual population movements associated with seasonal employment patterns. Some of these movements are from one rural area to another, others are rural to urban. In the arid lands of Brazil's Northeast, as well as in the African Sahel, migration to find wage employment is a recognized strategy for survival when the rains fail. Familiarity with such movements is essential when assessing the probable success of projects that presuppose the availability of a permanent labor force.

Income. This variable, so critical to our understanding of the benefits to be derived from development projects and their distribution among the project population, is also one of the most difficult to measure. In the first place, household income in developing countries usually includes both cash and non-cash components. Cash income from wage employment or sales of farm or craft products is the easiest to measure, although even here there are reporting problems. Most households produce extensively for their own consumption, some more successfully than others. In addition there is often a considerable amount of bartering of goods and exchange of services among households, as well as simple sharing, gift-giving and informal credit arrangements. Often it is not easy to place a market value on the goods and services which households obtain through such mechanisms.

Many households have more than one cash income source. Quite often rural households receive regular or occasional remittances from members employed elsewhere, in urban areas or even in other countries. This is one explanation for the relatively high population levels which persist in some apparently unproductive agricultural areas. For example, in Burkina Faso a large proportion of households living in rural areas depend on remittances from family members employed in Cote d'Ivoire. A similar relationship exists between rural households in Lesotho and wage earners in the Republic of South Africa. The degraded and inhospitable mountains of eastern Algeria support a strong rural economy based primarily upon war veterans' pensions and the earnings of migrant workers in Europe.

In turn, urban dwellers are often supplied with food and other farm products by their families in rural areas. The informal bartering of goods and exchange of services can be important sources of non-cash income in urban as well as in rural areas. Much of the so-called "informal sector" in urban areas operates on these principles. Even where cash is involved in such transactions, their contribution to urban household incomes may be difficult to trace. Furthermore, the purchasing power of rural and urban cash incomes should be compared, taking into account the fact that urban dwellers may have to pay cash to meet basic needs, such as housing, water and fuel, which are "free" (though certainly not costless) in rural areas.

Strong social forces are at work in developing countries to reduce income disparities and mitigate risk through collective consumption of individual surplus. These forces are directly opposed to the individualistic policies of deferred consumption, saving and investment which are fundamental to economic growth. In the developing world, household income is not a reliable indicator of social status, although it becomes more important as a country becomes more "modern." Similarly, apparent inequities in income distribution may need to be examined more closely before their social consequences can be determined.

Land Tenure and Size of Holdings. In rural areas, land is the key resource for agricultural production. Forms of land tenure are closely related to the incentives for project beneficiaries to adopt desired behaviors and to the expected distribution of the resulting benefits. The basic forms of land tenure are ownership, rental, sharecropping, and use rights. In situations where land is still abundant relative to population, as in much of sub-Saharan Africa, land tenure may appear to be a less critical issue than where land is a relatively scarce resource, as in Asia and parts of Latin America. However, recent research in Mali has shown that complex land tenure arrangements and land use rights are an essential part of the traditional system for managing marginally productive lands, even under conditions of low population density.

Some rural areas contain a significant landless population which has to survive through wage employment on other people's farms. In other areas, farms have been subdivided to such an extent that many families have holdings of less than subsistence size; they, too, have to supplement their production with outside wage income. Often, family farm holdings are in several small, scattered parcels, frequently held under different forms of tenure, at some distance from each other and from the homestead. Where slash-and-burn agriculture is still practiced, as in many parts of sub-Saharan Africa, small communities may need to control extensive areas in order to preserve soil fertility through a rotation period that may extend over as many as twenty years.

The distribution of land tenure arrangements and size of holdings, although not strictly speaking demographic data, are often available from the same sources. Such data can provide a useful indication of the distribution of real economic power in a rural community. Similarly, data on cropping patterns, use of fertilizer and other commercial inputs, and ownership of farm machinery or other household assets can give indications of emerging social distinctions within such a community.

In the absence of resources needed to collect appropriate data, the social analyst will need to be creative in interpreting whatever data are available to gain an understanding of potential project impacts.

Demographic Analysis

Definition of the Project Population. Project planners generally try to identify a "target" or "beneficiary" population. The term "target population" usually describes those people who are expected to be directly affected by the project or whose behavior is expected to change in some way as a result of the project. The "beneficiary" population may be more widely defined to include those who will presumably share in the economic benefits generated by the project. The issue of "Who benefits?" merits close attention by the social analyst, for it may well be that the presumed beneficiary population is quite different from those who will actually reap the rewards of the project. Another question to ask is "Who pays?" since the costs of a project may well be borne in part by persons who will not share in its benefits. The project population should be defined to include all those whose lives will be touched by the project in some way, within the bounds of a given geographic area and a given project lifetime.

Selection of Relevant Variables. The project population may be segmented in a number of ways. The choice of appropriate categories depends upon the range of possible impacts that have been explored during the "scoping" process. Generally, it is pertinent to know something about the age and sex distribution of the population, household size and composition, length of residence, educational status, health status, size of landholdings, types of tenure, and sources and amounts of income. Ethnic identity may be a critical factor, particularly in situations that involve potential conflicts of interest between members of different ethnic groups. If the project involves people moving from one place to another, the characteristics of both "newcomers" (those who will move) and "old-timers" (those who already occupy the area) should be considered.

Data Collection. Information on each of the relevant variables must be obtained from one or more of the sources listed above. This may involve inferences relating the project population to the population described by the existing data sets. For example, if census data available at the district level indicate that 85% of the population is literate, it could be inferred that most of the people in the project area are literate. However, other information may alter this conclusion, such as the availability of schools in the project area, or the knowledge that the particular group under study tends to have a lower than average literacy rate. Census data are often more useful to describe the social context within which a development project is to take place than to describe the specific characteristics of a target population.

Ideally, the demographer should use several data sources to "triangulate" the probable range of values for each of the variables in which he or she is interested. In practice, this approach often leads to confusion, as different sources may give widely differing estimates in developing countries. In this situation, most analysts end by selecting the data which seem most reliable and internally consistent, checking the values of a few key variables with data drawn directly from the project population.

Because the analysis of potential social impacts involves forecasting changes over time, it is important to collect data not only on the present situation but also on the immediate and more distant past, if possible. Too often development planners (and their critics) assume that projects represent the only change in an otherwise static situation. Secular trends are ignored and the evaluation of impacts is distorted by this assumption. Furthermore, the analysis of past changes may lead to a better understanding of indigenous adaptations and coping strategies, which can lead in turn to improved project design.

Construction of Indicators. Items of data from one or several sources may be combined to construct indicators of the social phenomena which are of greatest interest for the analysis. For example, agency data on the number of schools serving a given area may be combined with census estimates of the school-age population to give a crude measure of the level of educational service provision. It should be kept in mind, however, that the relationship between an "indicator" and the phenomenon which it is supposed to indicate is culturally defined. Thus, while the number of schools per capita may be meaningful to western-oriented planners, it may bear no relation at all to the perception of educational needs or benefits by the target population.

Trend Analysis. This may be the most difficult task in social impact assessment and the one which, in developing countries at least, is often the most subjective. The difficulty is largely due to the absence of large amounts of reliable, quantitative data permitting the construction of statistical models such as are used to evaluate potential impacts in the developed countries. Based on a few data points, on a variety of personal opinions among informants and colleagues, and on a kind of intuition which passes for professional expertise, the analyst is expected to predict the future social situation if the project does not occur, as well as the likely consequences of several possible interventions.

The simplest part of the task is to predict the future size and shape of the project population without any intervention. Planners generally assume a constant population growth rate, often broken down into urban and rural rates reflecting, in addition to births and deaths, the process of rural-urban migration. The assumed growth rate is often the intercensal rate, e.g. the average annual growth between 1970 and 1980. If significant reductions in mortality, especially infant mortality, have been achieved in recent years, these growth rates probably underestimate current averages. Urban growth rates may be inflated by the reclassification of small towns as urban centers once they pass a certain population threshold (often as low as 5,000 residents). Average rural population growth rates may also mask significant variations as farm households migrate from one rural area to another in search of better farming conditions. A check on such migration patterns may be made by looking at responses to census questions on place of birth or previous residence.

The dependency ratio (usually calculated as the proportion of population below the age of 15 or over the age of 60 to the population between 15 and 60 years of age) is an important indicator of project sustainability. The future evolution of this ratio can be predicted using simple cohort analysis and fertility and mortality rates by age groups, assuming that these will not change over time. A more sophisticated analysis would take into account the probable changes in age-specific fertility rates as a result of changing educational and employment patterns, as well as possible changes in age-specific mortality rates due to ongoing improvements in nutrition and medical care.

A related phenomenon is the formation of female-headed households and the corresponding movements of men into isolated one-person households, peripheral roles in extended families, or quasi-institutional settings. These events can be related to the distribution of educational and employment opportunities by sex and the relatively greater freedom of men to move between rural and urban areas. Consequently, a look at present education and employment patterns, combined with population pressure on available land in rural areas, may help to predict the future configuration of both rural and urban households.

Project Impact Assessment. From a demographer's point of view, direct impacts are those which will change the actual size and composition of project area population, by directly affecting fertility, mortality, or mobility rates. Population projects, of course, are intended to bring down fertility rates in the long run; however, this is usually approached by raising child survival rates in the short run, producing a temporary bulge in the population which will recur at regular intervals as each successive generation reaches child-bearing age. Health and nutrition projects are often targeted on major causes of mortality, especially infant mortality; this may have major implications for the future evolution of the dependency ratio.

Most projects, however, are not designed to have a direct impact on the demography of the project population. Such impacts may occur, but usually not by design. It is the task of the social analyst to assess the likely demographic and social consequences of the proposed project and to help planners and project beneficiaries to find ways of coping with these effects.

Development projects generally involve the provision of some combination of infrastructure (changes in the physical environment), services (changes in social organization), and information (changes in technology). These inputs are expected to produce certain behavioral changes on the part of the target population that will result in an improved quality of life, often measured in terms of greater material wealth. While each project is unique and must be analyzed on its own terms, it is possible to explore the types of demographic impacts likely to be associated with each of the elements in of this process.

Infrastructure projects involve construction of physical facilities and changing land use patterns. Small scale infrastructure projects utilizing local labor need not have major demographic impacts. However, by altering the pattern of economic opportunities (often in ways which are biased toward particular segments of the project area population), they may modify ongoing processes of social change. For example, irrigation projects that offer wage employment followed by increased productivity and cash incomes may have a major impact in reducing outmigration rates for younger men in rural areas. Larger infrastructure projects require a large and specialized labor force for construction and may require a reduced but even more specialized labor force for operation. This may well imply significant short-term growth in the project area population, followed by decline after the project becomes operational, with a more subtle shift in the long-term occupational structure of the area and associated patterns of leadership and local decision-making.

Social impact assessment of large infrastructure projects in the developed world has shown that small communities can be severely impacted by the "boom and bust" cycle associated with such projects. Short-term impacts include the requirement for rapidly expanding services, which in developing countries means new demands for food, fuel, water, and shelter; the introduction of new social problems associated with the arrival of a transient, mostly male group of construction workers; and possible conflicts between outsiders and the local population. Longer term impacts derive from the alteration in local employment and income patterns and associated social status and control systems. If an infrastructure project generates changes in land use, it may tend to displace project area residents in favor of migrants with greater skills and financial resources.

Service provision projects, such as health and education projects, have a more indirect effect on the demography of a project population. Like infrastructure projects in the operation phase, they introduce into the project area a new social element in the form of service providers (teachers, clinic workers, agricultural extension agents) who have new skills and whose status consequently needs to be defined. Outcomes may be different depending upon whether these "agents of change" reside in the community and find ways of bringing local people into the new social systems, or simply visit the area to conduct official business. Beyond this first-order demographic change, however, service provision projects may generate indirect impacts by altering behavior related to the demographic profile. In particular, by modelling the modern sector and improving awareness of the outside world, such projects are likely to accelerate rural-urban migration. Well-designed and effectively delivered social service projects can also help to improve the status of women and children and, in the long run, to reduce fertility rates.

Information or technology transfer components also have an indirect effect on project population. Through improved technology, people in the project area increase their mastery over the physical environment and make more effective use of local resources. This makes it possible to increase the size of the population which can survive on a given resource base. Such a sudden population increase can occur in two ways: (1) through natural increase, which implies a rapidly changing dependency ratio; and (2) through in-migration, which suggests a rapidly changing social structure. An increased flow of information to rural areas may also convey an expanded awareness of opportunities in other places and consequently may promote outward mobility among specific population subgroups.

Comparison of Alternatives. Ideally, one would seek to specify a set of mathematical relationships among all the possible outcomes that would enable one to predict and compare the full range of consequences for each development scenario, including the "do-nothing" option. Much work has been done on the development of such models for impact assessment of major projects in developed societies. Unfortunately, these models are most useful in dealing with aggregate data for large populations, and they can only address a limited range of variables. In most developing countries, their use would only lend an air of spurious accuracy to an analysis which is necessarily based on incomplete and partially subjective data.

A commonly used tool for approximating this comparison is the social impact matrix, in which the magnitude and direction (positive or negative) of each identified impact, compared to what will happen in the "do-nothing case," is assessed for each alternative on a scale ranging from high to low. This allows a rough estimate of whether the positive impacts outweigh the negative ones, and may be helpful in deciding which alternative should be adopted. It does not, however, solve the problem when two or more alternatives appear to be about equally desirable. In the end, the judgment is almost always made on the basis of a qualitative assessment, which may or may not involve the beneficiaries.

Conclusion

Demographic analysis is one of several methodological tools available to assist in the prediction and evaluation of social impacts associated with development projects. The identification and interpretation of demographic data in developing countries presents some particular challenges, but these can be met by taking a creative and pragmatic approach to make the best use of whatever data are available. Change is inherent in all development situations, and the definition of project impacts must take this into account. A project is socially acceptable when the positive impacts on human welfare outweigh the negative ones, when the balance between the two is more favorable than for any other alternative, and when provision has been made to minimize or mitigate negative social impacts, particularly as these may affect already disadvantaged groups.

6
Informant Interviewing in International Social Impact Assessment

William Derman

Introduction

As Briggs has remarked, "Interviews are not supposed to be conversations."[1] Instead, informant interviews provide a means to determine how individuals or social groups view themselves, their relationship to their environment, to others, and to agents and forces of change. Informants provide access into others' worlds. Those worlds are typically distinct, and the perspectives different from those of planners, developers, engineers, and others engaged in planned interventions. This is the case in domestic SIA and in international SIA. In both, informant interviewing permits the elicitation of perspectives, views, and attitudes in the informants own terms and context. It is this effort to understand "the other" that makes the interview (or other comparable methods) essential to SIA.

What makes social impact analysis (SIA) different from other types of enquiry is precisely *the social*. Other types of inquiry and analysis examine economic, environmental, administrative considerations, et al., but SIA takes seriously the views of the proposed beneficiaries and affected populations of any development activity. It renders visible the often invisible web of social groupings, stratification systems, social exchange, etc., to planners. Social impact analysis is generally carried out for the use of planners and policy makers, who typically are the ones who receive the analysis, reports and recommendations. However, there is a contemporary redirection toward participatory development to involve intended beneficiaries in different stages of an SIA process. Simultaneously it must be recognized that development activities always have their costs which means certain groups of people may lose out.

Not enough attention has been paid in the project literature to those whose lives are negatively impacted.

The international debate on participation parallels the North American debate on a policy neutral or a policy advocacy stance for SIA practitioners. In the international arena participation has become a popular and overused term and too often is economically defined: those working or participating in a project with no connotations of greater involvement or decision-making. Despite its overuse, the concept of participation nonetheless plays a central role in both the analysis of development and the implementation of projects and programs.[2]

Informant interviewing provides the window to explore and analyze not only what a given population thinks about a given course of action but also how to draw upon its knowledge.[3] My emphasis is upon the importance of understanding others' worlds in development practice both to provide voice and to utilize intended beneficiaries and affected populations to improve development projects and programs.

Interviewing of informants is critical in any social impact assessment, because it provides qualitative data about how people understand their own situation, their needs and their aspirations and quantitative information about types of households, flows of resources, allocation of labor, amount of time spent on ceremonies, etc. Often, it is only social analysts who take such concerns seriously and seek to understand them rather than dismissing them as the thinking and action of backward peasants. Respect, seriousness, tact, and humor are difficult to teach; but they are essential for conducting interviews with informants.

In cross-cultural analysis the use of informants and how to obtain their views on planned change raise many difficult methodological issues. This chapter identifies critical dimensions of interviewing including informant selection, language variables, sociocultural variation, question formulation, time and funding limitations, and ethics.

Ethnocentrism: Its Relevance for SIA

A major finding of anthropology (given lip-service in many other disciplines) is that we are all ethnocentric. Ethnocentric means regarding one's own group as superior. By implication ethnocentrism also means that one considers one's own values dearer and more normal than those held by others. There are degrees of ethnocentrism ranging from denying other peoples' humanity, to considering them inferior in mind or body, to viewing them as misguided, conservative, or uninformed. Ethnocentrism, which exists in most societies and is certainly not confined to westerners, may be manifested in how rural-urban differences, gender differences, or minority differences are understood. Ethnocentrism on the part of social impact investigators can affect the relationships established between interviewers and subjects and influence the quality of the information obtained. In some of my own interviewing in West Africa, the ethnicity of the interviewer was important in the kinds of questions that would be responded to. I have been part of several efforts to elicit information when informants would skirt the issue because they believed, as I later found out, that the interviewer was from an ethnic group with whom they had disagreements in the past and who, in their view, was condescending toward them. Often, that same re-searcher did not probe certain areas because he felt he already knew why this ethnic group lived principally in poverty. Interestingly, when he interviewed people who were related to his ethnic group in a neighboring village his energy level and intellectual interest dramatically increased.

One reason it is essential to discuss ethnocentrism in SIA is that a developmental paradigm emerged in the 1960s which despite some variations in the paradigm conceives of development as transcending cultures and continents. It is arguable that this paradigm continues to be as dominant today.[4] The assumption that those who undertake development—whether as analysts or practitioners—are the guardians of development and progress conflicts with a central proposition many anthropologists hold: that there are many ways to be human and that cultural change is a complex, multilinear, interactive process that usually involves a multiplicity of cultures. In contrast, much development theory and practice[5] assume that the "answers" are known; it is the people concerned who need to change and the developers do not. To combat this tendency, as many anthropologists have argued, we may adopt the principle of cultural relativism.[6] Werner and Schoepfle insist that cul-tural relativism predicates ethical standards and that: "It is the root of the greatest insights of cultural anthropology" (1986:313). It represents the best means we now have to avoid ethnocentric judgments. In my judgment, the methodological stance of cultural relativism, seeing other societies and cultures in their own terms as a first step in analysis, should be that of all social analysts. Furthermore, it is important to recognize variations within cultures. While in the past anthropologists often assumed that there was a single or a central view held in common by all members of another culture, recent studies have shown there can be a considerable range of perspectives and values within a society or culture. Therefore, methodologically, it is critical to search for both the commonalities and differences within the relevant units to be studied.

The methodological stance of cultural relativism is what I call the anthropological perspective. However, this does not mean that all an-thropologists hold this perspective or that it is not held by other social analysts but only that cultural relativism is most clearly enunciated in anthropology. In discussing informant interviewing I emphasize anthropology because anthropologists have given considerable thought to interviewing in cross-cultural contexts. Yet, anthropology has been appropriately criticized for its lack of generalizability, or at least the thin empirical basis it yields for generalizations. While the discipline is at its best in the analysis of small groups, its focus is certainly not restricted to them; and although historically anthropology has been associated with the examination of exotic cultures it is not inherently linked to them. The traditional anthropological subfield devoted to primary data collection is ethnography. Its methods can be and are used with all social groups, and are now emphasized by the social sciences as a whole.

A New Dimension of Interviewing
in the Third World

A relatively new and interesting methodological question has arisen in informant interviewing. Many social scientists envision relatively pristine situations, that is, they assume other investigators have not preceded them. Based on my and others' experiences, however, we greatly underestimate the degree to which people in developing nations have been the subjects of multiple surveys, investigations, and have had repeated contacts with their own government agencies doing similar kinds of work. In short, interviewing situations may be mildly or dramatically affected by the informants' previous experience and by how the interviewers were presented to, and understood by informants. In addition, there are a multitude of mechanisms by which both the rural and urban poor resist, most often passively, state authority.[7] One way to effectively interview such populations is to work with individuals known and trusted by such groups. They might be religious figures, political activists, or scholars who spent long periods of time in the area. If such people are not available then the alternative of having a researcher spend the time necessary to establish ties of trust might be required. This depends on the type of information being sought. The assumption made by many in development work that they are welcome because they are "doing good" is less and less defensible. People in the developing world increasingly perceive that those who are studying them and providing projects are doing so for their own reasons, motivations and goals. These may or may not be consonant with local objectives, and if they are not, local communities or individuals attempt to alter projects accordingly. Indeed, development projects viewed as failures from the donor's perspective may not be perceived in the same fashion from the local point of view, since benefits may have been obtained which fit with what local people thought attainable. If one drops the assumption that those informants being interviewed in social impact assessment view their interviewers as "bringing good" we will bring a greater realism to interviewing.

I would like to emphasize three points: First, many people in developing nations have extensive experience in being interviewed. Rarely will others not have preceded us inquiring about such diverse matters as soil erosion, deforestation, education, access to medical care, and so forth. Usually it will have been implied that the expressed needs and concerns of the interviewees would be taken into account, which often has not proved to be the case.

Second, many people are suspicious about the motives of interviewers due to their past experience with donors, their governments or a host of other possibilities. This wariness often leads to (1) non-responsiveness, (2) answers that will satisfy the interviewer so he/she will go away, (3) efforts to use the interviewer to obtain something for the individual or the larger group being interviewed, and/or (4) misinformation.

Third, many populations associate interviews with receiving benefits and seek to project themselves in such a manner that they might obtain something they want. It is difficult under these circumstances to obtain accurate information.

On the positive side, interviewing and interest in interviewees' concerns and perspectives, a willingness to present those concerns to planners and/or policy makers and, if possible, to report back to the interviewees the results of such interactions facilitate communication among intended beneficiaries, impacted populations, and policy makers and implementers.

It is clear from the experience of those engaged in international social impact work that the motivations for interviewers and subjects are likely to be different. The assumption that there is an identity of interest, and that the project or program being planned guarantees such a commonality cannot be taken for granted.

The Cultural Contexts of Interviewing

In my estimation, SIA should adopt from anthropology a concern for how people view themselves, think about their own society, and articulate with the wider world. To achieve access to this information, informants and interviews need to be utilized. The process of learning what people are thinking about a particular intervention or project or impacts has multiple dimensions. Three central dimensions are:

1. Language: The question of common meanings can be a problem even when the same languages are spoken by all parties and becomes more of a problem when different languages are used. The need for excellent translators whose behavior is appropriate to the situation is essential when speakers do not share the same language or culture.
2. Context: Creating the context in which an informant responds well[8] takes patience, tact, ingenuity and honesty. Direct questioning may not be the most appropriate technique for eliciting responses. Participation in activities followed by gentle questioning in someone's home, or several visits before asking if someone is ready to respond to certain kinds of questions might be necessary.
3. Contacts: Knowledge of a region and its culture is required to find the right contacts to set up the interview, to select the right time and the appropriate gift (not necessarily money), when to present it, how to ask appropriately so that an informant will answer freely and accurately.

Nationally and internationally, the interviewing situation may be understood or defined by interviewees quite differently from the way it is perceived by the interviewer.[9] For example, interviewers are seeking information and interviewees may be trying to obtain resources. In addition, there is the methodological point that interviewers and interviewees may not agree that what they are engaged in is a "speech event," one where the interviewer defines the rules and the questions, and evaluates the accuracy, informativeness and representativeness of the responses. Rather, interviewees fit interviewers into existing social categories of "outsiders," "experts," agents of a government or foreign visitors. The fit between interviewers and the kinds of questions they ask and the social categories that they are placed into directly affects whether the questions they ask "ought" to be answered to "strangers" or visitors, or non-believers, or other possible categories.

In general, there is always a trade-off between extensive and intensive social research. The former, which tends to permit statistically significant generalizations based on an appropriate selection of informants and a standardized research instrument, produces data on a larger geographical scale and can capture social variation in a district, region, or other appropriate unit. The latter, which relies heavily on a longer term and trusting relationship between the investigator and the informant, can lead to deeper insights into sociocultural practices which otherwise might remain obscure.

Intensive social research tends to be expensive, for it requires time to develop trust and rapport, language training, and a specific sense of the social universe to be investigated. In the past, criticisms of this method have emphasized the excessive reliance on too few informants or generalizing from one village or community to a larger category without a valid basis for doing so. In the best of worlds, both intensive and extensive research would enrich the results achieved. Central to the cluster of ethnographic methods that may be used is informant interviewing. The ethnographic field process usually is fairly long term, (more than one year) and requires that a social scientist learn the language of the people being studied.[10] This intensive approach, which is often not possible in SIA, has been modified into what are called rapid rural appraisals sometimes labeled "quick and dirty surveys." Perhaps one might alter the terminology and talk of rural appraisals, the time-frame being determined by the problem at hand. This is both closer to actual practice and would make "rapid" a relative term, not an absolute one. Under many circumstances the longer-term approach involving language competency, and a relatively deep knowledge of the community or communities is preferable but not possible. On the other hand, the problem or intervention to be carried out may not warrant the commitment of resources of more intensive study.

There are no tested recipes but only checklists of ingredients in preparing for interviews. Social analysts often will be frustrated in their endeavors at interviewing due to circumstances beyond their control. The possible reasons are infinite: they include the work schedules of informants, the wrong time of day depending upon the religion in the region, the wrong interviewer, travelling with government officials, lack of contacts, local leaders being unavailable and no one willing to answer questions, among others. Engaging social scientists who have previously worked in an area and can return for a short period, using their prior knowledge and contacts to do much useful work may provide a way to avoid some of these difficulties. However, some caution should be noted. Those who have previously worked in an area may themselves have strong viewpoints, or commitments to particular projects or interventions that may interfere with a more objective presentation. There is some value in also having those who may be less knowledgeable but more open.

There are no easy answers as to how to cope with these difficulties only for the analyst to be aware that they are an important part of a learning process. It bears emphasizing that there are no simple methodological tricks to handle these situations because interviews are at least a two-way interaction. The interviewer cannot simply command an informant to provide the "correct" information. While this may tax one's patience, there are the benefits from creating new tools, new ways of establishing relationships and recasting interviews to fit these chal-

lenging situations. Complex social interactions require channels of communication that are not easily established in a short period. The
emergent literature on participatory research, the growth of grassroots
organizations, and changes in donor organizations urge a shift away
from just regarding interviewees as subjects and to include change
agents' responsibilities to provide information and become subjects
themselves for interviewing by those to be impacted by development
interventions.

Informant Selection

The selection of appropriate interviewees will depend upon the
purpose for collecting information, the quantity and quality of information required, and the precision and accuracy needed. SIA in the
international arena has not yet achieved either the relatively clear
guidelines or the methodological complexity of SIAs discussed in, for
example, *Social Impact Assessment Methods* edited by Finsterbusch,
Llewellyn and Wolf (1983). AID's "social soundness analysis" emphasizes the "sociocultural fit" between a project's objectives and their
compatibility, feasibility, and replicability with a proposed set of beneficiaries rather than the steps outlined by Wolf (1983).[11] The article
on "Rapid Rural Appraisal" (this volume) suggests that data from
interviews ". . . are usually highly biased since most informants have
ulterior motives, or hidden agendas. . . ." Gow goes on to observe that
interviews can then be cross-checked to attempt to establish more
reliable information. In my experience the degree of confidence one has
in particular informants also depends upon the time and the nature of
relationships that one has. Longer-term associations, knowledge of both
the people and the area, are essential in assessing how to understand
and interpret different interviewees' perspectives. In all societies, there
is a range of expertise, and one has to know how this is distributed.
Among multiple considerations that need to be taken into account in
the selection of informants are:

1. The scale of information desired. Is the study to be a major social
survey or an impressionistic view of local strengths and weaknesses
regarding capacity to sustain a given project? What is the balance
between the kind of information needed to be "useful" (for whom?)
and the resources to be made available for the study?

2. The desired level of precision and accuracy of the data to be
collected. Is the study to be statistically valid as judged by the standards
of contemporary social science, or is it to be more qualitative? What
does one do when precision cannot be obtained because basic census
information is lacking, or out of date? There are significant variations

from nation to nation and region to region on the statistical base from which SIA can operate. While past projects or operating agencies may have some useable statistics to construct indicators of significant social phenomena, they may or may not be adequate. In general, one cannot overestimate the importance of basic demographic analysis for being able to identify potential impacts and therefore the groups from whom the analyst needs to select informants (see the article by Cook in this volume).

3. The resources available for the study and its purpose(s) strongly influence (if not determine) the number of informants, and their distribution in terms of gender, age, status, location, household type, wealth, etc. In my experience, too much reliance is placed on key informants, usually brokers between a village or town, the government and/or outside donors—who are engaged in what is perceived as successful "modern" economic activities. Frequently not enough attention is given to finding the poor in a given area and using them as informants.[12] In addition, inadequate knowledge of local social complexity may lead to various oversights, such as failure to interview second, third and fourth wives whose workloads and social position may be different than those of first wives.

4. Too often informants with high degrees of local knowledge are overlooked in designing, implementing, monitoring and evaluating interventions.[13] There is a large literature (often not taken seriously in developing nations) concerning the methodological importance of avoiding gender bias in informant selection. In addition, there are many subjects which cannot be pursued by men interviewing women but require female interviewers.

A specific suggestion that can be made to facilitate impact analysis is to explore in interviews past development experiences in the region (which is rarely done) and their successes, failures, and lessons from the perspectives of both the participants and implementers. Current analysis is largely ahistorical, that is, it does not include systematic study of past development interventions. In the selection of informants or interviewees I suggest that some of them be past participants in interventions or projects. For example, if an agricultural improvement project is being considered and such projects were undertaken previously these should be at least briefly examined and an effort made to find and locate those involved. In attempting to ascertain why participation in past projects was low or high and why objectives were or were not achieved, an understanding of past efforts may prove quite useful. By seeking to understand individuals' pasts, the interviewer indicates an interest in taking the community's experiences and knowledge seriously. Something, I might add, that is not done often enough.

Interviews and Interviewing

Inextricably linked to the selection of informants is the choice of the issues to be explored and the questions to be posed. Whatever the decision, there are numerous theoretical and methodological issues involved concerning the role of interviewers and the rules of interviewing. I am in partial agreement with Mishler's (1986) effort to move away from the behaviorist orientation dominant in questionnaire and interview formulation, which he aptly terms the "stimulus-response paradigm." The degree to which the interview itself, not to mention questionnaires, has cross-cultural validity is a significant matter. Interviews as situations can differ from one society to another. How they are conducted, understanding how to pose questions and when to write (or not write), tape (or not tape) responses is vital to communication and the validity of responses.

Among others, Mishler has noted that formal situations such as those characteristic of many interviews may represent a radical departure from everyday discourse for interviewees. This is so because: "respondent's answers are disconnected from essential sociocultural grounds of meaning. Each answer is a fragment removed both from its setting in the organized discourse of the interview and from the life setting of the respondent" (1986:23). Significantly, Mishler was referring to the interviewing process in the U.S. The difficulties can only be compounded in international work. This is due to the knowledge needed of different cultures and linguistic competence desired, to recontextualize the answers. The work of Briggs (1986) demonstrates both the complexity of interviewing and the need to incorporate flexibility in the process. In his inquiry about artisanal activities he found he could not use the formal interview process. Instead he had to work in an apprentice fashion side by side with artisans to be able to gain access to answers to his questions. Aside from the point that the site and context of interviewing varies, Brigg's work demonstrates how those being interviewed influence what questions will receive answers and the way in which the interview can be carried out.[14]

The critical methodological point is how to best determine the depth of knowledge required to carry out the SIA. This decision then guides the balance between intensive and extensive interviewing, between long- and short-term fieldwork, and the types of relationships that the researcher develops with impacted populations. There are now thousands of planned interventions in the developing world, ranging from improving maternal and infant health to changing cattle grazing patterns to advocacy of solar cookers. It is important to seek less-expensive and more rapid SIAs in order to minimize their time and expense which have implications for interviewing. The stance of social impact analysts should be to insist that the wise use of resources dictates as full an SIA as possible for benefit-cost reasons and to avoid, when possible, greater harm than necessary.

The Interviewing Process

Interviews often are described as scheduled and structured,[15] nonscheduled and structured,[16] and nonscheduled.[17] All these types have been used in international development and are used depending upon the purpose of inquiry. Whatever the interview's form, it is best that data be obtained in a manner acceptable to the informant. In addition, the demands placed on informants by the researcher should be kept to socioculturally accepted norms and within the scope of inquiry. Asking questions outside of the understood scope may lead to misunderstandings both with interviewees and with any accompanying agency, ministerial or national research personnel.

The settings in which interviews are conducted may vary, for example, large and/or small groups, mixed and/or single gender, formal, or informal one-to-one encounters. It has long been argued in the farming systems research literature that small group interviews are desirable because there will be no hesitation in answering since information discussed is common knowledge to all the farmers. Yet, if one is interested in sources and amounts of remittances, this cannot be so easily obtained in a group setting. Clear decisions need to be made about the importance of certain kinds of information, and the resources (including time) needed to obtain it.

The social interaction patterns that already exist in both rural and urban settings can facilitate or inhibit discourse. It is very difficult to generalize about these patterns because sociopolitical climates may be quite different. To ask poor peasants in El Salvador about the process of land reform may be virtually impossible, whereas such is not the case in parts of Peru. The rural poor may be unwilling to speak openly for a number of reasons: (1) fear of retaliation if they are in opposition to planned or ongoing changes; (2) fear of differing with government officials or technicians, who often accompany applied researchers; (3) belief that there is no use in communicating long-term and difficult problems to researchers who have no long-term commitment, or who have not demonstrated that commitment, to an area; (4) a desire to avoid public discussion of one's own poverty or difficult situation to outsiders; (5) an effort to tell the interviewers whatever they want to hear to facilitate their rapid departure; (6) the moral sense that they do not have the right to speak for a family or community to outsiders;

and (7) an embarrassment to speak publicly due to a lack of communication skills in an interview setting. To this list, other researchers
can add any number of items based on their experiences.

In sum, the larger issue concerns a culturally specific sense of when
and to whom what types of questions are appropriate. One technique
which has been frequently used is to move the informant to another
location to ask questions that are inappropriate in a given social context
(for example, because a junior cannot speak freely in front of an elder).
This may be effective but it entails risks because it may become
common knowledge that this has been done.

Interviews as social situations are complex social situations. Briggs
has observed that there are three more subtle components of these
social situations: First, "normative associations of social settings and
appropriate modes of verbal interaction are culture specific, and they
generally vary between social classes or subgroups as well" (1986, p.
45). In SIA one must consider the resources available and time required
to learn these appropriate modes and associations. An anthropologist
who will be spending a long period of time in one spot may want and
need to make the investment, but it is another matter for shorter term
researchers. It then becomes crucial to find a local person skilled in
assisting the interviewer to understand and to employ the appropriate
modes of verbal interaction. It must be recognized that much will be
missed and thus the importance of certain kinds of information has to
be assessed. The larger risk is always that what is predetermined to be
important or crucial information may turn out to be incorrect or partial.

Second, Briggs notes that the context affects the kinds and types of
responses. If one asks about certain ceremonial matters in a community
where there is religious conflict one is likely to obtain misleading or
even falsified answers, perhaps none at all if believers think such matters
should not be discussed with a non-believer. If one ignores these normative dimensions of a culture, one risks partial, misleading, or incorrect information. Lastly Briggs points out that speech is not simply
a "vehicle for describing nonlinguistic events" (1986, p. 460). It also
can create or transform a given state of affairs, that is, it has a
performative capacity. For example, a major focus of questioning among
interviewees in developing nations has focused upon obtaining village,
community, or individual expression of needs. Yet, responses typically
indicate clear choices on the parts of interviewees as to what they think
they might be able to obtain from their interviewers. Far from a
"neutral" description of what local people might like to have to resolve
their problems, responses may reflect both how they conceptualize the
interview as a social situation and what they hope (expect) will come
from their answers. In this connection Briggs comments on a more

difficult dimension of questioning, that of what people "will do" or "forthcoming" events. He could not collect data on the latter. "I eventually learned that members of semicollective groups of cooperating households never announce the imminence of such occasions to each other, let alone issue direct invitations" (1986, p. 460). (This is quite different than the experience of David Gow summarized in his article.) In short, in trying to determine the potential impacts of a project it seems so obvious to ask "what if" questions about the future, yet frequently these may most frequently need to be rephrased, translated, or in some fashion rendered both comprehensible and meaningful to the interviewee.

Ethics, Interviewing, and Informants

Leaving aside the broad social science issues involved in any discussion of ethics in social research, let us focus on a few ethical matters central to SIA: working in other nations subject to their laws, the lack of power or control on the part of the social scientists, and lack of knowledge about uses to which information obtained may be put, and therefore the degree to which a researcher can protect the privacy, anonymity and sometimes the safety of informants.

There has emerged through recent years both conventions and laws about social science research in North America and other nations. In most developing nations in contrast, there has developed a suspicion about social science research,[18] and conventions or laws regulating or controlling such research are lacking. Furthermore, many planners and policy makers may believe or suspect that what social researchers seek to do is block or delay particular projects or plans. Some nations have become suspicious of their own social scientists for a range of reasons[19] or do not feel that it is important to have social scientists (aside from economists).

It is often the case that national or regional policy makers and planners are not trained in social science. Depending upon the country, they may be unsympathetic to, or at least need to be convinced of, the value of social analysis in the accomplishment of particular projects and programs. This has clear methodological and ethical implications. Consequently, national guidelines for the conduct of social science research are lacking because the ethical issues central to the conduct of research may be considered as irrelevant in the planning and implementation of projects and programs.

One guarantee for ethical conduct, the free and open publication of research results, is not necessarily common practice everywhere. Leaving aside classified research, work carried out on behalf of developing nations' governments, even when paid for by bilateral or multilateral donors may not necessarily be public documents. Without detailing the various categories under which social research is conducted, reports provided to host governments (and their agencies) may be accepted, rejected, or simply received and govenments may not provide authorization for further distribution. Individual expatriate scholars may (depending upon the contract) draw upon that research for publication, but this could be more difficult for nationals involved in the research who might risk political retaliation.

The political and social contexts in which social research is conducted vary greatly ranging from relatively open environments and societies, to military or other dictatorships. In open societies, the ethics to be followed usually encompass respect for the rights and welfare of individuals, informed consent, and privacy. According to the Nachmiases (1987, p. 98), informed consent involves competence, voluntarism, full information and comprehension. They suggest as a rule of thumb or guideline that the more serious the risk to research participants, the greater becomes the obligation to obtain informed consent. This consent becomes difficult indeed when social survey methods are carried out which involve, for example, the continuous presence of a representative of a dictatorship or the member of a dominant group not substantially interested in the welfare of the groups to be interviewed.

There are no easy answers to ethical dilemmas or to the range of circumstances in which investigators may find themselves. For example, in a case involving resettlement of populations due to flooding of their lands it may be quite clear from the outset that building the dam will not be reconsidered; one must make the ethical decision as to whether to participate knowing that the die is cast. In this instance, one will clearly be identified by those to be resettled as part of the bureaucratic apparatus implementing what may be a highly unpopular decision. One's only choice may be to use interviewing to assist the affected population in making the move the least traumatic possible, rather than politically oppose or to refuse to participate in such a project.

In many nations, development projects and programs are part of a contested political terrain. What is one group's or region's development may be another's loss. For example, the building of dams or roads in Amazonia has different consequences for Brazilian Indians than other Brazilians. Brazilian Indians often actively oppose such activities. In many nations, opposition parties or organized nongovernmental groups are not permitted. When social impact assessment is carried out by such governments people who work in these situations may rightly or wrongly be associated with the government. It is part of the larger set of ethical issues that each individual researcher chooses in what countries to work, and with what kinds of agencies. In my estimation, not to develop knowledge about how different national agencies work, their relationships with intended beneficiaries, how project personnel will be hired and treated, and what may happen to those who may bear the costs of interventions will lead to a misunderstanding of what can and can't be accomplished with social impact assessment.

The appropriate use of interviewing for social impact assessment serves as a protection and voice for common people particularly in situations where either organizations are not permitted or a sufficient organizational capacity on the part of those to be impacted is limited. To be able to provide voice is to more deeply understand the concerns and worldviews of those to be affected by development interventions.

Notes

Ms. Susan Andreatta was of great assistance in the beginning stages of organizing and writing this chapter. Dr. Kurt Finsterbusch and Dr. Jay Ingersoll provided probing questions and suggested many helpful revisions. Dr. Ann Ferguson carefully read and criticized the revised chapter. Her critique was of great value and I hope that this version reflects some of her wisdom. The short-comings are mine alone, the strengths are due to the assistance that I have received.

1. Briggs (1986; p. 26). In this article I briefly discuss some of the conceptual and methodological issues involved in the nature of interviewing and interviewing as a process. These issues deserve greater consideration in international SIA than they have been previously been given. This chapter is only a tentative beginning.

2. By implication, the relevant questions are for whom the research is being done and the relationship of researchers to intended beneficiaries. One author who has articulated a thorough view of this process is Gran (1983). See especially his assessment of the nature of participation in the Philippines. For a review of the issues see Cohen and Uphoff (1977) and the other excellent papers on participation put out by Cornell.

3. The importance of both understanding other people's views of development practice and utilizing their knowledge to make projects and programs more efficacious have been elaborated in Michael Cernea (1985) and Brokensha and Warren (1983).

4. In my view this continues to be the case although there is greater diversity in the model on the one hand, while on the other, a developmental paradigm based upon the western model has achieved greater internationalization particularly due to the growing influence of the World Bank.

5. I hasten to add, not all. The recent work of Chambers (1986, 1988) provides a model of participatory approaches to development in general and poverty in particular.

6. Werner and Schoepfle (1986, p. 313). Bidney's book *Theoretical Anthropology* was originally published in 1955 and is an early and rich consideration
of the tensions and conflicts between cultural relativism and the implications
for belief and action if all value systems were to be considered as equal. This
debate emerged in anthropology during and after World War II in the analysis
of Nazi Germany and on what values could anthropologists objectively criticize
other cultures.

7. Rich details on how peasants resist are given in two exemplary works:
Scott (1985) and Hyden (1981).

8. A strong statement of the inherent problem in the interview process is
provided by Briggs (1986). He writes that interviewers often do not know that
they have been unable to "banish the native communicative norms that operate
in other environments" (p. 39) from the interview. Therefore there can be
genuine miscommunication about the nature of the event, how it is understood
and interpreted. Methodologically Briggs asserts that resultant errors from this
gap in the communicative process are systematic, not random, and therefore
". . . are not 'canceled out' through the standardization of questionnaires and
the application of sampling techniques" (ibid., p. 39). This is particularly
significant in areas where there have been long-standing contact between government agencies and/or expatriate agencies and the local populations being
interviewed. There are clear connections between the deeper methodological
issues of interviewing and social impact analysis.

9. There is neither time nor space to discuss the large literature on the
methodologies of interviews, and the analysis of them.

10. Space does not permit adequate discussion of a number of fundamental
aspects of translating interviews. These issues remain whether or not a researcher understands and speaks the language. Two recent books which consider
some of these issues have already been cited: Briggs (1986) and Werner and
Schoepfle (1986).

11. In his article "Social Impact Assessment: A Methodological Overview"
in Finsterbusch et al. (1983), Wolf lists eleven steps. These are not always
followed in North America but they provide a clear framework from which
analysts proceed.

12. For an eloquent discussion of "finding the poor," see the excellent book
by Chambers (1983), in which he discusses the multiple ways by which one
may miss the poor.

13. Cernea's edited volume *Putting People First: Sociological Variables in
Rural Development* provides multiple examples of the costs of not using local
knowledge and the benefits (and greater success rate) of doing so.

14. I cite Briggs because most other examples of which I am aware are
anecdotal. Briggs' book is important precisely because he is one of the few to
analyze interviewing as a methodology, and to provide examples from his own
work to discuss the limits of interviewing.

15. Questions, their wording, and their sequence are fixed and identical for
every respondent.

16. According to Nachmias and Nachmias (1987) nonscheduled and structured interviews have four characteristics: (1) Take place with respondents

known to have been involved in a particular experience. (2) Refer to situations that have been analyzed prior to the interview. (3) Proceed on the basis of an interview guide specifying topics related to the research hypothesis. (4) Focused on the subjective experiences regarding the situations under study. Thus, the interviewer while following a series of questions can pursue certain details, note emotional reactions, and the like.

17. Here, the are no pre-specified set of questions, nor a specific order. "The interviewer has a great deal of freedom to probe various areas and to raise specific queries during the course of the interview" (Nachmias and Nachmias, 1987:238).

18. There is tremendous variation among nations in terms of their social science capabilities. For example, countries like India and Mexico have both a long tradition of social research and carry out their own social analysis (although usually not within the social impact assessment tradition). Some small nations have no universities, while in many nations, social science is not emphasized in their national universities.

19. For example, in 1968 there was a major student strike at the University of Dakar (now Cheikh Anta Diop University). Sociology professors and students were thought to be part of the strike leadership, and the sociology department was disbanded and has not been reconstituted.

References

Bidney, David. *Theoretical Anthropology.* Reissued 1967. New York: Columbia University Press, 1955.

Briggs, Charles. *Learning How to Ask: A Sociolinguistic Appraisal of the Role of the Interview in Social Science Research.* New York & Cambridge: Cambridge University Press, 1986.

Brokensha, David, and Warren, Michael (editors). *Indigenous Knowledge Systems.* Baltimore: University Press of America, 1983.

Castillo, Jelia T. *How Participatory Is Participatory Development: A Review of the Philippine Experience.* Manila: Philippine Institute for Development Studies, 1983.

Cernea, Michael (editor). *Putting People First.* Oxford: Oxford University Press, 1985.

Chambers, Robert. *Rural Development: Putting the Last First.* Essex, U.K.: Longman Scientific & Technical, 1983.

_____ . "Normal Professionalism, New Paradigms, and Development." Institute of Development Studies Discussion Paper 227. Sussex, U.K., 1986.

_____ . "Sustainable Livelihoods, Environment and Development: Putting Rural People First." Institute of Development Studies Discussion Paper 240. Sussex, U.K., 1988.

Cohen, John, and Uphoff, Norman. *Rural Development Participation: Concepts and Measures for Project Design, Implementation and Evaluation.* N.Y.: Rural Development Committee, Cornell University, 1977.

Finsterbusch, Kurt, Llewellyn, Lynn, and Wolf, C. P. (editors). *Social Impact Assessment Methods.* Beverly Hills, Calif.: Sage, 1983.

Gran, Guy. *Development by People: Citizen Construction of a Just World.* New York: Praeger, 1983.

Hyden, Goran. *Beyond Ujamaa in Tanzania.* Berkeley and Los Angeles: University of California Press, 1981.

Mishler, Elliot G. *Research Interviewing: Context and Narrative.* Cambridge, MA: Harvard University Press, 1986.

Nachmias, David, and Nachmias, Chava. *Research Methods in the Social Sciences.* Third Edition. New York: St Martin's Press, 1987.

Scott, James. *Weapons of the Weak: Everyday Forms of Peasant Resistance.* New Haven: Yale University Press, 1985.

Werner, Oswald, and Schoepfle, G. Mark. *Systematic Fieldwork: Foundations of Ethnography and Interviewing.* Newbury Park, California: Sage Publications, 1986, in two volumes.

Wolf, Charles P. "Social Impact Assessment: A Methodological Overview" in K. Finsterbusch et al. *Social Impact Assessment Methods.* Beverly Hills, CA: Sage, 1983.

Part 3

Special Approaches and Methods

7
A Bayesian Perspective on Social Impact Assessment Data Collection
Kurt Finsterbusch

The objective of this article is to develop and apply a Bayesian perspective for social impact assessments (SIA) in Third World settings. It argues that the logic of Bayesian statistics is the appropriate logic for SIA's of development projects. It touches briefly on basic Bayesian statistics simply to identify its logic.

In 1763 Richard Price published Thomas Bayes' essay, "An Essay towards solving a Problem in the Doctrine of Chances," posthumously in *Philosophical Transactions,* Royal Society, London, Vol. 53, pp. 376–398. This paper was to become the basis for Bayesian statistics. Bayes' major contribution to probability theory was a computational method for combining prior estimates of probabilities with new evidence to produce posterior probabilities that are generally better guides to action than either of the components by themselves. When the new evidence is abundant it swamps the contribution of prior probabilities to the posterior probabilities. In such cases the results of Bayesian and classical computations of probabilities are identical. In other words Bayesian statistics are superior to non-Bayesian statistics only when relatively few new observations can be brought into the equation. However, SIAs usually are just this type of situation. Normally SIA budgets do not allow for extensive systematic data collection. When they do not, we argue, a Bayesian approach gives the best guidance for decision making.

The Bayesian Principle

Bayes' Theorem is:

$$P(A \mid B) = \frac{P(A \cap B)}{P(B)}$$

which means the probability of event A, given the occurrence of a second event B can be obtained by dividing the probability of their joint occurrence by the unconditioned probability of the second event B. This can be expanded into the Bayesian formula for calculating the probability of situation, event, or outcome "A" (versus the probability of "non A") as follows:

$$P(A \mid B) = \frac{P(A) \cdot P(B \mid A)}{P(A) \cdot P(B \mid A) + P(\bar{A}) \cdot P(B \mid \bar{A})}$$

The probability of both A ($P(A)$) and non A ($P(\bar{A})$) are prior probabilities and derive from past experience. B is the new information or new events. The formula computes the new probability of A given the new information that the condition B has occurred, i.e. $P(A \mid B)$. The key piece of information that it uses to calculate $P(A \mid B)$ is the probability of B given the prior probability of A, i.e. $P(B \mid A)$ (this is divided by the probability of B).

The importance of the Bayesian principle for our purposes is that it provides a useful methodology for decision making under conditions of limited information. It combines two approaches: the use of past experience to guide current decisions and the collection of new information on the decision situation. Although it seems obvious that the two sets of data are better than one, so often bills unwisely are passed and actions taken without first testing the concepts or actions in pilot projects or without taking past experience into account. It is rash to assume that our past experience is sufficient to figure out what needs to be done. It is also rash to take actions on the basis of current information without taking past experience into account. In the stock market these practices are quickly punished. It is unwise to invest either on the basis of past trends without considering current information or to invest on the basis of current information without considering past trends. The Bayesian investor would develop an estimate of the probability that a stock would rise significantly in the near future on the basis of past trends and then revise these estimates on the basis of current inquiries about the quality of the management, the opinions of experts about the strength of the firm's principal markets, the action of competitors, and the changing picture for other relevant factors.

We interpret Bayes' Principle to include the following interrelated ideas:

1. Knowledge is probabilistic rather than certain, and rational decision making involves uncertainty but tries to reduce it. In other words it tries to increase the accuracy of estimates of probabilities.

2. Past experience, empirical findings, or subjective estimates must always be checked against current data.
3. Research is the means for improving ones estimates of probabilities.

Knowledge is probabilistic rather than certain. This idea is widely accepted in principle but also is often forgotten. Statistics provides methods for determining the degree of confidence that apply to conclusions that are based on repeated systematic observations. It is now traditional to accept findings as facts when they have less than one chance in twenty of occurring by chance. The more cautious might insist on the criterion of one in a hundred. In either case the findings are thereupon considered facts and for practical purposes considered certain. Findings that fail to meet these criteria are not to be taken seriously because they are too uncertain. In our view, however, this operating procedure is poorly suited to many policy making situations, because most policy decisions must be made on information that do not attain these levels of certitude. Instead we propose a Bayesian procedure to be elaborated later which utilizes predictions based on past experience that are tested against current information to increase the accuracy and reliability of the predictions. It must be admitted that our procedure could be employed without a Bayesian rationale, but the Bayesian emphasis on the probabilistic nature of knowledge serves it well.

The polar opposite view is that knowledge should be certain and was the view of David Hume, a contemporary of Bayes. He argued that there is no rational basis for a belief in causation since all that can be observed is the repetition of sequence. One can not say A causes B but only that one repeatedly observes that A is followed by B. Hume is right and absolutely precise scientific statements will not use the term cause. Hume extends his argument to assert that the repeated observation of the sequence of A B does not justify the expectation of the repetition of the sequence in the future. His logic leads to the conclusion that "The supposition that the future resembles the past, is not founded on arguments of any kind, but is derived entirely from habit" (*Treatise of Human Nature,* Book I, part iii, section iv). In other words he is totally skeptical about the application of knowledge to the future and hence to decision making. The outcome of Hume's argument is radical skepticism as Russell (1946:698) points out in his summary of Hume's philosophy:

. . . he arrives at the disastrous conclusion that from experience and observation nothing is to be learnt. There is no such thing as a rational belief: "If we believe that fire warms, or water refreshes, it's only because it costs us too much pains to think otherwise" (*Treatise of Human Nature,* Book I, part iv, section ii). We cannot help believing, but no belief can be grounded in reason.

Hume's skepticism, however, is based on a concept of knowledge as absolute certainty. Everything short of this is irrational, from belief in God and miracles to belief that the sun will rise tomorrow. Those beliefs derive from habit not reason.

Hume's skepticism disturbed many people including both philosophers and the religious. In my judgment Bayes' principle is the answer to Hume's skepticism. Knowledge is probabilistic and not certain. The religious believer must admit that God does not give to him absolutely certain proof that God exists and is benevolent, etc. Rather, God gives him plenty of evidence (the traditional arguments for God which Hume showed were not absolute proof) but also God expects him to take a step of faith. Philosophers likewise must come to terms with the probabilistic nature of knowledge and construct philosophical systems that can accommodate uncertainty. Some like Carnap reject this view and equate philosophy with syntax or pure logic. Absolute certainty can be found in perfectly consistent logical systems but then nothing can be said about the real world. Most philosophers, however, are prepared to analyze the messy and uncertain world as it is. The pragmatists, for example, built their philosophies around uncertainty and had a somewhat Bayesian approach to knowledge. They recognized that their scientific and philosophical beliefs were not perfectly certain. They were convincing enough to act upon, however, even while they were subject to further testing.

The Bayesian approach uses the probabilistic or uncertain nature of knowledge as a rationale for a decision making methodology that seeks to assess the probabilities of the various possible outcomes as accurately as is reasonably possible given the time, money and information constraints. In practice this methodology translates into the injunction: "Improve the accuracy of your estimates of probabilities until you are prepared to act on them." For example, the evidence for the risk of cancer from smoking has been accumulating for many years and has greatly increased the accuracy of the estimates of the probabilities. Some people acted on the early estimates and some waited until recently to stop smoking.

The second idea that we believe is contained in the Bayesian principle is that past experiences, empirical findings or subjective estimates must always be checked against current data. For example, a new high yield seed may have been tested in climates and soils similar to a new area for its potential use but on site testing is always a good idea before making a total commitment to the new seed.

The third idea in the Bayesian principle is that research is the means for improving one's estimates of probabilities. The research might be journalistic if time is short, but scientific research is preferable if affordable in order to build a highly trustworthy interpretation of the situation. Nevertheless, the difference between scientific decision making and action decision making should be noted. Science is more interested in avoiding error than in publishing great quantities of weak findings, so only strongly supported findings are considered significant. Action decisions will use whatever knowledge is available, even weak findings, because decisions usually must be made before really good information is available. Sometimes scientists want to impose their decision procedures on policy decisions. They sometimes require a level of certainty that approaches Hume's skepticism. I have heard a doctor say that there is no real proof that smoking causes cancer. He probably is right if he means absolute proof, but he also is absurd if he continues to smoke because he thinks it is safe. If he wants to live long he better turn Bayesian, stop waiting for absolute proof and stop smoking, because the probabilities that smoking causes cancer are far greater than the probabilities that it does not. Our point is best made in two quotations. The first is attributed to Samuel Butler, "Life is the art of drawing sufficient conclusions from insufficient premises," and the second is attributed to Jose Ortega y Gasset, "Life cannot wait until the sciences have explained the universe scientifically; we cannot put off living until we are ready."

Bayesian Procedures

We have assembled a set of procedures that can carry out the Bayesian principle elaborated above. The procedures are grouped into the three steps of a Bayesian analysis: the identification of prior probabilities, the gathering of new information, and the deduction of posterior probabilities.

Prior Probabilities

The first step in a Bayesian analysis is to establish prior probabilities. This step requires a review of existing knowledge, the deduction of potential outcomes and the assignment of probabilities to the potential outcomes. The review of existing knowledge involves a review of the literature and data sources such as censuses, records and reports. Experts are another source of information about past cases or the background of the present case. The deduction of potential outcomes involves mainly common sense and the record of outcomes of past similar cases. It is best done by a multidisciplinary team in a work group session and then reviewed by experts and stakeholders for additional inputs and revisions. The assignment of probabilities to deduced potential outcomes involves calculating the distribution of outcomes in past cases and considering the special features of the current case that would make it deviate in a certain direction from the general pattern in previous cases. Since subjective judgments are involved multiple judges with a variety of backgrounds and points of view should be utilized. If the current case does not deviate clearly from past cases then the distribution of outcomes from past cases becomes the prior probabilities in the current case. Otherwise the judges set the prior probabilities by adjusting this distribution to take into account the special features of the current case.

New Information

The second step in a Bayesian analysis is the collection of new information. If extensive information can be collected by careful scientific procedures then the new information will probably overpower the prior probabilities in the calculation of posterior probabilities and the first and third steps would be unnecessary. The Bayesian approach is only appropriate when insufficient new information can be collected to determine the probabilities of outcomes. Otherwise the classical approach produces the same results and is simpler and cheaper to use. The amount and quality of new information that should be collected depends on two factors: the available resources and the level of confidence of the prior probabilities. When the research budget is generous and the prior probabilities have lower levels of confidence the gathering of new information should be as scientific and extensive as possible. When past knowledge is extensive and budgets are tight all that needs to be done is to test whether the past patterns are likely to apply to the present case and if not in what direction should the expectations be revised.

Posterior Probabilities

We have presented above Bayes' formula for computing posterior probabilities even though in most cases appropriate data will not be available to allow the formula to be used. It provides the logic for the general principle that we are proposing. The first step in computing posterior probabilities is to determine if the prior probabilities and the new information are comparable and therefore mergeable. If not, then the first step is to convert one set of data into the form of the other or to convert both into a third form, e.g. into the form of a set of survey results.

The second step in computing posterior probabilities is to weight, either objectively or subjectively, the old and new information relative to each other. We recommend that a variety of judges with different backgrounds and points of view should subjectively weight the two data sets. Then the posterior probabilities can be computed by merging them or using Bayes' formula. As an added feature we recommend that the judges should then evaluate whether the resulting posterior probabilities are appropriate in their judgment. If not, they should subjectively estimate the posterior probabilities. Finally, both the calculated and subjectively estimated posterior probabilities would be reported to decision makers.

The above procedures describe how to systematically follow the Bayesian approach. They produce the best estimates possible when only a little original research is feasible. Nevertheless, we recognize that Bayesian procedures may not be appropriate for public documents. Public documents tend to use non-numeric, and therefore, less precise language because this language is politically safer and more defensible. They use imprecise and vague terms such as few, many, most, probably, might, etc. Even if quantitative estimates are presented they would have to be portrayed as estimates with wide margins of error. In sum, we recommend using a highly quantified Bayesian approach including many subjective numerical estimates in the research and analysis stages but reduce the role of numbers, if necessary, in presenting the results.

Bayesian Methods

In this chapter we proceed from the Bayesian principle to Bayesian procedures to Bayesian methods in a progression of increasing specificity. In this section we briefly discuss methods for researching past experience and new information and methods for combining the two sets of data. Some of the methods are thoroughly discussed in other chapters and therefore only touched upon here.

Research Methods on Past Experience

Seven methods figure prominently in the research on past experience: literature review, review of primary recorded data, informant interviews, baseline data, standard information module, systematic case review, and probability estimation. Literature reviews, reviews of primary recorded data (censuses, reports of organizations and agencies, newspapers and media accounts, etc.) and informant interviews are standard social science research methods. Baseline data utilize these three standard methods for the purpose of developing an adequate description of the relevant history and current conditions of the current case. Some new information is usually added to complete the baseline description. Standard information modules, systematic case reviews and probability estimation are not standard social science methods yet so they will be described more fully.

A standard information module (SIM) organizes findings of the literature, the primary recorded data, and the informant interviews into descriptions of standard patterns. Then the variations in standard patterns are described for each major type of case and standard exceptions are identified and explained. For example, the literature on boom towns and rapid population growth would be reviewed to identify the standard patterns of change in boom towns. Then differences are identified in boom effects on towns with high levels of anticipation of and planning for the boom and on towns with no preparation. Next standard exceptions such as boom towns with crime rates that do not increase are identified and explained.

An excellent example of the SIM method is the *Report of the National Advisory Commission on Civil Disorders* (1968). It studied ten riots intensively and all known riots at some level. It had over 90 professionals worked on the report which produced the definitive SIM on riots in U.S. cities in the 1960s. For other examples of SIMs see *Understanding Social Impacts* (Finsterbusch, 1980) which develops SIMs for eight of the thirteen major social impact areas for public construction projects. For further discussion of the methodology of SIM see Finsterbusch and Hamilton (1978) and Finsterbusch (1985).

The systematic case review method (SCRM) applies a systematic and quantitative review procedure to a set of cases to determine the general patterns (SIMs) and correlations between variables. The cases should be of the same type as the current case, for example all cases being road projects. Important differences between the set and the current case should be identified so the significance of the findings for predicting the current case can be evaluated. For example, if the set of cases included 20 percent primary road, 60 percent secondary road, and 20 percent feeder road projects one would have to be cautious in applying the general findings to a feeder road project.

Information on the cases can be obtained from interviews or documents such as evaluation reports or case studies. Regardless, an information questionnaire is filled out for each case that describes all the important characteristics of the case. For example, for AID projects it would describe the background and history, need for and purposes, characteristics, inputs and outputs, constraints and opportunities, and micro and macro settings. We have performed a SCRM on 52 AID projects from post project evaluation reports (Finsterbusch 1984, Finsterbusch and Van Wicklin, 1987; 1989) and have identified the factors that are related to project effectiveness and the role of participation in the projects. We have also performed a SCRM on 13 agricultural research centers in Sri Lanka on the basis of interviews (Finsterbusch and Jogaratnam, 1984; Finsterbusch, forthcoming).

Once the number of cases exceeds five it is important to scale the information for statistical description and analysis of the set. As cases are added after the fifth, one can not keep track of specific details and conversion to numbers is necessary to prevent too much loss of information. Scales should therefore be created for coding all the important dimensions. We recommend five and six points scales of 5=very high, very many, very significant; 4=high, many, significant; 3=moderate, medium, moderately significant; 2=low, few, little significance; 1=very low, very few, very little significance; and 0=none (if none is an appropriate category). The scoring would be done by the informant or by two (or more) coders using reports, case studies or other documents.

The last method for utilizing past experience in SIA is probability estimation. Almost always estimation of probabilities will involve considerable amount of qualitative information so subjective judgments will be necessary. Four principles should guide the subjective estimation of probabilities (prior). First the estimations should be made by a multidisciplinary team. In other words, a variety of expertise and viewpoints should be represented among the judges. Second, the judges should become acquainted with the available information on past experiences. Third, they should carefully consider the comparability of the past experiences to the current case. Fourth there should be an exchange of ideas so individual judges can revise their first estimates. We recommend using the delphi technique (Delbecq et al., 1975) for obtaining these estimates but usually simpler techniques will have to do.

The product of the estimation process is a probability distribution among discrete categories for each estimated factor that averages the probability distributions of the individual judges. For example, the team's prior probabilities for the extent of farmer's acceptance of a new seed might be: 20 percent probability of high acceptance, 30 percent probability of moderate acceptance, and 50 percent probability of low or no acceptance.

Research Methods on Collecting New Information

The Bayesian approach demands that some new information be collected on the current situation. Past experience may provide excellent guidance for the current case but it is important to test the expectations that derive therefrom. For example, prior research had shown that displacement of lower class persons from their neighborhoods had more adverse social and psychological impacts than displacement of middle class persons. The lower class are more neighborhood oriented and more likely to have more of their close friends and relatives in the neighborhood. These findings are often used in SIAs for highway locations. However, for one highway location SIA we interviewed seven low income families and found that they hated their neighborhood. Their kids were being beaten up by older kids. Seven interviews are not enough to establish the facts about the identification of low income persons with their neighborhood along the highway corridor but they are enough to call into question the applicability of the general pattern (SIM) to that specific case. They could be used to revise the prior probabilities or to indicate the need for a more thorough study.

The full range of social science methods can be used to collect the new information, but we will discuss five methods that are much more important in the Bayesian approach than in social science research generally. First, experts are questioned for their knowledge and judgments. They provide information on the case and estimates of what will happen. Some experts are simply members of involved groups who serve as informants on their group. Other experts have disciplinary, professional or technical knowledge. The assessment team talks to many experts or knowledgeable people and tries to get representatives of various viewpoints. It finds out what the experts agree upon and what they disagree upon. The latter factors should be researched further.

The second and third special methods for data collection for SIA are workshops and group interviews. Workshops are discussed by Honadle and Cooper in Chapter 10 so we do not discuss them here. Kumar (1987a) describes when and how to conduct group interviews in Third World countries. He recommends bringing project beneficiaries or community members together and interviewing them in groups. The interviewer stimulates discussion on issues, experiences, ideas, insights and opinions by introducing topics or questions, encouraging more discussion with probes, and trying to prevent a few participants from dominating the discussion. Group interviews are useful for getting a sense of the thinking of the group without the time and expense of many individual interviews. Kumar also points out that many times they reduce participants' inhibitions to freely express themselves. On some topics people are more secure voicing their opinions in a group situation than when alone, especially their reservations about a program. Once one person speaks up others will join in who would not say anything negative by themselves. Of course in some situations and some cultures persons will be inhibited by the group in voicing their true opinions, so group interviews should be used selectively.

The fourth special method for gathering new information is the mini survey which is a survey of an unusually small sample of respondents, say from 20 to 80. Even 10 to 19 interviews give one an idea of which way the wind is blowing. Ideally the mini survey respondents are randomly selected from a good sampling frame just like in a regular survey. Since mini surveys are conducted to cut financial or time costs the quality of the sampling frame may be compromised somewhat. Nevertheless a random sampling technique should be used such as every ninth person contacted or every ninth household. Mini surveys are ideal for use in a Bayesian framework as explained in our previous work (Finsterbusch, 1976a, 1976b, 1977).

The fifth special method for gathering new information in a Bayesian framework is rapid rural appraisal. Gow presents the five steps of a rapid rural appraisal in Chapter 8 and discusses many related issues (see also Chambers, 1981). Honadle (1982) covers similar issues in his article on rapid reconnaissance for development administration but also has a section on rapid methods for organizational diagnosis. Kumar (1978b) presents a guidebook on rapid, low-cost data collection methods. Finally, de los Reyes (1984) presents a very thorough description of the rapid appraisal methodology that was developed for use by the Philippines' National Irrigation Administration for project selection and planning.

Methods for Combining New and Old Information

The last step in the Bayesian approach is to combine both old and new information into best estimates (posterior probabilities) of likely outcomes of proposed actions. This step is usually performed qualitatively but it can be made quantitative if subjective judgments are utilized. In this section we recommend three strategies for combining the two data sets: triangulation, Bayesian computations and error avoidance.

Triangulation simply refers to the use of multiple sources of data to investigate the same phenomena. The basic idea in triangulation is to strengthen the analysis by using congruent and complementary methods. Ideally, the problems or errors of one method are compensated by the strengths of the other methods. A common triangulation recommendation is to use both quantitative and qualitative methods (Greene and McClentock, 1985; Sieber, 1973). Our use of the concept of triangulation incorporates but also departs from the triangulation of quantitative/ qualitative methods. The data sources that we triangulate are the literature, experts and new information (see Finsterbusch and Hamilton, 1978, for a fuller discussion). The procedure that we recommend has eight steps: (1) review literature, (2) create SIMs and identify knowledge gaps, (3) consult experts for knowledge gaps and evaluations of the validity of SIMs, (4) consult experts on the applicability of SIMs to the new case, (5) formulate theories, hypotheses and estimates (probabilities) to be tested, (6) collect new information including mini surveys, informant interviews, field observations, and documents, (7) modify SIMs, theories, hypotheses and estimates in light of the new information, and (8) recycle through all or part of the process to fill remaining important knowledge gaps.

The above eight steps constitute a process of triangulation because the various data collection procedures are related to each other. The process is a dialectical interaction between the three corners of the information triangle: literature, experts and field study. Experts help identify the relevant literature, comment on the SIM derived from the literature, apply the SIM to the current case and help plan the field research. Since the field research usually must be considerably less than is needed to adequately estimate the social impacts of the project, it must be efficient. In our judgment the way to get the most useful information from a little field work is to use it to test the SIMs and the opinions of experts. It takes far less data to show that a SIM or expert's judgment is correct or incorrect in the current case than to establish from scratch what holds for the current case. In fact very little field data can give considerable confidence when it agrees with the literature and experts. It is also efficient to use the field study to fill in important gaps in the knowledge from the literature and experts.

The second strategy for combining new and old information that we recommend is Bayesian computations. The old information is used to create prior probabilities and the new information is used to revise the probabilities. Both types of information must be put into the same form, weighted relative to each other, and then combined to create posterior probabilities. These computations can utilize Bayesian statistics which can be rather complex with multiple categories and many kinds of data (see Finsterbusch and Weitzel-O'Neill, 1974) or they can use much simpler weighing and combining procedures (see Finsterbusch et al., 1975). The two methods are mathematically equivalent for the basic estimates but we recommend the simpler method for most purposes. For example, on the basis of the literature and the opinions of

TABLE 7.1

An Example of Bayesian Computations for Residents' Attachment to Neighborhood

Level of Attachment	Prior Probabilities	Col. 2 Given Weight of a Sample of 50	Sample n=7	Combined Sample	Posterior Probabilities
High	.50	25	0	25	.439
Medium	.30	15	0	15	.263
Low	.20	10	7	17	.298
Total	1.00	50	7	57	1.000

experts the research team might come up with the following estimates of the probabilities about lower class residents' attachment to their neighborhood: 50 percent probability of high attachment, 30 percent probability of medium attachment, and 20 percent probability of low attachment. If we drew a sample of 7 lower class residents and found all 7 with low attachment to their neighborhood as described in an illustration above, the posterior probabilities would be computed as shown in Table 7.1 if the prior probabilities were given the weight of a sample of 50.

In an earlier work (Finsterbusch and Weitzel-O'Neill, 1974) an interdisciplinary team judged that prior probabilities should not be given more weight than a survey of 50 respondents. A more average weight would be 25, which if used in the above example would result in posterior probabilities of .391 for high, .234 for medium, and .375 for low. However if there are only 15 low income households in the project area then much greater weight must be given to the sample of 7. Again judgments about weights must be devised and explained to complete the Bayesian computations.

The third strategy for combining new and old information that we recommend is error avoidance, and four methods of error avoidance are soliciting critiques, seeking contrary evidence, negative planning, and risk management. Because all estimates of social impacts will be uncertain, special steps should be taken to avoid errors of judgment and errors of actions. Errors of judgment are commonly avoided by having the judgments reviewed and critiqued by experts and this procedure should be built into all aspects of the Bayesian approach but especially the final product (the posterior probabilities). Another practice for minimizing judgmental errors is to look hard for disconfirming evidence. Much of the limited field research time should be used to talk to people who are against the proposed action or who disagree with the conclusions developed up to that time. Generally, more hitherto unknown information can be learned from opponents than supporters.

Negative planning is a simple method for reducing the risk of avoidable negative impacts of the proposed action (see Finsterbusch and Hamilton, 1978). In a brainstorming session a multiperspective working group identifies a range of possible negative outcome situations that should be avoided. Then the research is designed to get the information that is needed to plan how to avoid them. An obvious example for construction projects is to avoid relocating many residents by finding sparsely populated areas to locate the facility. Another locational example would be to imagine a malfunction at a nuclear power plant that requires evacuating the population within 50 miles. If the plant were on a peninsula it could block the evacuation for people on the end of the peninsula so the conclusion of the negative planning exercise is not to locate the plant where evacuation would be difficult.

A final method for error avoidance is risk analysis, evaluation and management. Risk analysis identifies potential negative impacts. Risk evaluation assigns values to the negative impacts as well as to the benefits for comparison by decision makers. Risk management entails actions to avoid, reduce or mitigate the negative impacts. Risk analysis is a burgeoning professional field (Covello, Menkes and Mumpower, 1986; Covello and Mumpower, 1985; Dietz and Rycroft, 1988; Lave, 1982). It emphasizes threats to life and health but can be and has been applied to all kinds of impacts. The assessment of risk is still an inexact science even though sophisticated mathematical calculations may be involved. Uncertainties abound so ranges of probabilities of risks are appropriate. Obviously a policy of error avoidance requires that probabilities on the high side should be selected for assessing potential negative impacts and planning mitigation measures.

Summary and Conclusion

The message of this chapter is that a logical method for many SIAs for drawing conclusions on the basis of very limited knowledge has been available for 225 years. It is the Bayesian principle which combines past experience expressed in prior probabilities with new information to derive estimates (posterior probabilities) of the likely outcomes of a planned action. We propose the Bayesian principle as the philosophical rationale for what most social impact assessors usually have to do in a trial and error manner. We also propose procedures for (1) estimating prior probabilities on the basis of past experience, (2) obtaining useful new information, and (3) combining both new and old information in SIAs. Finally we identify numerous methods to be employed in carrying out these procedures and briefly describe thirteen methods which are not widely reported in social science methods books. We are proposing the Bayesian principle, Bayesian procedures, and Bayesian methods as a highly productive framework for SIAs for projects in Third World settings. We also suggest that our Bayesian framework implicitly underlies the other chapters in this volume.

References

Bayes, Thomas. "An Essay Towards Solving A Problem in the Doctrine of Chances." *Philosophical Transactions,* Vol. 53, Royal Society, London, pp. 376–398, 1763; reprinted in *Biometrika,* 45, Parts 3 & 4, (December 1958), pp. 296–315.

Chambers, Robert. "Rapid Rural Appraisal: Rationale and Repertoire." *Public Administration and Development,* 1, 1, pp. 95–106, 1981.

Covello, Vincent T., Menkes, Joshua, and Mumpower, Jeryl (eds.). *Risk Evaluation and Management.* New York: Plenum Press, 1968.

Covello, Vincent T., and Mumpower, Jeryl. "Risk Analysis and Risk Management: An Historical Perspective." *Risk Analysis,* 5, pp. 103–120, 1985.

Delbecq, Andre L., Van de Ven, Andrew H., and Gustafson, David H. *Group Techniques for Program Planning: A Guide to Nominal Group and Delphi Processes.* Glenview, Ill.: Scott, Foresman and Company, 1975.

Dietz, Thomas and Rycroft, Robert W. *The Risk Professionals.* New York: Russell Sage Foundation, 1968.

Finsterbusch, Kurt. "The Mini survey: Underemployed Research Tool." *Social Science Research,* 5, 1 (March), pp. 81–93, 1976a.

_____. "Demonstrating the Value of Mini Surveys in Social Research." *Sociological Methods and Research,* 5, 1 (August), pp. 117–136, 1976b.

_____. "The Use of Mini Surveys in Social Impact Assessments," in Kurt Finsterbusch and C.P. Wolf (eds), *The Methodology of Social Impact Assessment,* Stroudsburg, Pa.: Dowden, Hutchinson and Ross, pp. 291–296, 1977.

_____. *Understanding Social Impacts.* Beverly Hills: Sage, 1980.

_____. *Statistical Summary of 52 AID Projects: Lessons on Project Effectiveness.* Final Report for the Office of Evaluation, Bureau for Program and Policy Coordination, Agency for International Development, Washington, D.C. (June), 1984.

_____. "State of the Art of Social Impact Assessment." *Environment and Behavior,* 17, 2 (March), pp. 193–221, 1985.

_____. "The Way Agricultural Research Centers Contribute to Sri Lanka Agriculture," in Kenneth E. Corey (editor), *Development in Sri Lanka: Recent Accomplishments, Problems and Future Prospects,* Riverdale, Maryland: Riverdale Company, forthcoming.

Finsterbusch, Kurt, and Jogaratnam, T. "Factors Related to the Success of Agricultural Research Centers in Sri Lanka." *Sri Lanka Journal of Agrarian Studies,* 4, 2 (December), pp. 65–79, 1983.

Finsterbusch, Kurt, and Hamilton, Mary R. "The Rationalization of Social Science Research in Policy Studies." *International Journal of Comparative Sociology XIX,* 192, pp. 86–106, 1978.

Finsterbusch, Kurt, and Van Wicklin, III, Warren A. "The contribution of Beneficiary Participation to Development Project Effectiveness." *Public Administration and Development,* 7, 1, pp. 1–23, 1987.

———. "Beneficiary Participation in Development Projects: Empirical Tests of Popular Theories." *Economic Development and Cultural Change,* 37, 3 (April), pp. 573–593, 1989.

Finsterbusch, Kurt and Weitzel-O'Neill. *A Methodology for the Analysis of Social Impacts.* Vienna, Virginia: Braddlock, Dunn and McDonald, August; especially see appendix A, 1974.

Finsterbusch, Kurt et al. *A Methodology for Analyzing Social Impacts of Public Policies.* Vienna, Virginia: BDM Corporation, May; especially see appendix B largely written by Lee Abramson, 1975.

Greene, Jennifer, and McClintock, Charles. "Triangulation in Evaluation." *Evaluation Review,* 9, 5 (October), pp. 523–545, 1985.

Honadle, George. "Rapid Reconnaissance for Development Administration: Mapping and Moulding Organizational Landscapes." *World Development,* 10, 8, pp. 633–645, 1982.

Kumar, Krishna. *Conducting Group Interviews in Developing Countries.* AID Program Design and Evaluation Methodology Report No. 8, Washington, D.C. (April), 1987a.

———. *Rapid, Low-Cost Data Collection Methods for AID.* AID Program Design and Evaluation Methodology Report No. 10, Washington, D.C. (December), 1987b.

Lave, Lester B. (ed.). *Quantitative Risk Assessment in Regulation.* Washington, D.C.: The Brookings Institution, 1982.

Report of the National Advisory Commission on Civil Disorders. New York: Bantam Books, 1968.

de los Reyes, Romana P. *Sociotechnical Profile: A Tool for Rapid Rural Appraisal.* Quezon City, Philippines: Institute of Philippine Culture, 1984.

Russell, Bertrand. *History of Western Philosophy.* London: George Allen and Unwin, 1962.

Sieber, Sam D. "The Integration of Field Work and Survey Methods." *American Journal of Sociology,* 78, pp. 135–159, 1973.

8
Rapid Rural Appraisal: Social Science as Investigative Journalism
David D. Gow

Much good RRA [Rapid Rural Appraisal] is little more than organized commonsense, freed from the chains of inappropriate professionalism and informed by continuous doubt and self-criticism.

—Chambers (1985:410)

Since rapid reconnaissance, like development administration, blends art with science, the challenge is to make the science more practical and the art more disciplined.

—Honadle (1982:645)

Introduction

In the fall of 1976, I participated in the design of an integrated rural development project in Afghanistan financed by the U.S. Agency for International Development (AID). As the social scientist on the design team, I was responsible for gathering much of the basic socioeconomic data on which the design would ostensibly be based. There appeared to be no limit to the resources made available: a team of male interviewers; a team of female interviewers; an Afghan anthropologist who came from the project area; and two expatriates who had spent ten years in Afghanistan and knew the country, the languages, and the people well.

The design team succumbed to the temptation which haunted much social science at that time: it confused quantity with quality. AID had made all these people available, therefore they had to be used. This would all have been fine had the design team three months rather than a mere seven weeks in which to design the project. The designing of the questionnaires took a minimum of two weeks: visiting the project area, pre-testing, typing, translating the questionnaires, checking the translation, running off copies, and explaining and discussing the questions with the interviewers. Two weeks were spent in the field which generated 17 group questionnaires, 138 household questionnaires, and 92 women's questionnaires. It took eight people a good two weeks to code all this material which left the design team less than a week in which to use the results in the final design.

With the benefit of hindsight, I must admit that much of the information generated was worthless (Gow 1976). First, the questionnaires were far too ambitious, since we attempted to find out a little bit about everything. Second, we spent far too much time trying to understand and code the very complex answers to our somewhat naive questions concerning land tenure and income. Finally, using questionnaires at all in such a highly stratified society, which viewed most outsiders with suspicion tinged with contempt, was foolhardy. Out of such fiascoes are converts born to rapid rural appraisal (RRA)—the subject of this chapter.

The Need for RRA

As development projects have grown more complex and ambitious, the demand for information and expectations about its utility for project decision making at all stages of the process—identification, design, planning, implementation, and evaluation—have risen accordingly. Yet there is ample cause for skepticism, because quantity is frequently confused with quality and methodology tends to overshadow the end uses of information. Despite considerable time, money, and other resources expended on these information activities, however, the returns to date often have been meager. Many projects continue to be managed poorly, which is in part attributable to information gaps.

To some extent, this is because information systems are compartmentalized inappropriately. For example, an artificial separation is often assumed to exist between planning, on the one hand, and monitoring and evaluation, on the other. If the planning process is considered to have ended at the time the project was approved, monitoring and evaluation activities will be used to measure compliance with, or deviation from, the plan laid out by the project designers. Yet most development projects involve a process of learning and adjustment that calls for modifications and replanning as implementation proceeds. This cannot be done effectively without information that is geared to the decision making structure and procedures of project managers and sponsors (Gow and Morss 1985:175–176).

Information Overkill

In the field of rural development, two polar extremes have dominated the gathering of information: the first is the "information overkill" syndrome and the second—to borrow Chambers' felicitous phrase—is the "rural tourism" syndrome. With the first, information has become confused with knowledge: more information is assumed to yield more knowledge. This can lead to an overemphasis on data collection and analysis, whereby information generation becomes an end in itself rather than a means to achieving an end—in this case better, more sustainable development.

Additional information is worthless unless the capacity exists to analyze, criticize, and reflect upon it (Deboeck and Ng 1980:10). This capacity has often been sadly lacking in the case of baseline surveys, usually justified on the grounds that project management needs the data the surveys produce for planning and evaluation. This justification has been roundly criticized on the grounds that the survey may be so broad that the information produced is too general to be of much use for planning. Equally important is the identification of who will use the information. What may be of interest to the academic researcher may hold little relevance for the development practitioner.

A further justification for such surveys is that the information generated may provide new ways of tackling implementation problems. This rarely happens since surveys do not produce new ideas. Such ideas evolve from different perceptions of those facts, rather than from the facts themselves. In fact, baseline surveys may ensure that there is less thought about the problems of development (Conlin 1979). In any case, survey results are often difficult to interpret—particularly with regard to the causes of social and economic change (Mickelwait 1979:199).

What such surveys can do, however, is provide some basic information with which to generate reasonable hypotheses about specific development issues which can then be tested through an iterative process. Furthermore, baseline surveys can be very useful if data are collected on key variables which are expected to change as a result of the development process. But is a baseline survey necessarily the most effective way of gathering this basic information—in terms of time and cost?

The data generated by census-type surveys on such crucial areas as population growth and agricultural production have proved important for planning, both national and regional. Nevertheless, the reliability and validity of such data are questionable in certain contexts. In Nepal, researchers, convinced by their experience that data generated by the

TABLE 8.1
Percent of Persons Aware of Family Planning and Contraceptive Methods

Questionnaire Category	Nepal Fertility Survey (N=5,940)	Survey (N=76)	Cross-Check (N=76)
Heard of family planning	22.4%	88%	97%
Heard of pills	12	63	93
Heard of loop	6	56	91
Heard of condom	4.8	45	95
Heard of laproscopy	13	53	91
Heard of vasectomy	15.7	58	95
Heard of abortion	5	64	100

Source: Stone and Campbell (1984:29).

Nepal Fertility Survey conducted in 1976 were inaccurate, decided to cross-check survey responses. The same questionnaire was administered in three villages known to the researchers by experienced interviewers who were strangers to the villagers they interviewed.

When the survey was completed, the researchers then went into each of the villages and cross-checked the information on the survey forms by using other methods, such as casual conversations and unstructured interviews with survey respondents and key informants. Finally, they checked the survey data with their cross-check information and measured the discrepancies, which proved to be considerable—as demonstrated in Table 8.1.

Much of this variation was due to non-sampling error—specifically cultural reinterpretation and contextual bias. With cultural reinterpretation, people respond not to the formal content of a question but to the meaning—the connotations and associations—which the questioner's concepts have for them. For many people, the context of the questionnaire interview itself is socially and linguistically awkward, a condition that can easily result in inaccurate survey data. In addition, survey research normally relies on only one context for the gathering of data. To claim that such data are valid entails the assumption that people's behavior and attitudes are consistent from one context to another (Stone and Campbell 1984).

Rural Tourism

In contrast to this "information overkill" syndrome, there is the equally prevalent "rural tourism" syndrome whereby the development experts—both national and expatriate—make fleeting visits to the countryside to perform cursory "reality checks." As tourism or public relations, such trips may have something to offer: as means of gathering data for development planning, monitoring, or evaluation, they are somewhat questionable. This syndrome is characterized by the following biases (Chambers 1980 and 1983a:10–23):

- *Spatial Biases—Urban, Tarmac, and Roadside:* The hazards of dirt roads, the comfort of the tourist, the location of places to visit and spend the night, dictate a preference for tarmac roads and travel close to urban centers. Urban bias concentrates rural visits near urban centers, particularly capital cities and large administrative centers. Tarmac and roadside biases direct attention towards those who are better off and away from those who are poorer.
- *Project Bias:* This is most marked by the showpiece—the nicely groomed pet project specially staffed and supported, with well-briefed members who know just what to say. As a result, visitors tend to ignore those areas immediately outside the project area. Non-project translates into unseen.
- *Person Biases:* Rural tourists talk with the elites, with the men, with the healthy, with the users and adopters of services and new technologies. Excluded are the poor, the women, the sick, the old, the infirm, and the insane.
- *Dry Season Bias:* It is in the dry season, when disease is diminishing, the harvest in, food supplies adequate, body weights rising, ceremonies in full swing, and people at their least deprived, that rural tourism is most prevalent. The poorest people are visible at precisely those times when they are least deprived, and least visible when things are at their worst.
- *Diplomatic Biases—Politeness and Timidity:* Urban visitors are often deterred by combinations of politeness and timidity from approaching, meeting, and listening to and learning from the poorer people in a village.
- *Professional Biases:* Specialization leads to narrow compartmentalization and the unwillingness and inability to view development problems from an integrated perspective.

A compromise approach, which lies somewhere in between these two extremes, is what has come to be known as "rapid rural appraisal" which is defined as (Beebe 1985:2):

a study used as the starting point for understanding a local situation; carried out by a multi-disciplinary team; lasting at least four days but not more than three weeks; and based on information collected in advance, direct observation and interviews where it is assumed that all relevant questions cannot be identified in advance.

This approach depends on an open-ended process of questioning and observation, conducted by qualified rural development specialists who concentrate the collection effort on key informants. The rationale underlying this approach assumes that it provides a way of rapidly synthesizing data into information, drawing on the analytical skills of the specialists (Mickelwait 1979:189).

The Guiding Principles

The salient principles for effective rural reconnaissance can be conveniently grouped under the following headings:

- Establishing priorities.
- Practicing process.
- Integrating disciplines.
- Including locals.
- Listening and learning.
- Being truly available.

Establishing Priorities

Depending on the job at hand, those responsible should specify what information is needed, why it is needed, who will use it, and how much it will cost to collect, process, analyze, and present. In this way one can limit the potential for informational overkill. For example, in the design of an effective management information system for a rural development project, the information requirements of each involved group of decision makers will have to be identified—ranging from individual farm families to the minister of agriculture—and their needs will be different (Gow 1980:33–34).

To make this process easier, Chambers (1981:99) preaches the practice of "optimal ignorance" and "appropriate imprecision." The former refers to the minimum information required to make reasonable decisions. The ability to determine just what this level is comes with experience. For example, in the use of RRA in assessing the productive potential of a particular farming system, an underlying assumption is that it is not necessary to know everything about the system in order to produce a realistic and useful analysis (Conway 1985:37). It often requires courage to implement, since the demand for excessive information may be an excuse for inaction or a buttress for caution.

Appropriate imprecision refers to the fact that—especially in surveys—much of the data has a degree of accuracy which is quite unnecessary. For RRA, the order of magnitude and the direction of change are often all that will be used. While imprecision is not a virtue, saving time and money is. The degree of precision depends largely on the nature of the question asked. For example, in a project to increase agricultural production, more precision might be desirable on information about non-traditional crops than, say, information on traditional crops.

Practicing Process

A process approach to rural development—whether in the design, planning, implementation, or evaluation phase—is characterized by flexibility, adaptation to changing circumstances, and a learning orientation that can digest previous mistakes (Honadle and VanSant 1985:92). For example, in the area of project design, this approach proceeds on the assumption that designers cannot know everything, must make decisions on the basis of available but limited information, and should be prepared to learn from both success and failure. Such flexibility and willingness to learn also imply a capability for using various approaches to obtain information and solve problems. Just as there is more than one way to skin a cat, so are there various ways of estimating agricultural production—including questioning, measuring, pacing, and observing.

Integrating Disciplines

While RRA can be done by a solitary individual working on his or her own, in its most effective form it implies a team approach in which individual members can complement each other's interests and skills, as well as provide a forum for discussing what has been learned during the day's investigations. One reason the development literature is ominously quiet about the dynamics of working together as a rural development team in the Third World is that development practitioners do not like to admit just how difficult and problematic this can be. At their best, such teams can be stimulating, challenging, and exciting—depending very much on the mix of personalities and the leadership provided. At their worst, they hold the potential for professional bedlam (Frank 1987).

Including Locals

One major criticism that has been levelled against RRA is that the emphasis is observational rather than capacity-building. That is, the focus is on cost-effective tools for external actors—national and expatriate—rather than on the generation and use of data by local institutions—such as public sector development agencies or private voluntary organizations—to improve their own performance and capacity (Honadle 1982:633). This can be addressed by inviting representatives of these institutions to be members of the RRA team—thereby satisfying two mutually reinforcing objectives: the external "experts" can provide on-the-job training for the local counterparts who, in their turn, can help interpret local realities to these outsiders.

Listening and Learning

One of the major contributions that anthropology has made to the practice of development is the importance of taking indigenous knowledge seriously and combatting the pervasive bias in favor of modern, scientific knowledge from the industrialized world, which only outside "experts" can provide. Local knowledge is obtained by the investigator through listening and learning and should be considered together with information obtained by more formal social science methods. The two sources of knowledge are complementary in their strengths and weaknesses.

An example of this successful fusion is provided by the International Potato Center in Peru concerning post-harvest losses of potatoes, the principal Andean cash crop. For the researchers, the problem was one of being able to store potatoes until prices rose. In contrast, for the farmers the storage problem was the difficulty of preserving seed tubers from harvest to the next planting (Werge 1980:15–16). The improved potato varieties, which were replacing the traditional ones in the region, produced long sprouts that had to be pulled off before the tubers could be planted, a labor-intensive, time consuming undertaking.

On the experiment station, reseach indicated that indirect light reduced sprout elongation and improved overall seed quality under Andean conditions. While impressed by the results, farmers were concerned about the cost of the seed trays. They began to experiment on their own, however, by placing potatoes under the verandah, by constructing a raised platform, and by building simple structures—methods which proved effective and much cheaper (Rhoades 1984:145–146).

Being Truly Available

Overcoming the pervasive biases of the rural tourist calls for a conscious decision to immerse oneself in the local society—to the extent that this is possible. This means overcoming one's initial fears and apprehensions, and being prepared to give a bit of oneself in the process: talking about family, pastimes, and personal interests; making vivid comparisons with one's own country; telling jokes and stories; and expressing interest, curiosity, and respect. The researcher must become available as a person, taking time for people. The visits take longer but they also get behind the public performance. Overnight stops provide an excellent opportunity.

By showing that he or she is eminently human, the researcher establishes good informal rapport in the process and encourages people to be more frank and forthright in the information they may provide. There are various ways of doing this—depending on the norms of the particular society involved:

> Luck, persistence, a sixth sense and palm wine are potential antidotes, but palm wine is probably the best (Richards 1978:8).

> Good, informal rapport can be established by moderate drinking, smoking, singing and particularly dancing or the playing of a musical instrument (Feuerstein 1979).

Doing RRA: The Five Steps

RRA is a relatively new, quick, cheap way to ask the key questions and obtain the critical data. RRA recognizes that the context of the data may be as important as the data itself, and that variations may be more revealing than the averages that are often the sole output of conventional surveys. Above all, RRA is intended as a highly iterative process through which learning takes place in the field as part of a dialogue with the farmers and the other members of the RRA team (Conway 1987:6). There is no one correct way of doing RRA: instead there are various alternatives as laid out by such practitioners as Chambers (1983a) and Conway (1985). Nevertheless, experience indicates that there are five important steps to be taken to satisfy the demands of RRA:

- Identify information needs.
- Select indicators and measures.
- Collect data.
- Conduct ongoing analysis.
- Present findings.

Step One: Identify Information Needs

Although RRA is premised on the impossibility of identifying all relevant questions in advance, this does not mean that one follows a purely inductive approach—a social science fishing expedition that allows the data to dictate the questions that are asked and the direction the appraisal will follow. In the case of project design, for example, not only are there problems to be addressed but also opportunities to be identified. Hence, the general categories of information that must be collected can, in fact, be specified beforehand.

In the case of an agricultural development project, for example, potential data requirements within the immediate project area could include the following (Sweet and Wiesel 1979:135–136):

- Project area environment: ecological and demographic factors.
- Farming systems: by ecological zone and differences in technology, division of labor and responsibilities within families, land tenure and access to land.
- Agricultural support system: research and extension, agricultural inputs, credit availability, marketing and pricing.
- Non-agricultural economic activities: existing enterprises and potential for new undertakings.
- Economic support infrastructure: transportation, communications, education and training, energy resources, physical infrastructure.
- Social support infrastructure: health care, nutrititon, potable water.
- Patterns of local organizations: description, inventory, actual and potential contributions to development.
- Equity: disparities in landholdings and income, and mechanisms for reducing these disparities.

Step Two: Select Indicators and Measures

Once the general categories of information have been established, indicators and measures must be determined for measuring them. For example, the most favored indicator of social status in the rural areas of the Third World is house type. In its crudest form, the number of tin roofs is used as a measure of the relative affluence or poverty of families or villages, either at one time or over time (Chambers 1985:406). But this has its limitations.

In the case of the Provincial Area Development Program in Central Java, Indonesia, two sets of indicators were compiled for determining the relative prosperity of beneficiaries (Soetoro 1979). The first set focussed on the standard items of material wealth that could be observed in and about the household compound, particularly the type of materials used in the construction of the walls, windows, floor, and roof. The second list concentrated on the perceptions of a particular group of villagers about who was and who was not prosperous. Although the first set was more amenable to quick checks by an outsider, the second set—which is displayed in Table 8.2—drew more heavily on the knowledge and values of the local population.

TABLE 8.2
Poverty Indicators in Central Java

A man is poor if he has no land, or if he has to rent out his land.

A man is poor if his house costs less than 10,000 rupiah ($16) to build and nobody wants to buy it.

A man is poor if he has to work as a paid laborer.

A man is poor if, when he wants to go somewhere, he has to borrow a bicycle.

A man is poor if he cannot live by farming alone and has to make handicrafts.

A man is poor if he has to mix his rice with cassava or corn.

Source: Soetoro (1979).

According to Honadle (1982:635–636), this second approach has the following three advantages:

- It has a higher probability of being continued as a yardstick after external project assistance is withdrawn because it is rooted in the local context.
- It improves the likelihood that locally defined social categories will not be overlooked by technical staff.
- It mobilizes local knowledge, articulates it, and begins a process of basing analytical categories on rural perceptions.

Step Three: Collect Data

To do an effective RRA requires the willingness and the ability to utilize and take advantage of a variety of ways of gathering data from a wide spectrum of sources and transforming it into information, including the following:

- Existing information.
- Aerial inspections and surveys.
- Direct observation.
- Interviews—individual and group.

Existing Information. For a rural area and its people, a wealth of information is often readily available for those who take the trouble to look for it. A consulting team in Rwanda, responsible for looking at health, education, and agriculture used 250 studies and reports available in-country during their assignment (Gow et al. 1986). Much can be learned from maps, aerial photographs, and satellite imagery about ecology, land use, settlement patterns, and communications (Chambers 1985:404). Additional sources include the national census, annual reports of government ministries, reports of village administrators, local credit offices, agricultural publications, administrative reports, and organizational bylaws (Shaner et al. 1982:72). The "clandestine literature" produced by consultants—feasibility studies, design documents, and evaluations—is also potentially useful, as are more academic sources such as journal articles and books. Such sources are, however, usually weak on actual behavior and the socioeconomic aspects of the local social and political system.

Aerial Inspections and Surveys. Aerial surveys from small planes can provide various types of information: vegetative cover, settlement patterns, land use patterns, irrigation distribution, and physical infrastructure. Surveys which provide the opportunity to get out and see the countryside and the people, to give one a flavor of the overall situation, can be extremely useful—especially as a precursor for the more detailed investigation to follow.

Direct Observation. The importance of walking, seeing, and asking questions cannot be overemphasized—commonsensical as it may appear. Although it should be the most natural way to collect data, observational skills must be developed and refined. Untrained observers often impute false meanings to people's actions, but trained researchers describe only what people do. Skilled observations can expose behavior that the actors themselves were unaware of exhibiting (Honadle 1982:641). Such observations can also pinpoint the contradictions between what people say they do and their actual behavior. They can also make the investigator aware of what previously may have been only lightly sensed.

This is particularly true when dealing with size of land holdings. In many societies, land is measured in terms of the labor inputs required to cultivate it. For example, in parts of the Andes crop land is measured in terms of the area that can be prepared by one man with a digging stick in a single day. Farmers never specify a fixed area since it is not a standardized measure. The area varies considerably depending on such factors as slope, soil type, presence of stones, and period it had remained fallow. The only way to find this out is by actually pacing out numerous plots, which were ostensibly all the same size, and asking informants to explain the differences (Gow 1976).

Individual Interviews. Data collected in interviews are usually highly biased since most informants have ulterior motives, or hidden agendas, which selectively present and actively interpret the information they possess. For this reason, cross-checking with a variety of informants is key. Four distinct types of informant—not necessarily mutually exclusive—can be distinguished: the individual respondent, the key informant, the confidential informant, and the resident gadfly.

Ideally, interviews are conducted with an opportunity sample of carefully selected "individual respondents," a cross section of the expected target population. In the case of an agricultural project, this might include: farmer leaders, farmers who have tried recommended technologies, innovative farmers who have successfully developed improved technologies, farmers who have chosen not to adopt recommended technologies, women farmers who are both members and heads of households, farmers who represent major cropping systems in the area, the landless and the nearlandless. Better information is collected from such individuals when it is clear to both respondent and investigator that questions concern only the individual's knowledge and behavior, and not what he or she thinks about the knowledge and behavior of others (Beebe 1985:17).

Key informants, on the other hand, are expected to be able to answer questions about the knowledge and behavior of others, especially about the operations of the broader systems of which they form a part. Key informants include bankers, landlords, government officials, local leaders, schoolteachers, extension agents, farmers, merchants, middlemen, and traders. Closely correlated with their broader knowledge is the tendency to be better-off, better educated, and more powerful. The biases this introduces need to be consciously offset by seeking out those who tend to be left out and uncontacted—women and the poorer people, who are often much better informed and articulate than outsiders are conditioned to expect. More generally, for any subject of interest, it is worth spending time asking which people or groups are most knowledgeable and then working with them (Chambers 1985:408).

Confidential informants are needed to obtain sensitive information. As one informant identifies someone who is deemed to be particularly knowledgeable on a certain subject, that person can be contacted and interviewed. The value of information produced by such confidential informants is high because often it is very sensitive. In Haiti in the mid-1970s, the only way one could get information about the "tontons macoutes," the president's private army, was through surreptitious conversations with those who were willing to talk. For example, we interviewed an expatriate priest who would only talk while swimming in the sea a good 25 meters from shore!

As Honadle (1982:641) points out, such confidentiality is not always possible. Even though the topic discussed is private, the visit may be well known. For example, an interview in a rice field may not be overheard, but its occurrence is in public view.

In every village, community, organization, or project, there is usually someone who can politely be termed the resident Cassandra—a combination of gadfly and nihilist who willingly criticizes everyone and

everything. Such Cassandras are an excellent source of information—
and stimulation—if handled correctly.

Group Interviews. Group interviews are one of the more demanding
ways of collecting data for a variety of reasons: the information can
be misleading; there is an element of theater and the hopes of promises
fulfilled; those who make the most noise may be the least important;
and a lone interviewer can easily lose control of the situation. Group
interviews tend to be rather formal and stilted and, hence, rather
artificial. Experience suggests that such interviews may reveal what
people believe are preferred patterns as opposed to what actually exists.

If not carefully planned, group interviews can very quickly degenerate
into a variation of official rural tourism. This may happen when a
village is informed that a design team wishes to visit and talk with
local authorities. To oblige, the local authorities turn out in force—
believing that the visitors may have some control over the allocation
of resources. This may well be the case if the team includes official
representatives from national and international institutions. In the design of a small business development project in Bolivia, for example,
the design team was accompanied by several representatives of AID,
including the head of the division responsible for financing the proposed
project. At one group interview, 35 people turned up to present their
petitions and grievances. For the design team, this experience provided
little information but lots of indiscriminate demands of the "shopping
list" variety (Gow, Kilmer, and Escobar 1986).

A final problem may arise when a solitary interviewer is confronted
by a feisty or demanding group which can quite easily inundate him
or her with their questions and demands. In a group interview, it is
much better—and safer—to have two people interviewing: such team-
work can keep up the momentum and also serve as a means of cross-
checking what was actually said—no mean feat if two or more people
are talking at the same time. The most stimulating, and potentially
most rewarding way of conducting a group interview is through a
variety of Socratic dialogue (Honadle 1982:640). This approach involves
a group of informed persons in a dialogue that exposes variations in
the interpretation of events, policies, or objectives. By pursuing a
gradually narrowing series of "What if?" questions, disparate responses
are refined into an increasingly coherent and accurate picture of actual
practices. Considerable skill is required for successful use of this approach. If the exercise begins with a hypothetical situation, it can
usually be transformed into an examination of real cases that reveal
actual past behavior. Moreover, the exercise itself may disclose much
about the interactions among those who participate in it.

Equally stimulating is the Village Dialogue approach practiced in Nepal in the design of local resource management projects. This approach follows three steps. The first is to survey and inventory the existing socioeconomic and biophysical resources. The second step expands the already established dialogue between developers and planners. To avoid co-option by the local elite, the planning team encourages local villagers to divide into representative groups for discussion, thereby fostering a better understanding of resource issues affecting all levels of the local society. After visiting proposed project sites, planners, technicians, and villagers discuss findings and draft a preliminary plan. In the third step, the plan is refined at the project office, returned to the village for final modification and approval, and incorporated into the District Development Plan (Messerschmidt 1987:387–388).

Step Four: Conduct Ongoing Analysis

Ideally, effective RRA is an iterative process, more akin to investigative journalism than conventional social science research for it is generally quicker and much more intense. Since a large amount of data is collected in a short period of time, it is important that members of an RRA team continuously analyze what they have learned during a day's interviewing, observation, and investigation. By using a multidisciplinary team, the hope is that more ground can be covered and the whole will be greater than the sum of the parts. The team members must be prepared to learn from each other and modify their approach accordingly.

Team members must also learn and understand the biases—both professional and personal—of their colleagues. And biases there most certainly are. Strong biases—sometimes verging on antipathy—are occasionally expressed against anthropologists by technicians. Anthropologists, not to be outdone, often accuse technicians of being practical but illiterate boors. And economists, not to be outdone, accuse the rest of paying insufficient attention to the "big picture"!

One of the major challenges facing a team leader is overcoming these types of biases through encouraging mutual respect, interest, and discussion. For RRA, this can be done by splitting the team up different ways on different days, having social scientists work with natural scientists. Equally important, the team should be forced to think through the implications of what they have learned during the day's interviewing, visiting, and observations. What lessons, implications, constraints, and opportunities have they discovered and what unanswered questions and priorities should they pursue the following day?

In leading a five-person team in Rwanda, consisting of a demographer, an economist, a human resources specialist, a natural resources specialist, I organized regular meetings around certain issues that had emerged from our numerous discussions. These discussions were often long and heated but they achieved three objectives: reaching a tentative consensus on the key issues, agreeing on general strategies for addressing them, and building mutual respect among team members. One member found these meetings too unstructured and rather boring since he was not overly interested in what his colleagues were doing. In drafting the final report, his work proved to be the weakest and was finally dropped.

Another way such ongoing analysis can be stimulated is through the use of workshops—discussed in more detail elsewhere in this volume. But to be effective, such workshops discard the traditional packaged approach that emphasizes giving standardized training to groups of unrelated trainees at a particular facility (Honadle and Hannah 1982). Such workshops should provide a forum for identifying the key questions, generating possible hypotheses, and providing tentative answers (Conway 1985).

In a similar manner, the preliminary results of the analysis can be presented in such a forum—thereby testing the intellectual credibility of the RRA team, while at the same time encouraging active participation from those most involved: beneficiaries, project personnel, and development bureaucrats. This was the case in the design of a small business development project in Bolivia, referred to above. The preliminary findings and recommendations were presented to the involved institution in draft form. Two days later a day-long workshop was organized with those professionals who would be implementing the project. As a result of the ensuing debate and discussion, important changes were made in the design before presenting a final version to the donor, in this case AID.

Step Five: Present the Results

The questions that must always be borne in mind before starting any information-gathering activity—and RRA is no exception to this generalization—are the following: *Who is going to use this information and for what purpose?* Third World rural development has spawned its own distinct subfield of development literature, produced by both consultants and technicians, that is seldom read or heeded. In theory, RRA is product-oriented, that is, the RRA team is expected to produce a report presenting its findings and recommendations. In fact, the report is incidental: more important is having its findings and recommendations accepted and acted upon.

According to Chambers (1983:15), the chances for RRA to influence decision makers can be improved by the following:

- Encourage full involvement of project staff.
- Integrate proposals with current programs.
- Give priority to what can be done soon.

But more is required than this. The RRA team, particularly the team leader, must continuously lobby for the ideas being proposed—starting early on in the process of information-gathering. While this is part of the analytic process, it is also part of the strategy of not surprising anyone. The most effective way of achieving this is through continuous consultation with those in charge. This is not to imply that the team leader has carte blanche to lobby for his own personal prejudices, biases, and unfounded opinions. On the contrary, he should lobby for those ideas agreed upon through consensus with the team. A team that speaks with more than one voice is doomed.

For example, the initial RRA on the design of a refugee resettlement project in Somalia indicated that it was too soon to design a project—since many important policy decisions had not yet been taken. Halfway through the design effort, a meeting was held with all those AID people most actively involved in the proposed project to resolve this issue. One faction favored more groundwork, while another was all for pressing on with the design. As team leader, the final decision was left to me. In consultation with my design team, I concluded that design was premature and communicated this to the AID mission director, thereby obtaining his official blessing. Had we left this until the last week, we would have been roundly criticized and accused of breach of contract!

Equally important is continuous contact with decision makers to ensure that some, at least, adopt the ideas proposed and assume some "ownership" of them, that is, they propose the ideas as if they were their own. This calls for regular conversation and dialogue at various levels of the project and/or institution involved. While it means the RRA team must have its own ideas clear, it also requires flexibility and openness to new information and differing interpretations of existing information.

When evaluating a range management project in Morocco, considerable time was spent discussing our findings and recommendations with the AID staff responsible for managing this project. As our evaluation was somewhat critical, our findings were not greeted with great joy. However, we spent considerable time discussing them with the involved individuals on an individual basis. During our final presentation to the AID director, who would make the final decision, he asked some pointed questions concerning our recommendations. It was his own AID people—and not the RRA team—that responded, so we concluded that the discussions were more important than the written report.

Although acknowledging the importance of the report, I agree with Hoben (1984:17) that:

> If you want your findings to influence the project do not rely on statements in your formal report to do so. They maybe ignored or toned down in editing. In any case, they will have little impact unless they are reflected in line items in the project budget, in site-selection criteria, choice of host-country implementing agency, mode of contracting (university, private firm, private voluntary organization), and in staffing.

A Final Word: Common Sense, Art, and Politics

This chapter started with quotations from two writers who have made significant contributions to RRA. Chambers refers to RRA as little more than "organized common sense" and, indeed, as I have tried to show, much of it is. But being commonsensical in what is often the nonsensical world of Third World development, differing agendas, and development bureaucracies is no mean feat. While technique, commonsensical or otherwise, is important, it is only half of the equation. The other half requires imagination, creativity, and intellectual curiosity. Interviewing is a case in point. One can teach people interview techniques but one cannot teach people to be good interviewers since so much depends on subjective factors, such as whether one really cares very much about the people one is interviewing. By the same token, one can teach people how to analyze data, but can one really teach them to make the necessary connections, say between last week's group meetings with farmers, yesterday's meeting with the regional governor, and today's meeting with the minister of agriculture?

Underlying the effectiveness of RRA—both commonsensical and creative—is a perspective on Third World development that is ultimately political, particularly the emphasis on equity and empowerment since both explicitly imply a redistribution of resources from those who have to those who have not. RRA is very much a people-oriented approach to information-gathering at all levels of the development process. It also accepts the inevitability of confrontation and conflict— hence the importance attached to lobbying and "ownership":

> . . . confrontation cannot be regarded, functionalist fashion, as no more than undesirable friction in an otherwise smoothly running social machine; as an irresponsible activity with a high opportunity cost. On the contrary, confrontation and conflict may not only be inevitable but also necessary in a process of development, while negotiation and bargaining

are reduced to being merely devices through which the strong decieve the weak (Bailey 1986:437).

It is for this reason that I view effective rapid rural appraisal really as a blend of social science and investigative journalism.

References

Bailey, F. G. "Unto Everyone That Hath Shall be Given." *Public Administration and Development,* 6 (4):435–444, 1986.

Beebe, J. "Rapid Rural Appraisal: The Critical First Step in a Farming Systems Approach to Research." Networking Paper No. 5. Gainesville, Florida: Farming Systems Support Project, 1985.

Conway, G. R. "Agroecosystem Analysis." *Agricultural Administration,* 20 (1):31–55, 1985.

Conway, G. R., Husain, T., Alam, Z., and Mian, N. A. "Rapid Rural Appraisal for Sustainable Development: Experience from the Northern Areas of Pakistan." Paper presented at the Conference on Sustainable Development, London, UK, 1987.

Chambers, R. "Rural Poverty Unperceived: Problems and Remedies." World Bank Staff Working Paper No. 400. Washington, DC: World Bank, 1980.

———. "Rapid Rural Appraisal: Rationale and Repertoire." *Public Administration and Development,* 1 (1):95–106, 1981.

———. *Rural Development: Putting the Last First.* New York: Longman, 1983a.

———. "Rapid Appraisal for Improving Existing Canal Irrigation Systems." Discussion Paper Series No. 8. Manuscript. New Delhi, India: Ford Foundation, 1983b.

———. "Shortcut Methods for Gathering Social Information for Rural Development Projects." *Putting People First: Sociological Variables in Rural Development.* Edited by M. M. Cernea. Pp. 399–415. New York: Oxford University Press, 1985.

Conlin, S. "Baseline Surveys: An Escape From Thinking About Research Problems and, Even More, a Refuge From Actually Doing Anything." Paper presented to the IDS Conference on Rapid Rural Appraisal, University of Sussex, Brighton, UK, 1979.

Deboeck, G. and Ng, R. "Monitoring Rural Development in East Asia." World Bank Staff Working Paper No. 439. Washington, DC: World Bank, 1980.

Feuerstein, M. T. "Establishing Rapport." Paper presented at the IDS Conference on Rapid Rural Appraisal, University of Sussex, Brighton, UK, 1979.

Frank, L. *The Development Game.* Granta (April):229–243, 1987.

Gow, D. D. "The Gods and Social Change in the High Andes." Unpublished PhD, University of Wisconsin, Madison, 1975.

———. "Data Gathering for Project Design: The Afghan Experience." Manuscript. Washington, DC: Development Alternatives, 1976.

_____. An Information System for the Rural Area Development-Rapti Zone Project. IRD Field Report. Washington, DC: Development Alternatives, Inc., 1980.

Gow, D. D., Blumgart, J., Busch, C., Greenham, J., Hoben, A., Kerven, C., Miller, C., and Sweet, C. Refugee Settlement in Somalia: A Discussion and A Report. Washington, DC: Development Alternatives, Inc., 1984.

Gow, D., Burzlaff, D., Duggan, W., and Martin, R. The Range Management Improvement Project in Morocco: An Evaluation. Washington, DC: Development Alternatives, 1985.

Gow, D., Dickie, A., Hoben, S., Jemai, Y., Ndoreyaho, V., Robins, E., and Wilcock, D. The Rwanda Social and Institutional Profile. Volume One: Context, Crosscutting Issues, and Recommendations. Washington, DC: Development Alternatives, 1986.

Gow, D., Kilmer, G., and Escobar, C. Market Town Capital Formation in Bolivia: Project Components and Project Analyses. Washington, DC: Development Alternatives, 1986.

Gow, D. D., and Morss, E. R. "Ineffective Information Systems." Implementing Rural Development Projects: Lessons from AID and World Bank Experiences. Edited by E. R. Morss and D. D. Gow. Pp. 175-198. Boulder, Colorado: Westview Press, 1985.

Grayzel, J. "Libido and Development: The Importance of Emotions in Development Work." Anthropology and Rural Development in West Africa. Edited by M. M. Horowitz and T. M. Painter. Pp. 145-165. Boulder, Colorado: Westview Press, 1986.

Hoben, Allen. "The Role of the Anthropologist in Development Work: An Overview." Training Manual in Development Anthropology. Edited by W. L. Partridge. Pp. 9-17. Washington, DC: American Anthropological Association, 1984.

Honadle, G. "Rapid Reconnaissance for Development Administration: Mapping and Moulding Organizational Landscapes." World Development, 10 (8):633-645, 1982.

Honadle, G. H., and Hannah, J. P. "Management Performance for Rural Development: Packaged Training or Capacity Building." Public Administration and Development, 2 (3):295-307, 1982.

Honadle, G., and VanSant, J. Implementation for Sustainability: Lessons from Integrated Rural Development. West Hartford, Connecticut: Kumarian Press, 1985.

Messerschmidt, D. A. "Conservation and Society in Nepal: Traditional Forest Management and Innovative Development." Lands at Risk in the Third World: Local-Level Perspectives. Edited by P. D. Little, M. M. Horowitz, and A. E. Nyerges. Pp. 373-297. Boulder, Colorado: Westview Press, 1987.

Mickelwait, D. R. "Information Strategies for Implementing Rural Development." International Development Administration: Implementation Analysis for Development Projects. Edited by G. Honadle and R. Klauss. Pp. 182-202. New York: Praeger, 1979.

Rhoades, Robert E. "Tecnicista Versus Campesinista: Praxis and Theory of Farmer Involvement in Agricultural Research." Coming Full Circle: Farmers'

Participation in the Development of Technology. Edited by P. Matlon et al. Pp. 139–150. Ottawa, Canada: International Development Research Center, 1984.

Richards, P. "Geography is a bottle of Heineken lager beer—How to be the most boring person in development planning and still get your facts wrong." Paper presented at the IDS Conference on Rapid Rural Appraisal, University of Sussex, Brighton, UK, 1978.

Shaner, W. W., Philipp, P. F., and Schmehl, W. R. *Farming Systems Research and Development: Guidelines for Developing Countries.* Boulder, Colorado: Westview Press, 1982.

Soetoro, A. "Prosperity Indicators for Java." Manuscript. Washington, DC: Development Alternatives, Inc., 1979.

Stone, L., and Campbell, J. G. "The Use and Misuse of Surveys in International Development: An Experiment From Nepal." *Human Organization,* 43 (1):27–37, 1984.

Sweet, C. F., and Weisel, P. F. "Process Versus Blueprint Models for Designing Rural Development Projects." *International Development Administration: Implementation Analysis for Development Projects.* Edited by G. Honadle and R. Klauss. Pp. 127–145. New York: Praeger, 1979.

Werge, Robert. "Potatoes, Peasants, and Development Projects: A Sociocultural Perspective from the Andes." Manuscript. Lima, Peru: Centro Internacional de la Papa, 1980.

9
Donor Agency Experience with the Monitoring and Evaluation of Development Projects

Annette L. Binnendijk

This paper reviews the experiences of the development assistance donor agencies with the monitoring and evaluation (M&E) of their projects in developing countries. First, the concepts and definitions of monitoring and evaluation are discussed. Then the paper traces the donors' early efforts to develop appropriate methodologies and procedures for M&E of development projects, and reviews the problems and issues that emerged during the 1970s. The final section discusses how these lessons from experience are leading to new M&E initiatives and reorientations among the donor agencies in the 1980s.

Introduction

The purpose of this paper is to review the past experiences of the major development assistance donor agencies with the monitoring and evaluation (M&E) of development projects in the developing countries; to highlight the lessons that were learned from these experiences; and to discuss the recently emerging trends and growing consensus among the donor agencies concerning more promising and practical approaches to M&E.

The paper provides a donor agency perspective, drawing primarily on reports and experience from the United States Agency for International Development (A.I.D.), from the Development Assistance Committee (D.A.C.) of the Organization for Economic Cooperation and Development, and from the World Bank and other international and regional development agencies.

The focus of the paper is primarily on monitoring and evaluation at the project level, although the paper also discusses the growing emphasis given during the 1980s to evaluation efforts beyond the individual project level and their relevance to broader sectoral programs, non-project assistance, and policy issues.

Definition of Monitoring and Evaluation

There has been considerable confusion and inconsistencies among the donor agencies, and even within donor agencies, regarding the distinction and the relationship between monitoring and evaluation. Most agree that M&E refers to analyses or assessments of project performance during or after project implementation, and not to ex ante appraisals done during the design stage of a project. A review of the many different concepts and definitions used to distinguish monitoring from evaluation suggests that M&E might best be thought of as a continuum along several dimensions.

This paper identifies four dimensions to be considered, including:

1. *the focus of the assessment*—with monitoring primarily concerned with tracking project inputs and outputs, and whether they are within design budgets and according to schedules, while evaluation focuses on measuring development results and impacts.
2. *the timing of the data collection and assessment efforts*—with monitoring typically involving a continuous, on-going process of data gathering and review, while evaluations are often considered as periodic, or even "one shot" efforts.
3. *the implementors of the assessment*—with monitoring viewed as a function implemented primarily by in-house project staff, while evaluation is frequently carried out by teams external to the project.
4. *the management uses of the assessment results*—with monitoring oriented primarily to serve the information needs of the project management to improve the project's implementation, while evaluation may serve the information needs of development managers above the project level; for example to provide guidance for broader program and sector level decisions.

By considering monitoring and evaluation as a continuum along these dimensions, it becomes less urgent to attempt to clarify the two as distinct and separate functions, and easier to recognize the multiple levels of objectives, the variations in data collection techniques and timing, the structural and organizational mixes, and the levels of management users that may be appropriate in these related assessment processes.[1]

Early History of Donor Agency M&E Approaches

During the 1960s the most popular approach to appraising and later evaluating development projects among the multilateral and bilateral donor agencies was estimating financial and economic rates of return. Given that most development projects in those days were large infrastructural and industrial projects seeking to maximize overall economic growth, this methodology was appropriate.

However, by the early 1970s a major bilateral donor agency, AID, was shifting its emphasis towards meeting the basic human needs of the poor. This new objective of development efforts was outlined in 1973 by the U.S. Congress in its "New Directions" legislation. Others in the development community followed suit. For example, the World Bank began to shift emphasis and resources towards agricultural and rural development efforts in improverished areas, including social services delivery, although not to the extent of AID's program. As a consequence, the evaluation technique of estimating financial and economic rates of return became increasingly insufficient. Problems with the methodology included its inability to deal adequately with the equity or distribution issue, and the difficulties involved in trying to assign a monetary value to all of the project's social benefits and other impacts.

While the World Bank and the other regional development banks began to adapt their economic analyses to accommodate the new equity objectives and the diversified program portfolios, the shift in AID goals and project approaches was so radical that for a while there was no clear preferred evaluation technique. An "investment banker's" approach to assessing development projects no longer seemed appropriate in the AID program context of the early 1970s.[2]

What emerged in AID in the 1970s was a conceptual framework for guiding project design, implementation, and evaluation efforts known as the Logical Framework, or the "Logframe". The Logframe solved a major evaluation problem by clarifying at the design stage the specific development objectives of the project, and how the elements of the project were hypothesized to affect those goals. The Logframe called upon designers to clearly identify project inputs, outputs, purposes (intermediate objectives), and goals (ultimate development impacts); to identify objectively verifiable indicators of progress in meeting these objectives; and to identify hypotheses about the causal linkages and assumptions about conditions in the project environment that must exist for the hypothesized linkages to occur.[3] Some other members of the DAC that also emphasized poverty alleviation and basic social service delivery in their assistance programs adopted the Logframe approach to project design and evaluation.[4]

The AID evaluation guidance of the early 1970s that accompanied the Logframe concept emphasized evaluation designs based on the "ideal" of experimental and quasi-experimental research designs, whereby impacts, or changes in the living standard and behaviors of the project beneficiaries could be measured and held attributable to project interventions. This methodology required that statistically representative sample surveys be taken as a baseline and periodically over the project's lifetime in order to track changes in outcomes (e.g. living standards, incomes, mortality rates, etc.) among project beneficiaries and control groups, and to prove scientifically that benefits were caused by the project.[5] The academic research community and other donor agencies were also advocating this approach to the evaluation of social and basic human needs-oriented projects during the early 1970s.[6]

Key Problems Emerging from M&E
Experiences of the 1970s

This "ideal" evaluation approach proved to be overly sophisticated, costly and impractical for the evaluation of most development projects. In fact, there was a wide gulf between evaluation precepts and practice. In practice, most evaluative reporting of many donor agencies were monitoring types of efforts, concentrating on implementation issues rather than on assessing development results. The emphasis upon this one "ideal" approach in the evaluation guidance of the 1970s unfortunately left a gap in terms of practical alternative methodologies for assessing development results and impacts that might have better served the information needs of development managers.

In the few cases where evaluation efforts attempted to assess project impacts, they tended to suffer from overly-sophisticated designs and too much emphasis in getting statistically representative proof of impact. These efforts, often based on quasi-experimental designs and multiple rounds of sample surveys, were very expensive and long-term, and ultimately suffered from methodological weaknesses, inconclusiveness, and an orientation of little practical usefulness or interest to project managers. Other complaints frequently heard about evaluation efforts were that they lacked focus, either collected too little data or too much data of poor quality, suffered from limited data processing and analytical capabilities, and were frequently left incomplete. In addition to the methodological and data collection problems encountered, M&E efforts of the donor agencies also encountered a host of management, organizational and other procedural problems.

Some of the key findings about donor agency M&E experience, emphasizing the problems and shortcomings that occurred during the 1970s, are highlighted below.

Conceptual Problems

Several evaluation problems facing the donor agencies involved conceptual issues.[7] These included:

- A frequent lack of clarity about the development objectives of a project and measurable indicators. The LogFrame was helpful in overcoming these problems.
- A second problem was uncertainties concerning the purposes and end-users of evaluation results. For example, evaluation purposes were not usually tied to managers' information needs for making operational decisions. As a result, evaluations were too frequently guided by the dictates of specific methodologies or frameworks rather than by management concerns.
- Other conceptual issues of concern to evaluators were how to deal with unexpected or unanticipated outcomes for which there was usually little data; with changes in project objectives over time or with conflicting objectives; and with over-optimistic targets typically found in project design documents.

Methodological and Data Collection Problems

Some of the most serious problems that donors have had with M&E of development projects during the 1970s were rooted in methodological and related data collection problems; in particular the use of the quasi-experimental design as the "ideal" standard.[8] The following highlights donor experience with this approach.

- *High Costs*: Formal impact evaluation designs based on quasi-experimental models and rigorous multi-round surveys have been very costly, often costing hundreds of thousands of dollars or even millions of dollars to complete.
- *Dependence on specialized skills*: This approach required rigorous statistical and data collection skills beyond the capabilities of indigenous and even donor staff. Reliance on external "experts" often resulted in evaluation issues and findings being oriented away from management needs.
- *Lengthy*: They required a long time frame to complete, frequently taking several years (and often beyond the funding life span of the project) before evaluation results were available. Because of this,

they were of little practical use to the project manager concerned with improving implementation, and were also hard to fund and complete within the context of a project. For these reasons, many of these efforts were never completed.

- *Methodological weaknesses*: There were inherent methodological weaknesses in attempting to apply experimental design standards to real-life development project situations where random assignment of treatments (e.g. project services) is typically infeasible and the alternative quasi-experimental design of carefully matching groups based on important characteristics is difficult to the point of being impractical. Furthermore, extraneous factors are constantly impinging on the project setting and differentially influencing the experimental and control groups. Because of difficulties such as these, the findings of some of these studies were inconclusive in terms of proving impacts and attribution, despite large expenditures on surveys.

- *Missed management concerns*: The findings of such evaluation designs (whether developmental impacts were statistically attributable to a project intervention) frequently missed many of managements' concerns regarding factors responsible for project success or failure. The design frequently treated these operational concerns (why and how processes occurred) as a "black box". Thus while the results were perhaps useful for "accountability" purposes (e.g. the donor agency could give examples of "successful" projects with proven impacts), there was little of operational value in the evaluation findings regarding lessons for improving project performance or future design of similar projects.

- *Overemphasis on quantification*: The method's emphasis upon quantification of outcomes could not be easily applied for certain types of project goals, such as those emphasizing institution building or encouraging community participation as objectives. Also, it tended to result in too much emphasis on easily measured impacts, and ignored unanticipated and difficult to measure outcomes.

- *Narrow scope*: The design approach frequently ignored other important evaluation issues, such as continued relevance of objectives, measuring intermediate effects, cost effectiveness, and sustainability issues in its concentration on measuring impacts, narrowly defined.

- *Not generalizable*: The findings of such studies were not transferable beyond its particular context. In other words, because a particular type of project had a proven impact in one geographical setting, it could not be concluded that similar projects would be successful in other countries or even in other locations within the same country.

Organizational and Management Utilization Problems

Different donors have taken different organizational approaches to the establishment of M&E capabilities at the project level. Even among projects supported by the same donor, organizational variation has been considerable. Not all donors have consistently followed the practice of planning and funding "built-in" evaluation as part of project designs; some have relied predominantly on centrally controlled, separately budgeted evaluations. This approach has sometimes suffered from disinterest on the part of project management in the evaluation function, which they perceived as separate from their information needs, or worse yet, as an external oversight function to be feared and avoided. Also, lack of on-going M&E systems at the project level frequently meant inadequate data collection on project performance and impacts.

Various donor agency reports on project M&E have cited as a major cause of failure of many M&E efforts during the 1970s to be a misperception on the part of project management of their roles, responsibilities, and objectives with respect to monitoring and evaluation efforts. Project managers were not using M&E system findings.

In addition, project managers sometimes viewed M&E units as surveillance agents operating on behalf of concerned ministries or donor agencies waiting to pass judgement on their performance, especially when the units operated outside of their direct control. Matters were made even worse when elaborate impact evaluation methodologies were imposed from the outside, which project management tended to view as irrelevant to their information needs. Under these circumstances, project managers typically took little interest or responsibility in guiding the activities of M&E units nor in utilizing evaluation information that was generated. They tended to leave M&E activities to the "experts".

Criticisms of M&E operations also indicated that insufficient attention and expertise was being given by project design teams to adequate planning of M&E systems, prioritizing information needs, and estimating M&E staffing and equipment requirements and costs. Follow-up technical assistance and training efforts for project M&E staff were also found to be lacking in many cases. Technical advisors assigned M&E responsibilities often lacked evaluation methods skills or pertinent experience. Even the so-called "experts" were a mixed blessing, since they often held unrealistic standards for rigorous statistical surveys and research design, and had little appreciation of the types of information required by management. Consequences of these shortcomings included massive data collection efforts with no focus, little capacity for data processing and analysis, and even less for presenting findings in a manner that drew management's attention and resulted in actions to improve project performance.

While some projects suffered from too much, indiscriminate collection of data others suffered from a lack of data. This was typically the case for projects that relied primarily on outside experts to evaluate the project and had little or no on-going M&E capability. The common refrain of returning AID evaluation teams of "there was no data" has led to an increasing emphasis in AID on data gathering internal to the project rather than external evaluation.[9] Another limitation of external evaluators included their frequent lack of understanding of the local context, sociocultural and policy aspects that can be important factors influencing project performance. On the other hand, some evaluation tasks of more interest to senior or central agency management, such as more comparative studies across projects or longer term impact/sustainability concerns, may be of little direct interest to internal project management and can best be coordinated at a central agency level. External evaluation teams may also be required where special methodological expertise or objectivity are of key importance.

Donor Coordination Problems

Little formal coordination existed in the 1970s among the various donors in terms of sharing evaluation findings or experiences with M&E methodologies and procedures. In part, this may have been because most donors were themselves still struggling with their first M&E efforts and because findings from individual project evaluations had not yet been sufficiently aggregated and synthesized to be of broad interest at higher program, sectoral, and policy levels. Furthermore, the differences among donors in development orientations, project portfolios, and evaluation techniques made coordination difficult.[10]

Host Country Commitment
and Collaboration Problems

Low host government understanding of and commitment to the M&E function was a frequently cited problem in donor agency reviews. Confusion of monitoring with an audit or "policing" function made it an activity to be avoided. Yet monitoring was in general more accepted by host governments than evaluation, which was frequently perceived as an expensive, externally imposed activity of little practical relevance to their operational concerns, except possibly in a threatening way when judgements on performance were negative. Such attitudes tended to result in effects such as resistance to establishing M&E units, delays in staffing, low priority given to such activities, and diversion of staff time to other functions. There were relatively few systematic efforts during the 1970s to educate host country personnel in M&E concepts, benefits, and utility. Other than routine internal monitoring and evaluation, most evaluation efforts were by external teams; collaborative evaluations were far too rare. For example, most donors did not include host country personnel on their ex post evaluation teams. Thus valuable opportunities were lost for building local evaluation capacities, for drawing on their special contextual expertise, for increasing host country understanding of evaluation efforts, and for enhancing the likely utilization of evaluation findings and recommendations by the host government.

From the point of view of recipient countries, different M&E data collection and methodological requirements by different donors were placing additional burdens on host country staffs. Moreover, the creation of separate M&E units at the project level was in some instances leading to competition for scarce local skills among the donors, and drawing them away from government service.[11]

M&E Lessons from Experience Applied to the 1980s

While the problems surrounding donor M&E methods and procedures of the 1970s were serious, there were growing signs of successful efforts by the 1980s. Lessons from past mistakes were leading the donors to new M&E initiatives and reorientations by the 1980s, including the following.

Recognizing Multiple Purposes for Project M&E

The multiple purposes and intended users of evaluation efforts are beginning to be clarified in the 1980s. Experience indicates that an evaluation's focus should not be dictated on the basis of some research design or framework developed by "outsiders" but should instead be based upon a dialogue with the intended management users regarding their actual evaluation questions and information needs.

During the 1970s, the over-reliance on the quasi-experimental design standard led to a tendency to focus evaluation efforts too narrowly on "impacts", usually defined as changes in the living standards or behaviors of the beneficiary population. In practice, this meant that other legitimate and important focuses of project evaluation were being ignored. By the early 1980s the focus of evaluations, and indeed the concept of impact evaluations themselves, were broadening considerably. It was increasingly being recognized that we knew little about concerns such as the longer term sustainability of projects or about their impact on institutional capacity or on the natural environment. There was also growing emphasis upon evaluating intermediate effects of projects since ultimate goals were so difficult to trace to projects. Evaluations were increasingly assessing the factors responsible for project performance, including the very important sociocultural context and policy environment.

Today, the project evaluation efforts of many donors cover this diversity of performance issues and examine more carefully than in the past the factors responsible. Below are some of the typical evaluation issues that are currently being addressed by the donors:[12]

- *Relevance*: The continued relevance of the project's objectives and approach may be assessed, in light of changing development problems and changing policies and priorities of the donor and host country.
- *Effectiveness*: Evaluations of project effectiveness usually examine whether the project's services, technical packages or other products are actually being utilized by the intended target group; whether there is equity or bias in access, and whether coverage of the target group is as planned in the project design.
- *Impact*: Some evaluations gather evidence regarding accomplishment of the ultimate development impact goal of a project. For example, whether the beneficiary group's socioeconomic status or welfare has improved as a result of the project. Unintended as well as intended impacts may be studied, as may any differential impacts among sub-groups. While traditionally such evaluations were done ex post of project completion, donors have been increasingly seeking ways to assess initial impacts during project implementation, using intermediate "proxy" indicators of results and also more qualitative, process-oriented evaluation approaches emphasizing beneficiary feedback.
- *Efficiency*: Evaluations that examine the results of a project in relation to its costs are concerned with efficiency. Cost-benefit analyses of economic investment projects are typically done by the multilateral banks and to a lesser extent by the bilateral donors. Cost-effectiveness analyses are more frequently being done for projects with social objectives, whereby the costs of achieving the same social objective by alternative project approaches can be compared. However, these cost-effectiveness analyses are still relatively difficult to do (they require a quantification of the social benefits of a project as well as costs) and are therefore rare. More intermediate indicators, such as cost per unit of output or cost per beneficiary reached, are more typically used as proxy measures of efficiency.

- *Sustainability*: There has been a growing concern among the donor community about the financial and institutional sustainability of a project's services and benefits after the donor's involvement ends. More evaluations are being undertaken several years after donors have completed projects to investigate their sustainability.
- *Special Performance Issues*: Evaluations are also increasingly addressing special concerns such as the impacts of the project on the environment, on women, or on the development of the private sector.
- *Factors Influencing Performance*: For evaluations to be operationally most useful, the factors that influenced a project's successful or unsuccessful performance should be identified. These factors may include aspects internal to the project and thus more within the control of project management, such as organizational and management approaches, the distribution system, the appropriateness of the technology or services being promoted, the extent of community participation, etc. Other factors influencing project performance may be external to the project and thus more difficult to influence, such as host government commitment to providing recurrent budget and counterpart support to the project and to creating a favorable policy environment, sociocultural attitudes of the target group, weather and other environmental factors.

Encouraging a Diversity of Methodologies and Data Sources

The 1970s clearly taught the limitations of universal application of the quasi-experimental design approach to project evaluation. Such rigorous statistical designs still have their place in the 1980s, but have been used far more selectively; for example, in experimental projects in limited "test" settings. It was recognized that for the vast majority of projects, monitoring and evaluation should be based on less rigorous and more practical techniques of data collection and analysis.

The 1980s saw a growing experimentation with multiple data collection approaches. The concept of one standard or "blueprint" methodology was replaced by a philosophy of using multiple data collection techniques and sources to address a variety of management-oriented questions. Sample surveys were replaced or accompanied by less representative, low cost, rapid reconnaissance techniques for gathering information about projects and their beneficiaries.[13] These approaches include:

- *Administrative records*: simple, yet carefully designed records systems can be used to regularly assess project progress and costs compared to design plans, targets and schedules. They can also be very useful for keeping basic information on acceptors of project services such as their socioeconomic status, whether they become "repeat" users, their repayment profile, and other pertinent information.

- *Small sample surveys*: inexpensive "mini" surveys with samples as small as 100 respondents can be used to measure the proportion of a population with access to project services, those adopting or not-adopting the services, and their initial responses and perceptions.
- *Proxy indicators*: Rather than attempting to directly measure changes in project outcomes, sometimes more intermediate, or proxy, indicators provide sufficient information on results at lower cost. For example, proxies for agricultural production might include changes in the volume of commodities passing through market, estimates of commodity supplies from traders or other key informants, and watching movements in prices as an indicator of supply movements.
- *In-depth beneficiary information*: Project experience has shown again and again that failures are often due to not understanding the perceptions and the local context of the intended beneficiaries. Informal methods such as use of key informants, holding focus group meetings or village meetings, and observing participants as "case studies" can be inexpensive and rapid feed-back approaches to gaining useful information for management's operational decisions. These methods emphasize understanding why and how the project implementation process is influencing beneficiary access, adoption, and response to project services. It is not overly concerned with measuring quantities. Thus, statistical representativeness is not critical, and in-depth interviews with 30–50 beneficiaries may be plenty to draw valid conclusions for management actions.

Locating M&E Responsibilities Organizationally Close to the Management Decision-Making Point

In the early 1980s there was a growing understanding based on experience that to increase the quality of evaluations and their relevance to management, the responsibility for various evaluation tasks should be functionally and organizationally as close as possible to the appropriate management decision-making point. In practice this meant that the responsibility for monitoring and evaluation systems of individual projects be decentralized to project management teams. Project M&E units were increasingly placed under the direct control of project management rather than "oversight" units. The 1980s saw a reorientation of M&E systems and reporting requirements to support project management's information needs.[14] An emphasis was placed on continuous, on-going evaluation as part of a project management information system and special interim evaluations timed to key management decisions. More emphasis was being given to explicit planning and funding of M&E activities at the project design stage, and of treating M&E as a special project component. In addition, there was growing recognition that M&E functions, just like other project components, required technical support and training to become institutionalized.

At the same time, there was growing awareness in the late 1970s that senior management levels of the donor agencies were not getting the evaluative information in the forms they required. The large volumes of individual project evaluation reports required further comparative analysis, and synthesis to be useful at higher management levels. Similar comparative syntheses were required to meet the needs of project designers interested in learning from accumulated experience. Final and ex post evaluations tended to be more useful for these types of information needs. For implementation of these types of evaluation efforts with broader program or policy focus, centralized evaluation staffs were generally found to be more appropriate.

Since the 1980s, some of the donors have increasingly been addressing evaluation concerns above the project level. Comparative evaluation studies that aggregate or synthesize findings across a number of projects have been useful to donor management for:

- influencing donor agency resource allocation decisions among sectors or project approaches
- influencing agency aid policies and procedures so that guidance reflects experience
- improving new project designs
- serving an accountability function of showing legislative bodies and constituents that foreign aid expenditures are achieving desired development results
- serving as a basis for policy dialogue between donor and host government officials.

Promoting Greater Coordination and Sharing of Donor Evaluation Findings and Experiences

During the 1970s most evaluations were at the individual project level and focused on implementation issues of little interest to other donors. However, as the focus of evaluation efforts broadened, the potential usefulness to other donors grew. Also, by the 1980s, the lessons learned by some donors about evaluation methodologies and procedures were also emerging that were potentially useful to other donors with less experience. By the 1980s, donors were less likely to be wedded to a particular evaluation technique and more open to searching for a variety of alternatives.

The perception in the 1970s of evaluations as judgments on performance meant that some donors treated them as confidential documents not to be openly shared. The trends in the 1970s focusing evaluations on practical management concerns and "lessons" with operational implications, made them both less sensitive and of greater interest to other donors. Another trend that promoted sharing of evaluation experiences among donors in the 1980s was the growth in computer automation and database management systems. The larger donors had relatively sophisticated, and easily accessible systems storing their evaluation documents.[15]

A D.A.C. expert group on aid evaluation was established in 1982 to strengthen members' exchange of information and experience; to contribute to improving the effectiveness of aid by drawing out the lessons learned from evaluation; and to seek ways of supporting developing countries' own evaluation capabilities. Recently this group has been making strides in the direction of further inter-agency sharing of experiences. For example, a compendium was published in 1986 that summarized the results of an internal survey of D.A.C. participants concerning their evaluation methods and procedures.[16] Also, the D.A.C. group has led collaborative donor assessments of evaluation issues in non-project assistance, rural development and several cross-cutting policy concerns such as project sustainability, impacts upon women and the environment.

Promoting More Collaborative Evaluation Efforts and Institutional Capacity of Host Countries

The growing volume of evaluation literature by the donor agencies is a potential force for exerting influence on developing country programs and policies. However, host country use of donor evaluation findings has generally been limited, due to their lack of involvement and misperceptions of evaluation efforts.

Host governments have often been involved in monitoring-type functions at the individual project level. However, involvement has been less typical with evaluations, especially ex post project evaluations, which frequently have been done by foreign donor teams.

The 1980s has seen growing efforts among some of the donor agencies to encourage host country involvement in evaluation efforts. Reasons for this increased emphasis on collaborative evaluation efforts include:

- A realization that local expert involvement can improve the quality of evaluation results by their superior understanding of important contextual and policy factors, as well as contributing local language skills.
- A recognition that host countries' involvement in evaluation efforts will enhance their institutional capacity to conduct evaluations in the future. Thus, not only is the project M&E function more likely to be sustained, but the benefits may go beyond the immediate project being evaluated, to benefit the evaluation efforts of other host country programs and policies.
- As donors undertake more "on-going" evaluation efforts within project management structures, the use of local staff becomes more and more necessary. An increasing concern with keeping the costs of evaluation efforts down has also led to a greater emphasis on utilizing local evaluation talent.

The commitment within many donor agencies to support the development of evaluation capacities in the developing countries is still limited, but collaborative evaluation activities have been growing. Some of these activities include:

- A variety of efforts to consult with recipients during the planning and implementation phases of an evaluation, or as part of the feedback process where results are shared and their implications are discussed.
- Some donors conduct joint evaluations, working with appropriate recipient agencies or having recipient staff participate on the evaluation team. AID, for example, includes recipients in more than half of its formal evaluations.
- Some donors have built recipient-operated monitoring and evaluation units into projects from the outset, emphasizing evaluation as part of an on-going redesign rather than an auditing process. Typically, technical assistance and training of counterparts were used to transfer skills in evaluation methods and concepts.
- In some instances, donors have supported institutionalization of data collection and evaluation capacity within government ministries or centralized statistical agencies not tied to specific project M&E functions. These efforts have the advantage of serving multiple project information needs, of focusing on broader program and policy concerns of interest to the recipient country, and probably are more sustainable than individual project M&E units.
- Donors may also support the evaluation capability of local nongovernmental institutions, such as universities, research institutes

and private consulting firms. This approach, which has been relatively underutilized, offers advantages of cost-effectiveness, objectivity, and knowledge of local conditions and languages.
- Donors have recently encouraged greater collaborative dialogue on
  evaluation with LDC counterparts, especially by holding special
  collaborative evaluation workshops.[17]

Summary

This paper has traced some of the key problems and lessons learned
by donor agencies in their efforts to monitor and evaluate development
activities in the 1970s. In summary, these problems included:

Conceptual and Methodological Problems

- Lack of clarity concerning the objectives of projects and the purposes of evaluation efforts caused conceptual problems for designing
  evaluations.
- Donor agencies tended to be at the extremes of too little or too
  much data collection, while the capacity for data processing and
  analysis frequently did not keep up with data collection.
- Experiences with rigorous statistical design approaches to evaluation, such as quasi-experimental models, were proving to be expensive, infeasible, and of low practical utility to donor agency
  management.

Organizational and Management Problems

- M&E functions were frequently not well integrated into project
  structures, and findings were not being used by management. Often
  M&E units were set up independently of project management and
  were consequently perceived as oversight units rather than as sources
  of useful information for project management.
- Management frequently failed to understand their role and responsibility regarding M&E, particularly in providing direction and
  defining the issues that the M&E system should address, and in
  applying evaluation findings to their operational decisions.
- M&E systems were not receiving enough attention or provision of
  resources at the project design stage. Implementation of M&E
  systems often suffered from inadequate follow-up technical assistance and training, late start-up, under-funding, and diversion of
  evaluation staff time to other project activities.

Collaboration Problems

- Insufficient sharing of M&E experiences and lessons among the donor agencies was another shortcoming. Also, donor coordination of M&E requirements at the country level was inadequate.
- Host country understanding, interest, and support for the M&E system components of donor projects were typically low, due to their misperceptions of evaluation purposes and inadequate collaborative evaluation efforts on the part of donor agencies.

While the problems surrounding donor agency M&E methods and procedures of the 1970s were serious, there has been growing evidence of more successful evaluation approaches being taken in the 1980s. Lessons from past mistakes are leading the donors to new M&E initiatives and reorientations with greater promise.

Conceptual and Methodological Lessons

- A recognition now exists of the diversity of possible purposes of project monitoring and evaluation efforts. Evaluation designs and issues are more clearly linked with management's practical information needs, not with some "ideal" research design. Evaluation may legitimately be interested in assessing various aspects of project performance, such as impacts, effectiveness, relevance, efficiency, and sustainability, as well as in analyzing the factors responsible for successful or unsuccessful performance.
- Encouragement is now given for exploring a variety of evaluation methodologies and data collection approaches. Emphasis on using one standard methodology has been replaced by a philosophy of using multiple data collection techniques and sources more responsive to and focused on management-oriented questions. Sample surveys have been replaced or accompanied by less representative but lower cost, more rapid appraisal techniques such as key informant surveys, mini surveys, group interviews, and analysis of existing administrative records.

Organizational and Management Lessons

- An understanding has developed that to be effectively utilized, M&E responsibilities are best located organizationally close to the management level requiring the evaluative information for decisions.
- This includes a reorientation and reorganization of M&E systems at the project level in support of project management's information requirements for operational project decisions.

- There is more emphasis upon explicit planning and funding of M&E activities at the project design stage, and of treating M&E as a special project component. As with other aspects of development projects, it is recognized that M&E functions require technical support and training to become institutionalized.
- Also, there is a recognition that some broader evaluation efforts, of interest primarily at more senior donor agency management levels, can best be coordinated and implemented by a centralized evaluation staff.
- A growing number of donor agency evaluations are now addressing concerns above the individual project level. For example, comparative assessments aggregating and synthesizing experience across multiple projects within a particular sector or focused upon a specific cross-cutting issue, are being undertaken to guide broad program, sector, or policy decisions facing a donor agency.

Collaboration Lessons

- More emphasis is given to coordination of evaluation efforts among the donor community and to greater sharing of M&E experiences and lessons.
- A greater effort by donor agencies is being made to promote host country collaborative efforts in evaluation, and to enhance local institutional capacity in data collection for monitoring and evaluation.

Notes

1. For a study that focused on a two dimensional continuum to distinguish monitoring from evaluation, see L. Sherwood-Fabre, "An examination of the Concept and Role of Program Monitoring and Evaluation," International Statistical Program Center, U.S. Bureau of the Census, paper prepared for the American Evaluation Association meetings in Kansas City, October 30–November 1, 1986. Other dimensions were drawn from discussions of monitoring and evaluation definitions by other donor agency papers' for example, see Dennis Casley and Krishna Kumar, *Project Monitoring and Evaluation in Agriculture,* A Joint Study of the World Bank, International Fund for Agricultural Development, and Food and Agriculture Organization of the United Nations (The Johns Hopkins University Press, 1987), Volume 1, Chapter 1; *AID Evaluation Handbook* (revised), AID Program Design and Evaluation Methodology Report No. 7, April 1987, pp. 18–21; Organization for Economic Cooperation and Development, *Methods and Procedures in Aid Evaluation: A Compendium of Donor Practices and Experience,* Development Assistance Committee's Expert Group on Aid Evaluation, 1986, p. 25.

2. For an interesting discussion of how donors' development objectives and "world-views" affect their evaluation techniques, see R. Hokeberger, "Approaches to Evaluation of Development Interventions: The Importance of World and Life Views," in *World Development*, Vol. 14, No. 2, February 1986, pp. 283-333. For discussion of the limitations of applying rates of return methodologies to poverty-oriented and institution-building projects, see *World Bank Experience with Rural Development, 1965-86*, Operations Evaluation Department of the World Bank, 1988, pp. 53-54, 83-85; and Robert Cassen and Associates, Does Aid Work?, Report to an Intergovernmental Task Force, Clarendon Press. Oxford, 1986, pp. 108-110; OECD, *Methods and Procedures in Aid Evaluation: A Compendium of Donor Practices and Experience*, op cit, p. 33.

3. *AID Evaluation Handbook*, May 1974, pp. 14-20.

4. For examples of frameworks adapted from the Longframe approach see Dennis Casley and Denis Luray, *Monitoring and Evaluation of Agriculture and Rural Development Projects*, World Bank (Baltimore: Johns Hopkins Press, 1981); B.E. Cracknell and J.E. Rendall, *Report on Defining Objectives and Measuring Performance in Aid Projects and Programs*, Evaluation Department, Overseas Development Administration, Great Britain, August 1986.

5. *AID Evaluation Handbook*, 1974, pp. 35-39; *AID Manager's Guide to Data Collection*, AID Program Design and Evaluation Methods Report No.1, November 1979, pp. 26-33.

6. See for example, Howard E. Freeman, Peter H. Rossi, and Sonia R. Wright, *Evaluating Social Projects in Developing Countries*, Development Center, Organization for Economic Co-operation and Development, Paris, 1979; Dennis Casley and Denis Luray, *A Handbook on Monitoring and Evaluation of Agriculture and Rural Development Projects*, Agricultural and Rural Development Department, World Bank, November, 1981.

7. For a discussion of conceptual issues in evaluation, see OECD, *Methods and Procedures in Aid Evaluation*, op cit.

8. For examples and discussion of the problem experienced in use of sample survey and quasi-experimental methods in evaluation, see Larry Cooley and Bruce Mazzie, "Use of Sample Survey Methodology for Project Evaluation," AID/CDIE unpublished paper, June 1983; Michael Hartz, "Lessons Learned in Evaluating AID Development Project Impacts," International Statistical Program Center, U.S. Bureau of the Census, paper presented at the American Statistical Association Meetings, Toronto, Canada, August 1983; Maureen Norton and Sharon Benoliel, *Guidelines for Data Collection, Monitoring, and Evaluation Plans for AID-Assisted Projects*, AID Program Design and Evaluation Methodology Report No. 9, August 1986; Dennis Casley and Krishna Kumar, op cit, Vol. 1, Chapter 8; World Bank, *Managing Information for Rural Development: Lessons from Eastern Africa*, 1980, and *Monitoring Rural Development in East Africa*, 1983.

9. Discussions of organizational and management problems, such as lack of "built-in" data collection and evaluation components into projects, and low levels of utilization of evaluation findings by management, can be found in

Maureen Norton and Sharon Benoliel, op cit; Chris Hermann, *Designing Monitoring and Evaluation Systems: Issues and Opportunities,* AID Evaluation Occasional Paper No. 14, 1987; World Bank, *Built-In Project Monitoring and Evaluation: An Overview* (restricted distribution), June 1985; Robert Cassen and Associates, op cit, p. 116.

10. See Robert Cassen and Associates, op cit, pp. 107–108

11. See OECD, *Methods and Procedures in Aid Evaluation,* op cit, pp. 48–52; OECD, *Evaluation in Developing Countries: A Step in a Dialogue,* Paris 1988; World Bank, *Built-In Project Monitoring and Evaluation: An Overview* op cit., Robert Berg, "Donor Evaluations: What Is and What Could Be," prepared for the International Conference on the Role of Evaluation in National Agricultural Research Systems, Singapore, July 7–9, 1986, cosponsored by IFARD and IDRC.

12. See OECD, *Methods and Procedures in Aid Evaluation,* op cit, pp. 28–31; *AID Evaluation Handbook* (revised), April 1987, p. 23; Dennis Casley and Krishna Kumar, op cit, Vol. 1, pp. 101–106.

13. For further references on rapid appraisal techniques being used by the donor agencies, see Dennis Casley and Krishna Kumar, *The Collection, Analysis, and Use of Monitoring and Evaluation Data,* A Joint Study by the World Bank, International Fund for Agricultural Development, and Food and Agriculture Organization (the Johns Hopkins University Press, 1988; Krishna Kumar, *Rapid Low-Cost Data Collection Methodos for AID,* AID Program Design and Evaluation Methodology Report No. 10, December 1987; Maureen Norton and Sharon Pines Benoliel, op cit., pp. 13–29 and Appendix B.

14. Emphasis on monitoring and evaluation as information systems serving project management's needs is the focus of the new *AID Evaluation Handbook.* It is also the philosophy of evaluation guidelines such as *Guidelines for Data Collection, Monitoring and Evaluation Plans for AID-Assisted Projects,* op cit. Chapter 3, and *Project Monitoring and Evaluation in Agriculture,* op cit., Chapter 1.

15. See Robert Cassen and Associates, op cit., pp. 107, 108, 309.

16. OECD, *Methods and Procedures in Aid Evaluation,* op cit.

17. OECD, ibid, pp. 48–52; OECD, *Evaluation in Developing Countries; A Step in a Dialogue,* op cit.

10
Closing the Loops: Workshop Approaches to Evaluating Development Projects

George Honadle and Lauren Cooper

Development projects have been castigated (Morgan, 1983), defended (Rondinelli, 1983), and examined for both strong and weak points (Honadle and Rosengard, 1983). At one time they accounted for the major portion of public sector aid flows to Third World governments. Today they represent a lesser portion of these flows due to the ascendency of structural adjustment and sector lending, but they still remain a major mechanism for development assistance (Cernea, 1986).

Evaluating international development projects is a task that shares all the difficulties of evaluating domestic service delivery programs and also adds some unique problems. One unique problem stems from the "development" nature of these projects—development involves building local capacities to deliver services at a future time and not just using a project to deliver them today. Sustainable projects build local knowledge and capabilities and internalize new ways of doing things within the community of affected people. Thus, a problem for evaluators is to ensure that evaluations are used as tools to help local organizations to learn. This is the problem of the learning loop.

A second unique problem stems from the "project" nature of much development. Projects enjoy funding levels and expert attention far exceeding the routine operations of government ministries in the Third World. As projects wind down their activities, the advantages they enjoyed during the period of flush funds and political protection begin to dissipate. Eventually project activities lose their identities as discrete endeavors and they merge into the stream of local activities. Linkages between project-initiated efforts and later activities quickly become lost. Thus, assessing the extended impact of a temporary and fleeting project presence can be a Herculean task.

This chapter addresses the two problems noted above. First, they are discussed and then specific roles for workshops are noted as ways to overcome them. Finally, the potential for workshop use is placed into the context of the purposes evaluations serve and the expectation that the contribution of workshops will vary depending upon those purposes.

Two Issues in Evaluating Development Projects

The two problems noted above represent key issues affecting development project evaluation methods. The first issue is concerned with the choice of a knowledge repository. The second is concerned with establishing the link between project activity and the development activity that flowed from, but was not an integral part of, the project.

The Repository of Knowledge

A common problem area in the domestic U.S. evaluation literature is that of "utilization" (Patten, 1978). That is, the failure to incorporate the results, lessons and recommendations of evaluations into implementation actions or policy thrusts is widespread. One reason for this failure is that evaluations are often conducted by outsiders who lack a vested interest in follow-through, an understanding of the subtleties of the situation, and access to methods to compensate for these weaknesses (Salmen, 1987).

Frequent use of outsiders as evaluators arose due to the need for levels of objectivity and analytical capability which were often scarce within the implementing units. At the same time, the need for managers and policy-makers to understand, support, internalize and act upon the findings has led to collaborative evaluation teams with both insiders and outsiders participating. This model is common in the field of international development where evaluation teams usually include donor staff, host country staff, and consultants. Even so, there is still a recognized need for improved collaboration in knowledge generation (Ross, 1988) and the problem of utilization persists.

The utilization problem, however, is part of a larger problem—the choice of an appropriate knowledge repository. International studies of rural development suggest that success is linked to the pursuit of a "learning process approach" (see Sweet and Weisel, 1979; Korten, 1980; Honadle and VanSant, 1985). This perspective rejects views that present development projects as just service delivery mechanisms or lock-step impositions of strategic decisions. Instead, it casts them as learning laboratories where organizations and communities gain the capacities needed to obtain some influence over their own destinies. An integral part of this process of empowerment and development is knowledge-building in local institutions.

For such an approach to work, there must be a local knowledge repository. The learning-feedback loop must be closed for development to occur. Formative, summative and impact evaluations must all take this into account.[1] In fact, loop-closing is not a one time affair. Rather, it is the cumulative effect of linking action to knowledge and then knowledge to action that indicates institutional development is happening.

The goal of institutional development requires that local institutions be involved in the process of evaluating development efforts and that local knowledge repositories be strengthened. For development projects, the evaluation feedback loop is an integral part of the implementation objective and a partial measure of its achievement. If they do not close feedback loops, development project evaluations do not contribute fully to the process of development. Evaluation procedures must deal with this issue.

The Engine and the Starter Motor

A project can be viewed as a sequence of transformation processes that begins with some set of *resources* such as money, people, equipment, information, facilities, and so forth. The first transformation occurs when management turns these resources into *goods or services.* For example, a farmer training program would result from management combining physical, human and monetary resources with technical knowledge in such a way that *x* number of farmers received training in the use of a new technique.

But the second transformation would be done by the trained farmers, not project management. Taking the knowledge and using it in the field would involve efforts by those exposed to the information. This second transformation results in *local action*—new behavior by the beneficiaries of the first transformation. This is the first level of project impact.

The second level of impact occurs when the farmers sell or consume the fruits of their labor. In this case, local action results in improved *welfare* as measured by increased income or nutritional intake. This transformation of local action into welfare (or "capacity" in terms of purchasing power, or health, or an improved environment) can be influenced by such non-project factors as culture, macroeconomic setting, pricing policies, weather, institutional performance, or social stability. Thus it is even further outside the control of project management than local action.

This sequence of RESOURCES—to—GOODS AND SERVICES—to—LOCAL ACTION—to—WELFARE AND CAPACITY comprises the set of direct transformations expected to emerge from project activities. But the achievement of sustained developmental impact only begins with improved welfare and capacity. Purchasing power and productive capacity are expected to generate, from other sources, new goods and services that support a self-sustaining cycle of further local action responses and capacity improvements. This is the main engine of development, fueled by a critical mass of social and physical capacities. The project serves only as a starter motor for this engine, which can be visualized as a loop of self-propelled local activities following the linear sequence of the elements of the project starter motor.

The perspective presented above is depicted by Figure 10.1, which shows the relative importance of the starter motor and the main engine. The challenge for impact evaluators is to determine whether or not the project activities furthered the development dynamics represented by the self-sustaining cycle of the impact loop; the challenge for formative evaluators is to keep management's eyes on the ultimate goal rather than the minutiae of day-to-day implementation; the challenge for summative evaluators is to identify outcomes throughout the starter motor sequence (see note 1 for explanations of the different types of evaluations).

Two objectives for the evaluation of development projects, then, are the building of local knowledge repositories to support sustainable development and the inclusion of information about the degree and type of project contributions to sustained, self-initiated, complementary development action. Achieving these objectives can be depicted as "closing the loops." Effective evaluation require tools to ensure that both of these objectives are met.

The Workshop as a Tool for Evaluation

The position taken in this chapter is that the workshop is an underutilized evaluation tool—workshops are useful both for evaluating the fit between a project and its environment and for improving that fit. Such a position, however, requires a clear statement of what a workshop is and what it is not.

Defining Workshops

The authors were once working in an Anglophone country in Africa where, as part of a reconnaissance and preparation mission, they attended a "workshop" on agroforestry. Upon arriving at the location,

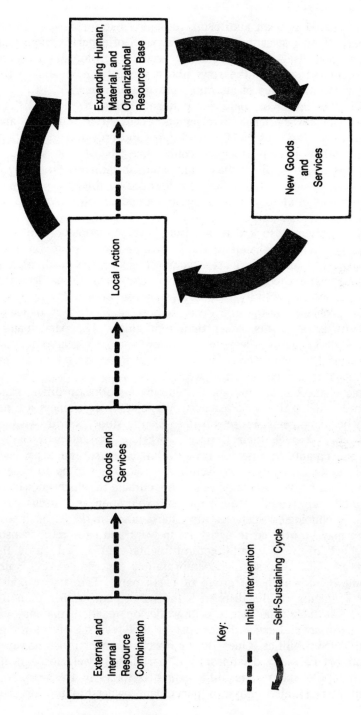

FIGURE 10.1 The Impact Loop. Source: George Honadle and Jerry VanSant, *Implementation for Sustainability* (West Hartford: Kumarian Press, 1985), p. 76.

they were ushered into an auditorium designed like an ancient Greek amphitheatre. Down at center stage was a panel of experts expounding on the definition of agroforestry and the need for agroforestry research in this country. Seated in the rows above were the members of the audience in various states of attention and inattention.

This was the dominant behavior pattern of this "workshop." The only concession to audience involvement occurred as question and answer sessions. This was NOT a workshop, and only someone totally unfamiliar with workshop processes could have labeled it as such.

Workshops are physically, behaviorally, and substantively far removed from the exercise noted above. They are founded on different principles and assumptions, and they have different immediate objectives than a lecture-cum-panel discussion.

Workshops attempt to create a climate where people of different disciplines and interests listen to each other and attempt to integrate relevant expertise and experience—technical, social, political, organizational, financial and economic. They involve minimal formal lectures, maximal participant activity, and extensive use of small groups for discussion, problem solving and decision making. The focus of workshop activity is on teams rather than individuals. The participatory operating style encourages learning by doing and it is geared to producing practical, action-oriented products and agreements that are directly relevant to the participants' work.

The role of those designing and conducting a workshop differs from that of traditional trainers or teachers. While teachers/trainers are assumed to be the experts whose job is to fill the students with wisdom and knowledge through their lectures, workshop facilitators recognize that the participants themselves bring valid expertise and experience related to the topic at hand. The facilitator's role is not to be an expert, but to create an active learning and sharing climate in which knowledge is discovered and created through mutual exploration and discussion.

Various technologies such as flip charts and markers, or laptop computers may be utilized to assist group work and capture consensus or divergence of insights and committments. But in all cases the approach assumes that adequate information concerning key issues exists somewhere within the group of participants. Primary responsibility for achieving results rests with the participants rather than the facilitators. At the initial stages of a workshop, participants may experience surprise and even discomfort at this reversal of traditional roles and responsibilities. Once the approach is understood, however, the discomfort normally disappears and participants welcome and appreciate the trust and responsibility which is theirs in the workshop. This shift in roles also enhances participant ownership of workshop outcomes. They quickly realize that they can use the event to deal with their own concerns instead of just serving the needs of donors.

Designing Workshops

The exact configuration of workshop participants, groups and exercises depends on the objectives and phase of the project and the circumstances in the field. In some cases, a series of workshops may be held. For example, a first workshop may involve a national level gathering with people from numerous ministries, followed by sector-specific or geographically-specific meetings that take the output of the first workshop and refine or adapt it. In other cases, it may be a series of gatherings that alternate between national and other levels of staff, or it may consist of a shifting mix of ministry, non-ministry, and private sector participants. The sequencing is designed so that each workshop builds on the outcome of the previous one.

A parallel approach is used within a single workshop. Exercises build on previous exercises. Sometimes two tasks may appear to be unrelated until they are integrated by an exercise that requires the output of both of the others. The integration may occur in small workgroups or it may be done in a plenary session involving all the workshop participants. Since workshops tend to alternate between workgroups and plenaries, either can be used, depending on the mix of people and the objectives the workshop is intended to serve.

Workshop designs must be both flexible and rigorous. That is, specific exercises may need to be redesigned during the workshop to accomodate to unforseen events, but the overall strategy linking the various exercises to an end product must be maintained. Step by step analytical procedures must be followed so that conclusions are based on a broadly accepted assessment of the situation under scrutiny. Closure is necessary.

This sequential rigor helps to keep the workshop effective in situations of extreme bureaucratic and political conflict. Although the facilitators may be under great pressure, the relentless logical march of the exercises keeps the effort on course. At the same time, the use of groups and group outputs protects individuals from exposure to political risk. Conclusions and recommendations are those of teams or the participants as a whole—not individuals. The small group work keeps much of the debate out of the larger public view, and the plenary presentations represent the conclusions of the groups—not the individuals doing the presenting.

Since each workgroup determines its own operating style, the workshop format also promotes culturally appropriate approaches to issue identification and problem solving. Thus a workshop embodies many advantages over more directive approaches to data collection and action planning under conditions of cultural plurality and political uncertainty. But the workshop method requires skilled and experienced organizers to work. It is not a tool easily used by neophytes. Indeed, both the ability to make appropriate in-course design corrections and skill at achieving the right mix of people in groups are attributes of good organizers, and these attributes usually emerge out of experience.

Some of the basic elements of workshop design can be easily mastered by the inexperienced, however. For example, arranging chairs and tables to support interactive discourse rather than a lecture takes awareness, not high-level training. Likewise, understanding that participants usually find alternating between plenary and workgroups to be preferable to a long string of either one requires no special insight. Another basic design element is the tradeoff between the number of workgroups and the number of people in a workgroup—more groups means more presenters and thus more time on a single topic in a plenary session, but more people in each workgroup may lengthen the time each needs to resolve an issue or produce a product. This tradeoff also is clear to beginners.

Absolute numbers of both participants and facilitators are also important. The rule of thumb for workshop size is keep it down to 35 people or fewer—any more are dificult to handle. The rule of thumb for small groups is no less than 3, no more than 5—fewer than three provides a poor base for group dynamics, whereas more than five extends the time needed and makes it difficult for all people to contribute effectively. For facilitators, the rule is never less than 2—there are always exhausting periods during the workshop when the baton must be passed to someone else and at least two heads are needed to catch nuances and develop effective midstream adjustments. In fact, it is best to have two experienced facilitators—the rule of two does not include apprentices. But the dictates of the situation often cause the rules to be broken. Purists do not do well in the area of development management, but at the same time it is sometimes necessary to just say "no." Too much is too much.

In terms of the time dimension, there is seldom enough. There is a tendency to try and do too much too quickly. Groups need time to learn how to work together. Inexperienced organizers try to push too many exercises into a set amount of time. It is better to have it underplanned than overplanned.

Another fairly clear tradeoff is between mixing agencies, regions, sectors and hierarchical levels in a small group versus keeping the group more homogeneous. When a particular exercise emphasizes sharing viewpoints and moderating extreme views, then the greater range makes sense (within local cultural parameters). But when the exercise objective is to develop an action plan or negotiate for resources with other units, or simply demonstrate the relationship between where you sit and what you see, then actual operating groups must be used. The logic of many workshops dictates a switch from cross-sectional to operational small group membership part way through the workshop. Some may begin with the mixed groups and some may begin with the "real" groups, but nearly all will contain some mixture of both and most will finish with the operational groupings. In any case, however, decisions concerning group composition for particular exercises must be consistent with the overall objectives and context of the workshop.

Three experienced practitioners of the workshop method have identified seven objectives for which the workshop has proven to be a powerful tool (Silverman et al., 1986). Those objectives are:

1. Identifying local perceptions of problems and constraints;
2. Revealing values and attitudes to which projects must be fitted;
3. Producing accepted procedural, analytical and operational frameworks for development activities;
4. Mobilizing support for development strategies;
5. Generating commitment and ownership among key actors in the implementation of an effort;
6. Starting a process for managing implementation teams; and
7. Improving management capacity.

To this list we would like to add two elements:

8. Identifying impact dimensions that are not obvious; and
9. Sharing knowledge in such a way as to enhance local knowledge repositories.

The choice of objectives will influence the design of the workshop. Moreover, a number of these objectives can be applied directly to a project evaluation exercise. Exactly where the workshop is used in the exercise will determine the relative importance of the various objectives.

Using Workshops for Evaluation

Workshops can play key roles at four points in the evaluation process. First, they are helpful for developing assessment methods and preparing teams to go to the field. Second, they can be used to inform and select organizations bidding on evaluation contracts. Third, they are useful for "closing the loops" during the field assessment. And fourth, they are practical for testing draft reports and study conclusions with clients and field teams. Each role is discussed below.

Team Preparation. Workshops are helpful for building the interview instruments to be used in the field. Draft questionnaires can be used as the basis for group discussion, key data requirements and data collection approaches can be outlined, and reporting formats can be agreed upon. Underlying issues can also be raised. These include "closing the loops" considerations or others such as the primacy of project evaluation versus confidentiality versus country program level assessments or other areas of potential disgreement within the team(s). Particular needs of the institution funding the study and major emphases of the substantive disciplines represented on the team(s) can also be dealt with at this time and incorporated into the methodology.

There is also a process dimension to preparation workshops. Teambuilding can begin before field work and those who will collect data can be involved in determining the how and what of data collection. Even logistics can be planned as part of this workshop. In fact, a common design for preparation workshops is that of a "funnel," with broader themes dominating the beginning and detailed instruments and schedules emerging from the end of the exercise (see DAI, 1985; OTA, 1988).

When teams are staffed primarily by nonlocals, preparation workshops are usually held in the home location of the donor. But staging such activities in institutions located in third world countries and including locals on the teams could contribute directly to closing the feedback loop and building local knowledge bases and organizational capabilities. Hiring local firms or universities and funding preparatory workshops at their facilities would serve multiple objectives.

Bidder Information. Another use for workshops involves informing organizations that intend to compete for the chance to conduct either an entire evaluation or a part of an evaluation package. This informs the potential contractors of the meaning and intention behind the terms of reference (TOR) and it can help to adjust the TOR to local circumstances. This is especially useful when indigenous firms will be contracted to perform the evaluation.

Such an approach was used in an AID effort to evaluate the impact of participant training in Nepal. The multi-pronged evaluation included survey research, country-based historical data, and case studies of organizational performance. The design for the organizational case studies was presented to, and modified by, Nepali social scientists representing firms interested in obtaining the contract. The workshop informed in both directions—to the bidders and to the funders. The collegial and interactive nature of workshop processes compressed a high volume of high quality information flow into a very short time period of two days. This resulted in an improved study design and the acquisition of knowledge by the parties involved.

Using workshops for informing bidders has numerous advantages over using simple meetings to answer questions. The workshop exposes potential bidders to the perspectives of the competition and raises general awareness of different approaches to issues, it provides much better information in both directions, and it often results in improving the original TOR.

Field Assessment. Strengths and weaknesses of workshops for field data collection have been noted in discussions of rapid rural appraisal (Honadle, 1982). These characteristics are compared with those of other methods in Table 10.1.

Workshops are generally underutilized during field assessments for two major reasons. First, the logistics involved in identifying appropriate participants and venues often stagger the consciousness of those planning the field phase of the evaluation. Compressed time frames, budget limitations, and lack of prior familiarity with the projects to be studied add to this tendency to steer clear of workshops. Second, evaluation teams are seldom staffed by experts experienced in conducting workshops. Without such people as facilitators the probability that the workshop will add significantly to the results of other data collection approaches is very low. In fact, a workshop can backfire if it is poorly run.

But these are surmountable problems. The potential contribution of workshops during field assessment is great, especially when the issues of the two loops are integral to the exercise.

Workshop exercises can be structured so that local experts, merchants, public officials, and villagers generate and assimilate new data about the connections among project investments, complementary program-level efforts, and post-project development. But identifying and assembling the right people requires advance work by a knowledgable person. This adds to the cost and the logistical complexity. The potential returns for assessing the impact of the starter motor have yet to be fully tested, but when the main engine involves such elusive dimensions as institutional change, organizational performance and attitudinal shifts, then workshops are likely to be more cost effective than when the impact dimensions are predominantly physical infrastructure related.

The value of workshops for involving local institutions and benefitting local knowledge repositories is more firmly established. For example, twinning arrangements linking local and external institutions have been combined with workshops during evaluation exercises (Cooper, 1984). Although workshop use in impact evaluations is negligible, they

TABLE 10.1
Workshops Compared to Other Methods of Reconnaissance

Data Collection Approach	Advantages	Disadvantages
Record examination	Language barrier is lessened Documents can be reviewed at convenience of interviewer; does not disrupt staff activities	Records are often inaccurate, or inappropriate Difficult to estimate sample bias Limited range of variables covered Can be very time consuming
Direct observation	Provides primary data Does not disrupt routine bias Can expose data not anticipated by investigator Low cost	May be confounded by investigator's presence Susceptible to misinterpretation by researcher May contain seasonal bias Lack of representativeness
Confidential interview	Protects informer Allows access to examples of actual dynamics Increases extremes and range of perspectives	Usually highly biased Emotionally taxing Requires leads from other informants If interpreter is required, protection is lost, interpreter may filter information Sample may be limited or confidentially impossible in some settings
Key informants	Useful in clarifying issues, testing conclusion of the investigator Acts as filter to avoid culturally objectionable questions or data gathering techniques Key informant linked to key decision-makers can help prepare atmosphere for report Involvement in process can build skills of informant	Bias or perspective of key informants may have undue influence on results Excessive time may be required to identify the best informants Some informants may alienate potential actors who are key to implementing recommendations Rapport between key informants and evaluators is essential

(continues)

TABLE 10.1 (*continued*)

Data Collection Approach	Advantages	Disadvantages
Informal delphi	Facilitates participation and exposes interpersonal dynamics Increases accuracy of meanings imputed by researchers Increases sample representativeness Generates data beyond interview design Low cost Can begin dialogue among participants	Minimizes extremes and range of perspectives by inducing consensus Emotionally taxing May require interpreter Exposes view of informers Susceptible to domination by a strong personality Disrupts staff activity
Workshop	Builds capacity as well as serving as information collection technique Promotes investment in and receptiveness for results on the part of participants Can lead directly to identification of strategies to improve situation Communicates information to decision-makers as simultaneous part of collection process Can produce formal commitments, recommendations or analyses based on group effort	Costly in terms of staff or beneficiary time and effort Requires scarce facilitative skills for evaluators Status difference among participants may affect attendance

Source: George Honadle, "Rapid Reconnaissance for Development Administration: Mapping and Moulding Organizational Landscapes," *World Development,* vol. 10, no. 8, 1982, pp. 641, 642.

have been employed successfully in design and implementation based assessments in Africa, Asia and Latin America.

Another established use of workshops during field evaluations involves the staging of mini-workshops within evaluation teams at the end of the field assignment. This helps to build consensus on findings or highlight the reasons for diverging conclusions. The results have been very positive.

Development projects usually contain a major component of technical assistance. Given this, both donor and recipient institutions are concerned about the impact of this assistance. Two illustrations of workshop usage in evaluating technical assistance performance and impact can demonstrate some of the points made above.

As part of the assessment of the impact of technical assistance (TA) on institution building in the irrigation sector in an Asian country, four one-day workshops were held. The objective was to identify where and how the TA was working or not working, develop strategies for remedying deficiencies, and gain commitment to improvement. The participants were different in each workshop, and included headquarters staff of the implementing ministry, headquarters staff of the ministries of finance and planning, field staff responsible for irrigation project implementation, local and foreign consultants conducting feasibility studies, and field staff supervising the work of the consultants.

In the first workshop participants identified 61 problems which were then clustered into six categories. Two priority problems were selected from each category and then working groups were used to outline strategies for resolving or reducing those problems. At the second and third workshops spokespeople from each of the workgroups at earlier workshops presented their groups' findings and then these became the starting point for the next round of analysis and planning.

By the end of the fourth workshop, 184 problems had been identified, of which only a small percentage could be resolved by that group alone. This quickly became apparent and served to lessen the tendency to blame a single group for problems that were clearly attributable to more than one source. The workshops enabled key stakeholders—implementing agency staff, consultants, and donor staff—to identify explicitly the problems each was experiencing in relation to the others and to then appreciate the need for different strategies to deal with different problems. The result was that different assumptions and expectations about roles and responsibilities surfaced, resource deficiencies were specified, and the incentives and disincentives affecting TA performance and institutional development became clear.

In another Asian country an international donor agency evaluated the effectiveness of TA to the 31 projects it was supporting in that country. The evaluation consisted of: a review within the donor organization of the content, cost and perceptions of the TA experience; questionnaires to the staff of the local implementing agencies; interviews with key host country actors; discussions with other donors concerning their TA experience in that country; interviews with selected consultants who had provided TA in the country; and, a two-day evaluation workshop held in the capital city.

Over 30 people from 17 different ministries and organizations attended the workshop. Using data generated from the questionnaires and interviews, as well as personal knowledge, they identified an array of issues, reached consensus on four priority points, and identified lessons and strategies for future application to the management of technical assistance.

Due to the limited time of the workshop, the level of detail appearing in the strategies was less than optimal. But one of the suggestions provides a good example of the kind of subjective issue which commonly surfaces and which, if not addressed, can create stress and resistance to the "real" work at hand. That suggestion came from local people. It was to reduce the number of donor agency staff visits from two or three to only one per year per project. Discussion of the problem revealed that the hosts felt compelled, by their cultural standards, to spend much time and money taking donor staff around and out to dinner throughout each visit. But the constant stream of people to be hosted was proving to be exhausting from the local perspective. From the donor's viewpoint, two or three visits per year are essential to supervise project implementation, but the labor-intensive, financially costly "escort services" provided by their hosts were not necessary and they were far beyond the level of hospitality accorded to them in other countries. Because the workshop provided a culturally acceptable way for host country nationals to raise this issue, a resolution was obtained.

A workshop approach had not been used in this country prior to this event. Some donor agency staff were concerned that it would not work, that it would not be possible to get host country staff from 17 agencies together in one place and have them discuss openly the problems they faced, and that there would be resistance and discomfort with this different way of doing things. But in the participants' evaluation of the workshop they said that the workshop provided them with a rare opportunity to exchange experiences with other departments and that not only did they benefit from this, but the donor also was given a much better understanding of their situation. They felt that the workshop enabled the two sides to put forth their respective views without reservation and that a mutual understanding was achieved. Indeed, another "loop" was closed.

Although these two examples deal with technical assistance evaluation, the range of emphases appropriate for workshop use goes far beyond this one focus. Nevertheless, the comparative strength of the workshop method is with the assessment of subtle, non-physical dimensions of project impact. Institutional development and policy reform efforts are apt to be major investment categories where the workshop method is most likely to prove its worth.

Report Testing. Workshops have also been used as part of the process of constructing and testing the final draft report or report series. One model is to bring together the members of field teams to review their case studies and critique drafts of the synthesis of lessons and issues extracted from those cases. This is a final attempt to harness the creative energies of team members and to obtain a synergistic product. It has been useful (see Kettering, 1986).

Another model is to structure a workshop so that the client for the study channels its concerns, concurrence, and suggested report modifications to the organization contracted to do the study. This allows a much faster turnaround than when the client responds on its own initiative. It promotes effective resolution of conflicting recommendations, and it generates clearer communication of underlying issues than written comments on a draft report. The workshop also forces client staff to become familiar with the report, and the group interaction may greatly improve the dissemination of the findings within the client organization. Greater internalization of those findings may also result.

The interactive nature of workshop small groups and plenary sessions helps both the client and the contractor to understand more fully the perspectives and operating constraints of the other. That improved understanding can make the difference between the study becoming just another document gathering dust or the study becoming a blueprint for improved policies, procedures and practices.

Conclusion

This chapter has identified two concerns of development project evaluation that can be addressed more adequately through increased use of workshop methods. These two concerns have been labelled the two loops—the learning loop and the impact loop.

Some experience using workshops has been reviewed and workshops have been found to be commonly employed in team preparation and report testing. They have been used less commonly in field assessment and bidder information, but workshop use in these activities is increasing due to a growing awareness of the valuable roles they can play. Concern for the learning loop and the impact loop support this trend. Moreover, projects focussing on institutional development and policy reform may be most able to benefit from such increased usage and, indeed, the learning loop is integral to institutional development and the impact loop represents the rationale for structural adjustment.

But the use of workshops as evaluation mechanisms will also depend upon the purpose the evaluation itself is intended to serve. Closing the loops will have different priorities and be viewed in different ways when different ends are served.

For example, evaluations and evaluation systems may be used primarily to *generate support for an organization or policy thrust.* When a donor agency is using an evaluation system to gain support and demonstrate accountability, then project-level evaluation workshops may seem peripheral. But an occaisional program-level workshop including key people exercising control over the agency and outside professionals might be useful. Or if a Third World government and donor together are trying to build a broader base of support for a structural adjustment program that is forcing short-term sacrifices among some segments of the population, then a workshop component bringing key members of those segments into the analytical process may help to serve this end.

A second evaluation function is *policy testing.* Policies and projects can be viewed as hypotheses, and evaluations can be constructed to test whether they did or did not work and why. Workshops can contribute to this exercise during the team preparation and report testing phases of the evaluation and under some circumstances they can be useful during field assessment. But for policy testing to work, the organization doing the evaluation must be more knowledge-driven than ideology-driven. This is a characteristic that cannot be implanted merely through workshops.

A third evaluation function is one of *managerial intelligence and institutional development.* Here the lessons of field experience are expected to be fed back into the leadership and managerial levels of the executing agency so that future performance can be improved. Workshops of a report testing or dissemination nature can support this end. The inclusion of managers in such workshops can help an organization to internalize an expanding knowledge base.

Workshops are useful tools for development project evaluation because they can capture subtleties connecting project activities and the legacies they leave behind, and because they can directly further the objective of building local institutional capacities. When closing the loops has high priority, then workshops are both powerful and practical. But when other priorities hold sway, then the issues are far more fundamental than whether or not to employ workshops as evaluation tools for development projects. That challenge is addressed elsewhere.

Notes

1. Formative evaluations are conducted during the implementation of a project to identify key shortfalls and areas of success in time to make adjustments and perhaps even redesign the project. Summative evaluations occur at

the end of implementation (the end of the donor funding period) to examine how well the project performed throughout its life cycle. Impact evaluations are done usually five or more years after the end of donor funding to judge the sustained contribution made by the investment.

References

Cernea, Michael. *Putting People First.* New York: Oxford University Press, 1986.

Cooper, Lauren. *The Twinning of Institutions,* World Bank Technical Paper no. 23. Washington, DC: World Bank, 1984.

Development Alternatives, Inc. *Development Management in Africa: Workshop Proceedings.* Washington, DC: DAI, 1986.

Honadle, George. "Rapid Reconnaissance for Development Administration: Mapping and Moulding Organizational Landscapes," *World Development,* vol. 10, no. 8, 1982.

Honadle, George, and Cooper, Lauren. "Beyond Coordination and Control: An Interorganizational Approach to Structural Adjustment, Service Delivery and Natural Resource Management," *World Development,* vol. 17, no. 10, 1989.

Honadle, George, and Rosengard, Jay. "Putting Projects in Perspective," *Public Administration and Development,* vol. 3, no. 4, 1983.

Honadle, George, and VanSant, Jerry. *Implementation for Sustainability.* West Hartford: Kumarian Press, 1985.

Kettering, Merlyn. "Synthesis of Lessons and Guidelines for Development Management in Africa," Development Program Management Center, U.S. Department of Agriculture, 1985.

Korten, David. "Community Organization and Rural Development: A Learning Process Approach," *Public Administration Review,* vol. 40, no. 5, 1980.

Morgan, E. Philip. "The Project Orthodoxy in Development: Reevaluating the Cutting Edge," *Public Administration and Development,* vol. 3, no. 4, 1983.

Office of Technology Assessment. *Grassroots Development: The African Development Foundation,* OTA-F-378. Washington, DC: U.S. Government Printing Office, 1988.

Patten, Michael Quinn. *Utilization-Focussed Evaluation.* Beverly Hills: Sage, 1978.

Rondinelli, Dennis. "Projects as Instruments of Development Administration," *Public Administration and Development,* vol. 3, no. 4, 1983.

Ross, Lee Ann. "Collaborative Research for More Effective Technical Assistance," *World Development,* vol. 16, no. 2, 1988.

Salman, Lawrence. *Listen to the People: Participant-Observer Evaluation of Development Projects.* New York: Oxford University Press, 1987.

Silverman, Jerry, Kettering, Merlyn, and Schmidt, Terry. *Action-Planning Workshops for Development Management,* World Bank Technical Paper no. 56. Washington, DC: World Bank, 1986.

Sweet, Charles, and Weisel, Peter. "Process versus Blueprint Models for Designing Development Projects," in G. Honadle and R. Klauss, eds., *International Development Administration: Implementation Analysis for Development Projects.* New York: Praeger, 1979.

Part 4

An Application

11
Tropical Deforestation and the Threat to Biodiversity: New Directions in Social Assessment

Lynn Llewellyn

Introduction

Listening to the Silence of the Watchdog in the Night

Among the less well known Sherlock Holmes stories by Sir Arthur Conan Doyle is a tale about the mysterious disappearance of a race-horse, Silver Blaze, and the murder of its trainer. According to the story, Silver Blaze was heavily favored to win a high-stakes race. Just a few days before the event was to take place, the horse vanished despite being closely guarded by a team of stable boys and a very reliable watchdog. Shortly thereafter, Sherlock Holmes was called in to see if he could solve the crime. While making his initial investigation, Holmes was joined by Inspector Gregory.

"Is there any point to which you would wish to draw my attention," inquired the Inspector.

"To the curious incident of the dog in the night time."

A perplexed Gregory responded: "The dog did nothing in the night time."

"That," replied Holmes, "was the curious incident."

Sherlock Holmes, it seems, had correctly concluded that the watch-dog's inaction did not necessarily imply that nothing of any consequence had happened. Another possibility was that something quite significant had occurred. As Holmes surmised, the thief who stole Silver Blaze did not draw a bark because he was well known to the dog.

Perhaps the analogy between the silent watchdog in "Silver Blaze" and the threat to biodiversity posed by the destruction of tropical rainforests seems somewhat remote. However, Charles Warren, former Chairman of the President's Council on Environmental Quality and the source for this story, makes the connection with relative ease: "We should listen carefully to the mute testimony of species that are being snuffed out in this biological night time man has created. They cannot speak for themselves, but the sound of their silence should fall on our ears as a most eloquent alarm" (Warren, 1978, p. 9).

Overview

Prior chapters in this volume have dealt primarily with mechanics of social analysis—the methods and techniques, the important DOs and DON'Ts. In most instances, only a few examples of site-specific application were mentioned to illustrate how these techniques have been used successfully in Third World countries. The present chapter is a somewhat radical departure from the earlier contributions, focusing as it does on a single, highly complex natural resource issue—tropical deforestation and the threat to biodiversity. In this specific context an attempt is made to show how various tools of the social scientist have been used singly, or in combination with the methods employed by other disciplines, to search for solutions to one of the most pressing environmental problems of our time. The chapter begins with a discussion of some of the many factors that are contributing to the destruction of tropical forests and to species extinctions. Some of the information is drawn from journalistic sources as well as technical studies. In the final section, examples are provided of the use of social science techniques such as surveys and informant interviews in Latin America, Asia and Africa. Of primary interest here is the "hands-on" work being done to preserve endangered and threatened species while, at the same time, assisting indigenous people and other local populations.

Tropical Deforestation and Human Needs

Third World Problems
and the Impact on Biodiversity

The fate of the world's tropical forests, and the myriad of species that inhabit them, is inextricably intertwined with that of millions of indigenous people, indeed, perhaps all humankind, if one accepts the cataclysmic "greenhouse" scenario proposed by some environmental theorists (see, for example, Rifkin's article printed in *The Washington Post,* July 31, 1988). Consider that 54 percent of the species on the globe occur in seven "megadiversity" countries: Brazil, Colombia, Mexico, Zaire, Madagascar, Indonesia and Australia (*The Economist,* June

4, 1988). All seven countries are partly in the tropics where there is an abundance of heat, sunlight and water. Taken together, these countries contain roughly 40 percent of the world's mammals (four-fifths of its primates), 60 percent of its birds, and 50 percent of its plants. Unfortunately, with the exception of Australia, these countries also share to a greater or lesser degree problems rampant in the Third World: population growth, poverty, debt, and massive environmental degradation.

Despite attempts in recent years to suggest that world population growth is not as serious a problem as it was once thought to be, Haub (1988) disagrees. He argues that another 90 million people were added to the world's population in 1987, more than any other year in history. Moreover, Third World countries do not appear to be undergoing declining fertility rates some experts had predicted, and family planning programs are losing support in some instances. As a result, the most rapid growth in population is occurring in countries that can least absorb it. For example, as Haub indicates, developing nations in Africa, Asia and Latin America now contain 3.9 billion people, many severely undernourished, and yet fertility levels remain anywhere up to seven children or more per woman. As former World Bank President Barber Conable states: "Poverty on today's scale prevents a billion people from having even minimally acceptable standards of living. To allow every fifth human being on our planet to suffer such an existence is a moral outrage" (*The Washington Post,* September 28, 1988).

The conflict between human needs and species preservation in developing nations is of paramount concern among conservationists. In a recent article concerned with African peoples' attitudes toward wildlife, Abrahamson (1983) writes:

An estimated 10 million large mammals remain on the continent's great savannas and its broad river valleys. But human populations, which have almost doubled since the early 1960s, are likely to double again . . . by the turn of the century. Already Africa contains 21 of the world's 45 poorest nations, and by the year 2000, Africans are expected to be able to provide just 25 percent of their own food. Pressed to feed themselves, these impoverished people are pushing wild creatures and wildland to the limit. For both animals and people, it is a desperate struggle for survival (p. 38).

Evolving Awareness of Tropical Deforestation

Concern about tropical deforestation is nothing new. However, it is only within the last fifteen years that the magnitude of the problem has been fully appreciated. For example, just over a decade ago, the

U.S. Department of State and the Agency for International Development sponsored a Strategy Conference on Tropical Deforestation. In addition to sounding the alarm about the accelerated pace of forest loss near and within tropical latitudes, the Conference underscored critical gaps in knowledge, some of which are still with us today. Among these are: (1) the nature and impact of forest removals at the local, regional and global levels; (2) the character and value of species being lost; and (3) whether or not tropical forests can be effectively and economically sustained (Council on Environmental Quality, 1979). Similarly, early in 1980, E. O. Wilson offered the following:

> During the next thirty years, fully one million species could be erased. The current rate is already by far the greatest in recent geological history; it is vastly higher than the rate of production of new species by natural evolution. Furthermore, many unique forms that emerged slowly over millions of years will disappear. In our own lifetime humanity will suffer an incomparable loss in aesthetic value, practical benefits from biological research, and world-wide environmental stability. Deep mines of biological diversity will have been dug out and discarded carelessly and incidentally in the course of environmental exploitation, without our even knowing fully what they contained (Maryland Nature Conservancy, 1988).

According to some estimates, tropical forests provide habitat for approximately half of all the species of animals and plants that exist on the earth. Today, these same forests are being destroyed at an unprecedented rate. At one time, tropical forests covered about 10 percent of the earth's surface. This area has already been reduced by a third. Each year, in fact, roughly 29,000 square miles of tropical forest—an area larger than West Virginia or Costa Rica—are destroyed. The number of species that vanish each year as the forests disappear is conservatively estimated at about 10,000.

While it is easy to dismiss such estimates as "doomsday predictions" by a small band of Chicken Little disciples, data collected from satellite photographs and on-the-ground research conducted by teams of biologists are more difficult to refute. As Wolf (1988) suggests:

> Many scientists believe that a larger share of the earth's plant and animal life will disappear in our lifetime than was lost in the mass extinction that included the disappearance of the dinosaurs 65 million years ago. It is likely to be the first time in evolution's stately course that plant communities, which anchor ecosystems and maintain the habitability of the earth, will also be devastated (p. 102).

Competition for a Vanishing Resource

To say that tropical forests are central to the economies of many Third World Nations would be a commonplace. Various estimates by the World Bank and other authorities (World Resources Institute, 1986; Denslow and Padoch, 1988) suggest that as many as 200,000,000 people earn their livelihoods directly from tropical forests. Of these, perhaps one-fourth are traditional forest dwellers; the remainder are there as the result of government policies (e.g., see Davis, 1988, for a discussion of planned land settlement in Indonesia), political turmoil, exploding populations, or as environmental refugees.

As Russell Train has noted in a presentation to the American Bar Association's Standing Committee on Environmental Law:

> One of the great ironies of our global condition . . . is that soils in large areas of many tropical countries are poor, and prevailing farming methods will not produce crops on a sustainable basis. For example, in much of the Amazon Basin, the nutrient elements essential to all life are found principally in the trees. Nutrients are much less available in the soil (p. 16 ELR 10256).

Train goes on to say that poor people, in order to grow crops on the land, chop down the trees and then burn them. The ashes provide some nutrients to the soil, but slash-and-burn agricultural methods provide good crops for only a few seasons before yields quickly decline. Because of the absence of tree cover, torrential tropical rains leach the nutrients from the soil and wash them away. When this happens, the poor generally give up their homes and move to a new location where they can slash and burn another area, and the vicious circle continues. By some estimates, approximately 250 million people in Asia, Africa and Latin America are engaged in slash-and-burn agriculture.

Brazil, for example, which encompasses nearly one-third of the world's remaining tropical forests has actively encouraged transmigration into the Amazon through large subsidies and promises of free land. Over the years, a network of TransAmazon highways has been built, providing a conduit for thousands of settlers fleeing landlessness and poverty. The result has been a "moving frontier" of slash-and-burn cultivation, exploding populations, and new settlements that have for the most part been unsuccessful. According to *The Economist* (1988), 70 percent of the rural population does not have title to the land, and slightly less than one percent of the farms account for 43 percent of the land area. The ecological damage to the region has been enormous. During July-October 1987 alone, about four percent of the Amazon forest was destroyed in this manner. As recently as September, 1988, forest burning was continuing at an unprecedented rate. If projections were accurate, eighty thousand square miles—an expanse of tropical forest larger than Austria, Belgium, Denmark and Switzerland combined—were lost by the end of the year (*The Washington Post*, 1988).

Slash-and-burn agriculture is a key factor, but far from the only contributor to tropical deforestation. In Central America and Brazil, conversion of forests for the purpose of grazing cattle has accounted for a substantial amount of forest loss. If present trends continue in Central America where the amount of pasture for cattle ranching increased by a factor of three from 1950–1980, there will be no forest remaining by the year 2000. Frequently condemned as one of the worst alternative land uses in tropical regions, conversion of Brazilian forests to grazing land continues at an alarming rate because of the ample availability of credit and the increasing value of the land itself.

Extraction of timber for commercial purposes also has contributed mightily to the rapid depletion of tropical forests on a global scale. As Schmink (1988) indicates, in Brazil, a combination of government subsidies designed to promote wood production for export, and a road system financed by multinational banks in many cases, has shifted the locus of logging investment dramatically. For example, in the Brazilian state of Pará, the decade of the 1970s saw an increase in wood production of 4000 percent. A government measure designed to keep down the price of logs for domestic uses—prohibiting the export of unprocessed timber—has also had an adverse impact on the way timber is harvested. Loggers typically extract only the better parts of felled trees and leave the rest. Specialization in only a few varieties such as mahogany and cedar has led to wasteful burning of lesser known but valuable species in areas converted to agriculture and ranching.

A similar situation in Southeast Asia has been described by Brookfield (1988). Thirty years ago, when individual trees were felled with an axe and saws were used immediately, minimal damage occurred to other trees. With the advent of the logging boom, and the introduction of new technology (i.e., chain saws, bulldozers, log hauling vehicles, etc.) much larger areas were depleted or degraded. To maximize profit against the cost of using more expensive equipment, "concessionaires" sought out the best trees, cutting primarily those of highest value in the most expeditious, least expensive way; and, in the process, doing extensive damage to the surrounding forest before moving to a new location.

Logging, such as that described above, often has additional adverse ecological impacts. Large bare areas permit little water penetration and promote rapid water run off. Not only does the resulting erosion uproot more trees creating even more erosion, but the runoff promotes siltation.

Streams and rivers that carry the eroded materials become shallow, changing the water flow in ways that eventually cause some areas downstream (e.g., irrigated croplands) to dry up while, at the same time, creating conditions that promote widespread flooding in others. For example, the devastating floods that occurred in Bangladesh in 1988 were thought to be correlated with the intense deforestation taking place in Nepal and northern India (Weintraub, 1988).

Other factors threatening tropical forests include (1) hydroelectric dams needed to meet the Third World's growing energy needs; (2) mining, particularly in the Amazon, where large deposits of iron, tin, copper and manganese wait just beneath the soils that support the trees; and (3) the intense use of wood for fuel in developing countries. While hydroelectric dams cause large expanses of forest to be flooded, mining creates other problems, particularly iron ore. Pig iron factories like those being built in Brazil require vast amounts of charcoal obtainable only from the forests. According to Train (1986), approximately 80 percent of all wood cut in developing countries is used as household fuel.

Before closing this section, it is interesting to note that almost half the modern medicines in use today are derived from the natural world, largely from tropical forests according to The World Resources Institute (1986). Among these are reserpine, quinine, curare and ipecacuanha. Recently, a small periwinkle plant native to Madagascar has been found to produce a substance useful in the fight against certain strains of leukemia. Elsewhere, a variety of snail was discovered to contain a substance that helps to reduce blood pressure. In all likelihood, countless other valuable drugs await discovery in plant and animal species rapidly disappearing and largely unknown outside tropical societies.

Much more could be included in the present discussion of forces that are contributing to the demise of tropical forests. However, it is important to move on to some examples of the way in which social science is broadening our understanding of how people perceive and react to the natural world, first in a more global context, but more importantly in efforts to preserve biodiversity in various areas of the Third World.

Assessing Attitudes and Beliefs
About the Natural World

The Global Connection

Earlier chapters in this volume (see especially Buzzard, Derman and Gow) have discussed at some length the many problems associated with doing survey research. While one would do well to heed their thoughtful advice, surveys and structured interviews provide broadly based information in certain situations that would be extremely difficult to collect in any other fashion.

Turner Smith, addressing the American Bar Association's Standing Committee on Environmental Law, offered the following: "We have had in this country a widespread adoption in public attitudes of the conservation ethic. We should ask what has brought that about in our culture and whether that ethic is compatible with the various social and cultural attitudes in other parts of the world" (*Environmental Law Reporter,* 1986, 16 ELR 10255).

It is useful to note that a decade earlier, George Gallup (1976) reported the results of the first "global" public opinion poll. According to Gallup, the survey, which included 10,000 personal interviews in 70 countries on six continents, was designed to "assess the happiness, ambitions, worries and problems of the world's inhabitants, and to probe their attitudes toward issues of global concern" (p. 132). One of the more interesting findings was that nine out of every ten people interviewed favored increased conservation of animals and fish. Somewhat surprisingly, the results were very much the same in every country. At the same time, however, two-thirds of all those interviewed in Latin America, Africa and the Far East were "worried most of the time" about meeting family expenses. Fifty percent or more reported insufficient money to provide their families with food, clothes or medical needs.

Gallup (1976) also found that, when asked what the ideal number of children in a family should be, better than 25 percent of those interviewed in Latin America and the Far East indicated at least four children. Two-thirds of the Africans thought the ideal number should be five or more. These figures contrasted sharply with the responses in more advanced nations where no more than two children were desired by a majority of interviewees. People in developing countries (as well as those in more prosperous countries) felt that the best ways to improve their lives was through greater industrialization.

While it would be easy to dismiss the importance of Gallup's global survey for any number of methodological reasons, the results do underscore basic similarities and differences in the way conservation and development issues are perceived by the nations of the world. It is unlikely that any attitudinal survey of this magnitude will be undertaken again in the near future; however, there have been other efforts worthy of mention.

In 1977, the U.S. Fish and Wildlife Service provided a grant to the Yale University School of Forestry and Environmental Studies to begin work on the most comprehensive study of American attitudes toward wildlife ever undertaken. Based primarily on 3,100 personal interviews with adult Americans in the 48 contiguous states and Alaska, the study was concerned with how people perceive and relate to wildlife and natural habitat issues. (See in particular, Kellert, 1979, 1980; Kellert and Berry, 1980.)

Among other things, the results strongly supported Kellert's concept of a typology of attitudes toward animals. The typology comprises nine identifiable attitudes that collectively reflect how people orient themselves toward animals in terms of feelings, beliefs and basic perceptions. One of the key findings reported by Kellert and Berry (1980) was that the most prevalent attitudes toward animals in the United States are the humanistic, moralistic, utilitarian and negativistic attitudes. The humanistic attitude (primary interest and strong affection for individual animals) and the moralistic attitude (concern about the right and wrong treatment of animals including strong opposition to cruelty and exploitation) also were found to be the most pervasive attitude types among 10–12 year old schoolchildren based on a national sample of over 3,000 fifth and sixth graders (Westervelt and Llewellyn, 1985).

As important as Kellert's pioneering work has been in understanding the tenuous relationship between man and wildlife, the full study has yet to be repeated in the United States to determine what trends might still be present, and what changes might have occurred in more than a decade since the original data were collected. More importantly, it would be extremely useful to see the typology of attitudes toward animals used in a Third World context, particularly in areas of deforestation where species are being lost at such an alarming rate. One might hypothesize, for example, that a more favorable orientation toward species preservation would be occasioned by a better balance between naturalistic (strong interest and affection for wildlife and the outdoors) and ecologistsic (concern for the environment as a system) attitudes, on the one hand, and utilitarian (concern for practical and material value of wildlife and habitat) or negativistic (indifference, dislike or fear of animals) attitudes, on the other (Kellert and Berry, 1980).

Latin American Projects

Surveys and structured interviews are being used in support of localized efforts in Latin America to preserve species and natural habitat. One of the more innovative uses of these techniques has been described by Dietz (1988) and Kleiman et al. (1986). The focus of these efforts has been the community conservation education program for the golden lion tamarin, a small primate and one of the most endangered animals found in the Brazilian Atlantic Coastal Forest. Only 400 golden lion tamarins are thought to remain in the wild; all are located in small forest patches within the Poco das Antas Federal Biological Reserve in the state of Rio de Janeiro. Once hunted for the zoo and pet trade, today the biggest threat to the animal and other species that live in this tropical ecosystem is the rapid destruction of habitat. Less than two percent of the golden lion tamarin's original forest habitat is still standing, and what remains is being converted into cattle pastures and rice fields, or sold for commercial firewood (Dietz, 1988).

The target group for the conservation education plan is the 89,000 residents of the rural region surrounding the Reserve. In 1984, structured interviews were conducted with over 500 adults in the area, and mailed questionnaires were sent to a sample of absentee landowners. In addition, all local school children in the third grade and above filled out written questionnaires. The purpose of the data collection effort was to determine the extent of local people's knowledge about the forest, and their attitudes and behaviors regarding the Reserve, endangered species, conservation activities and the forest itself. The data also were the basis for planning educational activities, determining the optimal ways for communicating with people in the region, and for evaluating the results of conservation education strategies after the first two years based on comparisons with similar interviews and questionnaires.

Preliminary findings showed little in the way of negative attitudes toward the golden lion tamarin; however, local people were not very knowledgeable about forest conservation, indigenous wildlife, or hunting laws, and were basically unaware of the existence of the Reserve. Based on the results, the education program focused in part on building a broader knowledge base concerning the long-term effects of human activities on the local environment, and the interconnectedness of man, wildlife, and natural habitat. Another goal of the project was creating pride in local natural resources. Initial findings suggest that the conservation education program has been a success.

Another Latin American project that seeks to strike a balance between man and the natural environment is Bolivia's Beni Biosphere Reserve (Ortiz, 1988). The diverse forest habitat and open savanna grasslands support over 500 species of birds and 13 of Bolivia's 18 endangered animal species. When first established the Beni Reserve comprised 334,200 acres; however, as the result of an unprecedented debt-for-nature swap, an additional buffer area of 3.7 million acres was added in 1987. Conservation International purchased $650,000 of Bolivian foreign debt in exchange for the government's agreement to establish three conservation and sustainable use areas. Bolivia also agreed to designate an additional $250,000 in local currency to administer, manage and protect the reserve.

The Beni is home to over 500 Chimane Indians—nomadic hunters and gatherers. Prior to establishing the newly acquired protected areas, which include the Chimane Indian Forest Preserve, anthropologists contributed to the planning process by conducting a human needs analysis focused on local populations. Their findings helped document the extreme poverty and critical health needs of the Chimane. Through sustainable development in the buffer zone, including improved forest management practices, local populations should benefit economically and improve living standards without disrupting cultural traditions thanks to the assistance of the anthropologists.

Asian Projects

A recent study by Machlis (1987) clearly illustrates the variety of ways social science can contribute to species conservation. Machlis was a member of an interdisciplinary team in China seeking ways to slow the rapid pace toward extinction of the giant panda. For many years the primary habitat of the giant panda—the mountainous forests of bamboo found in southwest China—has been steadily reduced as the result of forest removal, agricultural expansion, road building and other forms of development. Further adding to the problem is increased poaching (a panda skin may be worth as much as $2,500 to a panda poacher, or about eight times as much money as the average urban Chinese earns in a single year). According to the World Wildlife Fund (1988), Chinese officials reported the recovery of 146 pelts in 1988 in Sichuan Province—a figure representing approximately 15 percent of the pandas thought to be left in the wild. Others are inadvertently caught in snares set for musk deer, another highly endangered species killed for its musk gland used in traditional medicines as a supposed cure for impotency.

In 1983, the plight of the panda worsened in one preserve area when a major species of bamboo flowered and died, part of a cycle that occurs every 15–120 years according to the World Wildlife Fund (1988). For thousands of years pandas had dealt with this problem by moving down the mountains where the die-off was occurring, crossing the valleys below, and eventually climbing to unaffected bamboo forests. Now as the result of human encroachment, they could no longer do so. Many were threatened with starvation because they would not cross agricultural development in the valleys. Machlis (1987), working with Chinese officials, assisted in a strategy for relocating some of the people in the valley to permit the pandas a new access corridor. The move itself involved tribal, cultural and social problems that had to be resolved including how and where to move people in the least disruptive way. According to Machlis, the Chinese had never before considered "asking" the affected settlers where they might want to go. Without belaboring the point, as Machlis notes, the significance of this work is that biologists are actively seeking social science assistance to better the lot of people as well as preserve endangered species. Somewhat belatedly in some instances, sociological models are now being considered along with ecological and habitat models.

Work to save Sri Lanka's wild elephant population threatened by agricultural development has been reported by Moran (1988). Her efforts were largely concentrated on a herd of 800 wild elephants that was being destroyed as a result of human encroachment on their traditional habitat. As more people moved into the area, the elephants began raiding farms for food, posing a threat to family safety and otherwise disrupting development progress. Using a combination of methods, Moran examined ways in which traditional cultural management practices could be employed to conserve elephants while exploiting their commercial value through capture and domestication. Part of Moran's research involved the use of observational methods, interviews and questionnaires, initially with elephant keepers and later with elephant owners. A strategy evolved that included monetary incentives for farmers who provided logistical information on troublesome elephants that was used to facilitate capture. Rather than killing off elephants as pests, farmers were encouraged to aid in their conservation. As Moran indicates, the results of these efforts demonstrate that traditional cultural practices offer potential solutions for contemporary natural resource management. In the case of Sri Lanka, elephant capture and domestication evoked a sense of pride in traditional ways while satisfying the goals of conservation and development.

African Projects

In Kenya, the effects of tourism and transportation-related behavior on wildlife conservation have been examined through the use of surveys and observational techniques (Western, 1988; Henry and Western, 1988; Henry, 1989). As Western (1988) points out, since the turn of the century the human population in Kenya has increased ten fold while animal populations have been reduced by 80 percent. During World War II, a considerable loss of wildlife occurred, which hastened the creation of national parks and game reserves. It was not until the 1960s, however, that tourism became a central component of the Kenyan economy. Since then, areas such as the Amboseli, a small park on

Kenya's southern border with Tanzania, have become much in demand by international tourists because of their wildlife and scenic resources. With increased tourism, however, came the fear that traditional conservation objectives might be compromised.

Visitor behavior and its impacts on the Amboseli were examined through observing vehicular movement (virtually all transport and access to wildlife in the Park is vehicular) while visitor reactions were surveyed separately. The results showed that seeing and photographing wildlife in their natural surroundings was one of the most satisfying aspects of the Park visit. Also mentioned was the chance to see rare and endangered species and unusual animal behavior. Among the things that disturbed the visitors were habitat destruction and drought, and the perceived scarcity of animals in the park. Most of those surveyed also were disturbed by damage caused by unregulated tourist vehicles and by the sheer number of vehicles in the area, particularly when trying to view lion and cheetah. The latter were thought to be especially vulnerable because hunting behavior and success were found to be adversely affected by vehicular activity (Henry and Western, 1988).

Competition for the land in and around Kenya's parks and game reserves is fierce. Wildlife populations are steadily losing out to local people seeking land to till or to graze cattle. To the Masai, for example, "wildlife" equates with "government land" (Western, 1988). The Masai appear to appreciate the value of wildlife-related tourism, but have little interest in giving up cattle. A similar problem exists in Tanzania where support for the concept of conservation among the people is offset by the perceived absence of benefits to local populations. Abrahamson (1983) cites an attitude survey sponsored by the Africa Leadership Foundation that showed 85 percent of Tanzanian school children felt too much land was being devoted to reserves and parks. Moreover, such areas were thought to be set aside primarily for the benefit of foreign tourists. In the words of one African wildlife management expert: "Europeans speak of conserving wildlife for posterity. To an African, what is posterity? What is the future when you have nothing but an empty stomach" (Abrahamson, 1983, p. 38).

Clearly, it is imperative in cases like those cited above, that revenue obtained through wildlife-related tourism demonstrably benefit the local people living near the parks and reserves. As Henry and Western (1988) point out:

> When it can be argued that the gross annual worth of each of the lions in Amboseli is $27,000 or the worth of an elephant herd is . . . $610,000 per year (based on visitor viewing times and expenditures), the argument becomes more convincing to developing countries such as Kenya where

the alternatives for wildlife are often death by poaching or elimination of their habitat for farming (p. 8).

Other projects under the auspices of non-governmental organizations (NGOs) such as Conservation International, The Nature Conservancy, and the World Wildlife Fund's Wildlife and Human Needs Program show great promise. For example, the lowland tropical forests of the Central Africa Republic still contain the highest density of elephants found in African forests as well as many other species such as chimpanzees, gorillas, and forest buffalo. According to Stone (1989), new parks and reserves are being created to offset increasing pressure from logging interests, diamond mining and illegal hunting. Also affected by outside encroachment are the Babinga pygmies who have lived in the forests for countless centuries. Creation of the proposed Dzanga-Ndoki National Park and the Dzanga-Sangha Forest Reserve will promote sound conservation measures and, at the same time, permit the Babinga to maintain traditional lifestyles in harmony with rural development and increased tourism. Stone also cites another example in which rapid rural appraisal (see Gow) was used in an attempt to assist indigenous people in the Kilum region of the Cameroon to move away from slash-and-burn agriculture. The hope is that such practices will be replaced by reforestation of steep mountain slopes, and that crop diversification will reduce pressures on local forests.

In Zimbabwe, a program has been underway for several years that emphasizes the involvement of local communities in the management of wildlife. In the Omay, three NGOs including the Centre for Applied Social Sciences at the University of Zimbabwe provide sociological, economic, ecological and institution building assistance to locals. In parts of Zambia, a program of sustained yield management and the revenue it yields is being used to finance and train park guards to catch poachers, probably the greatest single threat to Zambian wildlife. Recently President Kenneth Kaunda of Zambia made the following observation:

> Our wildlife sanctuaries, which in some cases have for generations existed side-by-side with human populations, have not been established for prestige reasons or indeed for the sake of affording the wildlife a better protected life than that led by human beings. Rather, it should be understood that wildlife is part and parcel of our cultural heritage and hence we have a duty to protect it (Stone, 1989, p. 7).

Final Observations

In summary, despite the less than rosy outlook for the world's tropical forests and the species that inhabit them, some hopeful signs are beginning to appear. Conservationists are becoming increasingly aware that the concept of vast, pristine areas of tropical forest are no longer viable. With the assistance of social scientists, usually serving as members of multi-disciplinary teams, there is a better understanding of the compelling human needs in the Third World, and that sustainable development may be a key to forest survival. Similarly, no nature preserve can survive if the surrounding areas are destroyed. As Mott (1987) has noted, conservationists traditionally paid much more attention to park and nature preserve "visitors" than to their "neighbors"; today, rather than trying to push indigenous people aside, we had better start thinking about forging a social pact with those neighbors. Russell Train (1986) sounded the proper word of caution recently when he stated that, given present trends, in ten years time wildlands not in the "hearts of the people" simply will not survive.

A few years ago, a British ecologist compiling a list of species living in a remote area of Indonesia happened upon an old picture of the Sangir flycatcher, an exotic bird found only on a small island south of the Philippines. An ornithologist was sent to see if he could find the bird. Instead, he found that the island had been sheared of its tropical lowland forest, which was now covered with coconut plantations. The ornithologist could find no trace of the bird and concluded that it was extinct since there was no longer any forest habitat. As the account states, no one had noticed its existence was threatened, and no other picture of the bird, probably a female, is known to exist. The ecologist noted: "It's kind of sad, really . . . we've lost it, but we don't know what we've lost" (*The Chronicle of Higher Education*, 1986, p. 4).

There is an object lesson in the account of the Sangir flycatcher. Someone once said that we do not understand the web of life sufficiently to risk unravelling it by sending species to oblivion. And, as Caws (1987) suggests: "It would be ironic, but we would never know, if the very organism we had needed for the cure of AIDS had been plowed under by the bulldozers of some multinational conglomerate" (p. 5). By the same token, we also must heed the words of Moreira (1989) who talks in terms of the immense social debt owed those still deprived of the fruits of progress. It is imperative that we find the delicate balance between these two polarized but not irreconcilable points of view.

In *The Hollow Men,* T. S. Eliot wrote: "This is the way the world ends, not with a bang but a whimper." Should that be the case, then one might ask: when it becomes our turn to follow the course of the Sangir flycatcher, who will note on our behalf the silence of the watchdog in the night?

References

Abrahamson, D. "What Africans Think About African Wildlife." *International Wildlife,* July-August, 1983, pp. 38–41.

Brookfield, H. "The New Great Era of Clearance and Beyond." In J. Denslow and C. Padoch (Eds.), *People of The Tropical Rain Forest.* Berkeley: University of California Press, 1988, pp. 209–224.

Caws, P. "Nature: Preserve It for Science." *The Washington Post,* August 9, 1987.

"Conable Urges Curbs on Population." *The Washington Post,* September 2, 1988.

Council on Environmental Quality. *The President's Environmental Program: 1979.* Washington, D.C.: U.S. Government Printing Office, 1979, pp. 53–56.

Davis, G. "The Indonesian Transmigrants." In J. Denslow and C. Padoch (Eds.), *People of The Tropical Rain Forest.* Berkeley: University of California Press, 1988, pp. 143–153.

Denslow, J., and Padoch, C. (Eds.). *People of The Tropical Rain Forest.* Berkeley: University of California Press, 1988.

"Destruction of Tropical Rain Forests Alarms Scientists." *The Chronicle of Higher Education,* September 17, 1986, p. 4.

Dietz, L. "Community Conservation Education Program for The Golden Lion Tamarin, Brazil: Building Support for Habitat Conservation." Paper presented at the National Zoo, Smithsonian Institution Symposium: Culture— The Missing Element in Conservation, Washington, D.C., April 8–9, 1988.

Gallup, G. "What Mankind Thinks About Itself." *The Reader's Digest,* October, 1976, pp. 132–136.

Haub, C. "Standing Room Only: The Population Peril Isn't Over—It's Worse." *The Washington Post,* July 24, 1988.

Henry, W. Personal communication on The Masai Mara Survey, June, 1989.

Henry, W., and Western, D. "Tourism and Conservation in Kenya's National Parks: Planning for a Better Partnership." In E. Krumpe and P. Weingart (Eds.), *Management of Park and Wilderness Reserves.* Moscow, Idaho: University of Idaho, Wilderness Research Center, 1988, pp. 1–9.

Kellert, S. *Public Attitudes Toward Critical Wildlife and Natural Habitat Issues.* Washington, D.C.: U.S. Department of the Interior, Fish and Wildlife Service, 1979.

Kellert, S. *Activities of The American Public Relating to Animals.* Washington, D.C.: U.S. Department of the Interior, Fish and Wildlife Service, 1980.

Kellert, S., and Berry, J. *Knowledge, Affection and Basic Attitudes Toward Animals in American Society.* Washington, D.C.: U.S. Department of the Interior, Fish and Wildlife Service, 1980.

Kleiman, D., Beck, B., Dietz, J., Dietz, L., Ballou, J., and Coimbra-Filho, A. "Conservation Program for The Golden Lion Tamarin." In K. Bernirschke (Ed.), *Primates: The Road to Self-Sustaining Populations.* New York: Springer-Verlag, 1986, pp. 959–979.

"Lawsuit Helps Protect Imperiled Pandas." *World Wildlife Fund Letter,* 1988, 2, pp. 1–8.

Machlis, G. "The Fate of China's Giant Panda: An Applied Problem for Rural Sociology." Paper presented at the Annual Meeting of the Rural Sociological Society, Madison, Wisconsin, August 14, 1987.

Moran, K. "Traditional Elephant Management in Sri Lanka and Its Implications for Conservation and Development." Paper presented at the National Zoo, Smithsonian Institution Symposium: Culture—The Missing Element in Conservation, Washington, D.C., April 8–9, 1988.

Moreira, M. "Brazil: Facing Up to The Debts." *The Washington Post,* July 29, 1989.

Mott, W. Remarks presented at The World Wildlife Fund Conference: Partners in Conservation, Washington, D.C., September 17, 1986.

Ortiz, M. "The Beni Biosphere Reserve." Paper presented at the International Forestry Seminar, Rosslyn, Virginia, February 28, 1988.

Rifkin, J. "The Greenhouse Doomsday Scenario." *The Washington Post,* July 31, 1988.

Schmink, M. "Big Business in The Amazon." In J. Denslow and C. Padoch (Eds.), *People of The Tropical Rain Forest,* Berkeley: University of California Press, 1988, pp. 163–171.

Smith, T. Remarks before the American Bar Association's Standing Committee on Environmental Law. In "The Global Environment: Challenges, Choice and Will." *Environmental Law Reporter,* 9, 1986, pp. 16 ELR 10255–10268.

"Species Extinction—A Problem of Ruinous Proportion." *Maryland Nature Conservancy,* 1988, 12, 3, p. 7.

Stone, R. "The View From Kilum Mountain." *World Wildlife Fund Letter,* 1989, 4, pp. 1–8.

Stone, R. "Zambia's Innovative Approach to Conservation." *World Wildlife Fund Letter,* 1989, 7, pp. 1–10.

"The Other Group of Seven." *The Economist,* June 4, 1988, pp. 73–74.

"The Vanishing Jungle." *The Economist,* October 15, 1988, pp. 25–28.

"Thousands of Amazon Acres Burning." *The Washington Post,* September 8, 1988.

Train, R. Remarks before the American Bar Association's Standing Committee on Environmental Law. In "The Global Environment: Challenges, Choice and Will." *Environmental Law Reporter,* 9, 1986, 16 ELR 10255–10268.

Train, R. Remarks presented at the World Wildlife Fund Conference: Partners in Conservation, Washington, D.C., September 17, 1986.

Warren, C. "A Dog in the Night-Time." Remarks presented at the Annual Meeting of the American Association for the Advancement of Science, Washington, D.C., February 17, 1978.

Weintraub, R. "Deforestation Linked to Flood in Bangladesh." *The Washington Post,* September 10, 1988.

Western, D. "The Impact of Economic Development on the Environment." Paper presented at the National Zoo, Smithsonian Institution Symposium: Culture—The Missing Element in Conservation, Washington, D.C., April 8–9, 1988.

Westervelt, M. and Llewellyn, L. *Youth and Wildlife.* Washington, D.C., U. S. Department of the Interior, Fish and Wildlife Service, 1985.

Wolf, E. "Avoiding a Mass Extinction of Species." *State of The World—1988: A Worldwatch Institute Report on Progress Toward a Sustainable Society.* Washington, D. C.: Norton, 1988, pp. 101–117.

World Resources Institute. *World Resources—1986.* New York: Basic Books, 1986, pp. 70–72.

About the Editors
and Contributors

Editors

Kurt Finsterbusch is a sociologist at the University of Maryland. He is active in the field of social impact assessment and has published *Methodology of Social Impact Assessment,* edited with C. P. Wolf; *Social Impact Assessment Methods,* edited with Lynn Llewellyn and C. P. Wolf; *Social Research for Policy Decisions,* with Annabelle Bender Motz; and *Understanding Social Impacts.* He is currently working on issues of sustainability of Third World development activities and has published *Organizational Change as a Development Strategy* with Jerald Hage.

Jasper Ingersoll is an anthropologist at Catholic University in Washington, D.C., and a consultant for development organizations. His publications have focused on Buddhism, Mekong River basin development, and social analysis of development projects. He is currently writing *The Drama of Development: Struggling for Well-Being in Village Thailand.* His interests include project analysis, systems analysis, river basin development, and resettlement.

Lynn Llewellyn is a senior social psychologist and Assistant Chief, Policy and Directives Management, U.S. Fish and Wildlife Service. His current research interests include social impact assessment, public attitudes toward the natural environment, and the human dimensions of wildlife management. He was a co-editor with Kurt Finsterbusch and C. P. Wolf of *Social Impact Assessment Methods* and recently collaborated with William R. Freudenburg on an article appearing in *Society and Natural Resources* entitled "Legal Requirements for Social Impact Assessment: Assessing the Social Science Fallout from Three Mile Island."

Contributors

Annette L. Binnendijk presently serves as Chief, Division of Program and Policy Analysis, Agency for International Development (AID). Among her current research interests is impact evaluation of child survival in Egypt. One of her most recent publications is *Rural Development: Lessons from Experience,* Highlights from the Seminar Proceedings, AID Program Evaluation Discussion Paper no. 25.

C. Hobson Bryan is professor and chairman of the Department of Sociology, University of Alabama. His research interests include social implications of natural resource issues and environment/resource policy. He has worked for the U.S. Forest Service and was awarded a Fulbright Senior Research Fellowship to New Zealand in regard to natural resource and social impact assessment issues.

Shirley Buzzard is an applied anthropologist and independent consultant in Washington, D.C. She has conducted research in thirty countries mainly in the areas of health, small business development, and institutional development. Her research emphasizes participatory methods and rapid rural appraisals.

Cynthia C. Cook is a sociologist in the Environment Division, Africa Region of the World Bank. Her responsibilities include managing project environmental impact assessments, assisting countries in the preparation of environmental action plans, and supervising regional studies. Her latest publication is *Agroforestry in Sub-Saharan Africa: A Farmer's Perspective* (with Mikael Grut), World Bank Technical Paper no. 112.

Lauren Cooper is an independent consultant in Washington, D.C. Her publications reflect her interest in management processes and methods for delivering goods and services to Third World clienteles. She has worked in Africa, Asia, and the Caribbean.

William Derman is an anthropologist at Michigan State University. His publications include *Social Impact Analysis and Development Planning in the Third World* (co-edited with Scott Whiteford) and *Serfs, Peasants, and Socialists: A Study of a Former Serf Village in the Republic of Guinea.* His interests include economic anthropology, development anthropology, SIA, and systems of food production, especially in west and south Africa. He is currently doing field research in Africa.

David D. Gow is an anthropologist at Development Alternatives, Inc., in Washington, D.C. His publications include: *Implementing Rural Development Projects: Lessons from AID and World Bank Experience* (co-edited with Elliott Morss) and "Development of fragile lands: an integrated approach reconsidered," in John Browder (ed.), *Fragile Lands of Latin America: Strategies for Sustainable Development.* His interests include project analysis, sustainable agriculture, natural resources management, and resource sustainability.

George Honadle is a visiting professor of administration at George Washington University in Washington, D.C. He has worked in twenty-two countries. In addition to fifteen articles, he has published *International Development Administration, Implementation for Sustainability,* and *Putting the Brakes on Tropical Deforestation: Some Institutional Considerations.* His current interest is in managerial and institutional dimensions of natural resources management.

William L. Partridge is an anthropologist in the Asian Environmental Division of the World Bank. His publications include *Training Manual in Development Anthropology* and *Human Ecology of Tropical Land Settlement in Latin America.* His major interests are community development, human ecology, and environmental risk assessment.

C. Nicholas Taylor is currently a private consultant and was formerly a research officer at the Centre for Resource Management, Lincoln College, New

Zealand. He also is an adjunct professor of sociology at the University of Canterbury. His research in rural sociology, rural development, and social impact assessment has focused on the social effects of New Zealand agricultural aid projects in the South Pacific, coal development, and the sociology of resource communities.